Managing Business Relationships

Second Edition

Managing Business Relationships

Second Edition

David Ford
Lars-Erik Gadde
Håkan Håkansson
Ivan Snehota

WILEY

Other Wiley Editorial Offices

John Wiley & Sons Inc., 111 River Street, Hoboken, NJ 07030, USA

Jossey-Bass, 989 Market Street, San Francisco, CA 94103-1741, USA

Wiley-VCH Verlag GmbH, Boschstr. 12, D-69469 Weinheim, Germany

John Wiley & Sons Australia Ltd, 33 Park Road, Milton, Queensland 4064, Australia

John Wiley & Sons (Asia) Pte Ltd, 2 Clementi Loop #02-01, Jin Xing Distripark, Singapore 129809

John Wiley & Sons Canada Ltd, 22 Worcester Road, Etobicoke, Ontario, Canada M9W 1L1

Wiley also publishes its books in a variety of electronic formats. Some content that appears in print
may not be available in electronic books.

Library of Congress Cataloging-in-Publication Data

Managing business relationships / David Ford ... [et al.] — 2nd ed.
     p. cm.
   Includes bibliographical references and index.
   ISBN 0-470-85125-2 (pbk. : alk. paper)
   1. Strategic alliances (Business) 2. Business networks. I. Ford, David, 1944-

   HD69.S8M327 2003
   658'.044—dc21

                                                          2003050058

British Library Cataloguing in Publication Data

A catalogue record for this book is available from the British Library

ISBN 10: 0-470-85125-2 (PB)

ISBN 13: 978-0-470-85125-8 (PB)

Typeset in 10/12pt Goudy by Mathematical Composition Setters Ltd, Salisbury, Wiltshire.
Printed and bound in Great Britain by Antony Rowe Ltd, Chippenham, Wiltshire
This book is printed on acid-free paper responsibly manufactured from sustainable forestry in which
at least two trees are planted for each one used for paper production.

CONTENTS

ABOUT THE AUTHORS

The IMP Group

The IMP (Industrial Marketing and Purchasing) Group was formed in 1976 by researchers from five European countries. The Group's first work was a large-scale comparative study of industrial marketing and purchasing across Europe. Results from this study were published in *Industrial Marketing and Purchasing: An Interaction Approach*, John Wiley, 1982. This interaction approach has been the cornerstone of the Group's work since then. It is based on the importance for both managers and researchers of understanding the *interaction* between *active* buyers and sellers within continuing business *relationships*. The Group has carried out a number of studies into business relationships and the wider *networks* of which they form part. This work has been published in numerous books and articles. A selection of recent examples can be found in *Understanding Business Marketing and Purchasing*, third edition, International Thomson, 2002. The Group has also published an easily accessible introduction to business marketing in *The Business Marketing Course*, John Wiley, 2002. Further details of the Group's work and its publications can be found at www.impgroup.org. The Group holds a major conference in September of each year in Europe, in addition to separate events elsewhere.

The Authors

David Ford is Professor at the University of Bath in the UK.

Lars-Erik Gadde is Professor at Chalmers University of Technology, Gothenburg in Sweden.

Håkan Håkansson is Professor at the Nordic School of Management, BI, Oslo, in Norway.

Ivan Snehota is Professor at the University of Lugano in Switzerland.

PREFACE

When the first edition of this book was published in 1998, the IMP Group had spent over twenty years researching into business marketing and purchasing. This work had led to a number of research books and many academic articles but until then we hadn't produced a book, based on our research that would help practising managers and students of business to develop their ideas on managing business relationships. The first edition was intended to fill that gap and had the following aim:

> To help managers and students of management to understand the reality of business markets and the tasks of managing the complex relationships in which all companies are enmeshed and on which they rely for competitive success.

We anticipated that the book would be purchased by some managers and individual students, but in fact it was adopted as a recommended text by many lecturers and by the Open University and was subsequently translated into Japanese. So the publishers asked for a second edition of the book, "with some modifications". But research and ideas have moved on a great deal in the past five years and so this second edition is almost completely new.

The book still has the same aim of helping managers and students to understand the reality of business markets. But the major difference between the two editions is that this one takes a much stronger *network* approach. All companies are becoming more dependent on their relationships with those around them. And all these companies and relationships must cope with pressures and capitalise on opportunities from wider afield in the network. This means that we can only understand a business sale or purchase by looking at the relationship in which it takes place. But also, we can only effectively manage what happens in that relationship by understanding the wider network of which it is part.

The book starts by explaining some of the ideas of the IMP Group on what we see as the reality of the world that businesses find themselves in. It then tries to provide a structured way to understand what business networks are all about *and what their effects are on the practising manager*. Business networks are complex and difficult to understand. It is tempting to cope with this complexity by trying to simplify them to produce an easier, but deceptive structure, or on the other hand to try to make sense of a mass of confusing information and simply get lost in the detail. We try to steer a middle course in this book by explaining the underlying dynamics that are common to all business networks and the options that they create for all companies.

Following from our analysis of the manager and the network, we examine the nature and development of business relationships. We then deal with the specific cases of customer, supplier, distribution and technical development relationships.

The book then presents a simple model of managing in networks, that builds on these general ideas and specific cases. This model provides a structure for the activities and choices for the manager and tries to give some new perspectives on business strategy. Finally, the book tries to bring things together by explaining what it all means for the practising purchasing or marketing manager. We have tried to make the book suitable for a managerial and student audience and so the emphasis is on explanation and academic argument and we have included examples wherever possible to illustrate particular points.

Producing the book has been great fun and we have all learned a lot through the process. We hope that it will be useful to others. As always, we acknowledge that many of the ideas in the book have come from others in the IMP Group or elsewhere and we are grateful for this. Thanks also to Stephanos Mouzas for having the patience and courage to read the chapters and provide constructive comments.

Note on the Text

We have varied the use of he and she throughout the text when discussing the business marketer as, obviously, marketers can be female as well as male.

David Ford
University of Bath
January 2003

IMP AND THE INTERACTION APPROACH

Aims of this Chapter

- To outline some of the ideas of the IMP Group on the nature of the complex networks in which business companies operate.
- To help students, managers and instructors try to understand the Group's approach to business marketing and purchasing in these networks.
- To outline a number of myths that we believe condition the way that business in general, and marketing and purchasing in particular, are analysed and practised. We refer to these myths as the Myth of Action; the Myth of Independence and the Myth of Completeness.
- To describe the Group's alternative views in order to form an introduction to the analysis of business relationships in the remainder of the book.

Introduction

This book is part of the output from the research of the IMP (Industrial Marketing and Purchasing) Group.[1] The original group came together in 1976 and has now developed into a large, informal network of researchers throughout the world, all trying to make sense of the relationships between companies in the complex *networks* in which they operate as they buy, sell, co-operate and compete with each other. The Group's work has been based on a number of core ideas developed or borrowed over the years, that have become known as the "Interaction Approach" to understanding business marketing and purchasing.

Over the years, the Group has sought to counter a number of myths that we believe condition the way that business in general and marketing and purchasing in particular,

---

[1] The Group's Website is www.impgroup.org. A selection of the recent work of the Group can be found in Ford (2001).

are analysed and practised. We refer to these myths as: the Myth of Action, the Myth of Independence and the Myth of Completeness. These myths and the Group's alternative approaches can be outlined as shown below.

The Myth of Action

This myth has its origins in traditional ideas of marketing. According to these, marketing is built on the "marketing mix" – the set of variables that marketers are said to manipulate and direct at the market. The mix is composed of the product; the price that is charged for it; the way it is promoted and the distribution methods that are used (or the "place" in which it is sold).[2] Consumer marketing managers are charged with building and modifying the mix for their brand to achieve growth in market share and profitability. At the same time, marketing research aims to assess the effectiveness of each mix variable and deals with questions such as the best ways to set prices, or which promotional techniques would bring the best response from the market.

This idea of the mix also underlies approaches to business marketing. This is often regarded as a "special case" of general marketing, where the mix is likely to emphasise personal selling more than advertising and where after-sales service is likely to be important. Many business purchases seem to be rather complex processes. So marketing researchers have tried to categorise different types of these purchases; to map the "stages" that are involved in each; to determine which functions within the customer's management are likely to be involved in each case and what the most effective mixes are that a seller could use to get the desired response from the market. We believe that this way of looking at consumer and business marketing has developed into the Myth of Action.

According to this myth:

- *The supplier* acts *and the customer* reacts: The supplier is the active party in marketing and it assembles the mix and directs it towards the market. The role of the customer is passive and limited to choosing whether or not to respond to the supplier's mix that is launched at the market as a whole.
- *Marketing is what* manufacturers *do:* Distributors and retailers are selected by a manufacturer to be part of *its* mix and to promote and make offerings available as part of *its* strategy. Each intermediary responds passively to the manufacturer's action.
- *Each customer is individually insignificant:* Each is part of a relatively homogeneous and faceless market, or market segment.
- *The marketing actions of a supplier and the purchasing reactions of a customer can be analysed* separately *from each other:* Further, each purchase is an isolated event and can be examined without reference to other purchases or other aspects of either companies' experience.

---

[2] For example the 11th edition of Philip Kotler's *Marketing Management* (2002) starts with the mix as the basis of a marketing program by a marketing company (p. 15).

The IMP approach

The IMP Group's approach to understanding business markets is based on the idea that this myth does not relate to what really happens in business markets. In particular:

- *Business markets do not consist of a large number of individually insignificant customers*: Customers vary widely in size, requirements and importance. Some of them are bigger than their suppliers and marketers have to deal with many of them individually.
- *Business markets do not consist of active suppliers and passive customers*: Often a customer, faced with a particular problem, has to seek out a suitable supplier, assess its abilities and persuade it to help solve the customer's problem. This is likely to be difficult for the customer if the problem is a tough one or if the volume of its purchases is small.
- *Customers are not looking for a product from a manufacturer. Instead they seek a* solution *to their* problem *from a* supplier: Business purchases are problem-driven. A *problem* may relate to the customer's need to carry out its basic activities efficiently and economically. Examples include the problems of wastage of material, poor utilisation of staff or an unacceptable failure rate in components. We refer to these as problems of "rationalisation". A problem can also arise for positive reasons, such as when a company is trying to develop relationships with new customers or enhance the performance of a product. We refer to these as problems of "development".

    There are many possible *solutions* to most business problems. Rarely are these provided by a simple product or service alone. Instead, interaction between a customer and different suppliers may lead to various offerings from the suppliers, each consisting of a combination of the elements of *product, service, advice* and *logistics*. The supplier's offering may include adaptations to some or all of the elements, when compared with the supplier's standard offering to suit an individual customer's requirements.

Companies combine the offerings of their suppliers with their own resources and abilities to provide offerings for others. Suppliers of offerings are neither faceless nor homogeneous and vary in the extent to which they provide the different elements of their offerings themselves, or subcontract to others. Many suppliers, including those conventionally called manufacturers, do little or no manufacturing, but buy in the product element of their offerings from others. Some suppliers will produce most elements of their offering internally. Their offering may then be combined by their customers with the offerings of many other suppliers to produce a new offering for their customers. Some of the elements of an offering, such as logistics, may be provided by the customer itself. Both customer and supplier *together* may be involved in developing or adapting the supplier's offering. Sometimes the customer will have to adapt some aspects of its own offering or its operations to suit the supplier.

The following are elements of relationship management:

- *Lots of people from different functions in* both *companies are likely to be involved in the processes of developing and fulfilling the offering that is traded between them*: Business marketing and purchasing are not confined to sales people, marketers and buyers. People from design, development, operations, finance and logistics in both companies may be involved. Business marketing is not a process of *action* by the supplier and *reaction* by the customer;[3] it is one of *interaction* between them.

- *Each business sale and purchase is not an isolated event, but part of a continuing relationship between a supplier and a customer*: Sales and purchasing people in business markets do not usually just meet, make a deal and then never see each other again. Sometimes, for such things as the purchase of a piece of capital equipment, there may be many interactions between a number of staff before a purchase takes place – months of initial meetings, negotiations, product and production development. This purchase may also be the forerunner of others, often taking place infrequently over many years. In other cases such as the supply of production components or business services, deliveries are likely to be continuous, perhaps for several years, involving frequent contact between operations and logistics people in both companies as well as marketing and purchasing. Some other purchases will not be very important to supplier or customer and both will try to reduce the costs and time involved in them. In these cases the interaction between customer and supplier may be limited to a phone call each time a purchase is made.

  But in all cases both the customer and the supplier will interact on the basis of their experience of any previous purchases between them and on their expectations of any possible future purchases. So each interaction between a customer and a supplier is a single *episode* in the *relationship* between them. Each episode, whether the exchange of product, service, finance, advice, information or social interaction, is affected by the relationship of which it forms part and each interaction, in turn, affects the relationship itself. We can only understand each interaction and each purchase or sale in the context of that relationship.

- *Many business relationships are close, complex and long term*: This does not mean that the parties know everything about each other, or that they always act in each other's best interests. Other relationships centre on a single important transaction, such as the purchase of a power station that could take months or years to complete. Sometimes the supplier or customer may dominate a relationship or there may be conflict or deceit. The two companies involved in the relationship will almost always have different ideas of what they want from the relationship or about what they or their counterpart should be doing in it. Some relationships simply become inert or end in divorce. Others are only brief encounters, such as when one of the companies takes short-term advantage of the other. Both companies are likely to be highly involved in some of their relationships, but others may be more distant and the only contact between the two companies is impersonal, by advertising or mail. In this way they approximate to the situation in many consumer markets.

- *Each relationship is part of a network of relationships*: No business relationship can be understood in isolation. Each is related to the other relationships of the two companies

---

[3] Nor vice versa. An alternative form of the Myth of Action that is implicit in some of the purchasing literature is that it is the customer that acts and the supplier that reacts to its requirements.

and through these it is linked to numerous other relationships elsewhere in a wider "network". Within this network the offerings of each company are developed, bought, sold, added to, refined, combined and sold on to others until they reach a final consumer. The relationship between a single customer and supplier anywhere in the network will be affected by that customer's relationships with its own customers and the supplier's relationships with its suppliers. The relationship will also be affected by the relationships between each of those suppliers and customers and their other customers and suppliers. A business network does not exist for the benefit of a single company or to solve a single problem. It is far more than the supply-chain or distribution channel of a single company. No one company controls the network, although some may be powerful members of it.

- *No single type of relationship is "right" for either buyer or supplier in all circumstances*: Hence there is no single measure of the "quality" of a company's relationships. Business companies cannot just develop a marketing or purchasing strategy that includes a single "design" for all of its relationships and expect it to be acceptable to all its counterparts. The central task of both business marketing and business purchasing is to manage a *diverse* portfolio of relationships over time to maximise the long-term value from them for their companies.

Relationship management involves analysis, investment in relationships and a clear view of the wider value that can be gained from each relationship and which extends beyond the straightforward features of the product that is exchanged.[4]

The Myth of Independence

This second myth has its origins in ideas on business strategy. These ideas developed from the rather simple view of "strategy as plan" that were current in the 1960s and 1970s (e.g. Ansoff 1965), to the view of strategy as something that "emerges" within a company through a combination or "pattern" of conscious and unconscious evaluation within the company over time (Mintzberg 1985, 1987; Araujo and Easton 1996).

"A strategy is the *pattern* or *plan* that *integrates* an organisation's *major* goals, policies, and action sequences into a *cohesive* whole." (Quinn 1996: 3; authors' emphasis)

We believe that this way of looking at consumer and business marketing that centres on the idea of the "entrepreneurial firm" has developed into the Myth of Independence. According to this myth:

A company is able to *act* independently. It can carry out its own analysis of the environment in which it operates, develop and implement its own strategy based on its own resources, taking into account its own competences and shortcomings.

---

[4] We will return to this wider concept of value in subsequent chapters.

The IMP approach

The IMP approach builds on the interaction that takes place between active customers and active suppliers in relationships. The companies in these relationships are *interdependent* for sales, supplies, information, development and for access to other companies elsewhere in the surrounding network:

- *The management process in any company is interactive, evolutionary and responsive.* Companies have a restricted view of the surrounding network and limited knowledge of the aims and intentions of their counterparts. They have limited freedom to act independently and the outcomes of their actions will be strongly influenced by the attitudes and actions of those with whom they have relationships. Management involves lots of reacting to the actions of these others. "Strategising", or the process of thinking strategically involves identifying where there is scope for individual action and working within the constraints of the network. It includes reacting to, or coping with the actions, intentions or requirements of others and working with, through, in spite of, or against them.

    For example, companies are frequently affected by technological developments controlled by others with whom they have little or no contact, elsewhere in the network. Or they may have a small number of critical customers, suppliers or distributors on which they must depend, at least in the short term. Some of the changes made by others may be anticipated, but others cannot be foreseen, or have effects that may be beyond the company's ability to control. Also, changing the company's portfolio of relationships or what happens in them may take a long time and will be dependent on the views of those in counterpart companies or elsewhere in the network.

- *Strategising is not simply concerned with competition.*[5] The essence of strategising is in coping with and taking advantage of relationships with surrounding companies *in their entirety.* These companies include suppliers, customers and competitors. Co-operation and competition are not a simple dichotomy for companies. Instead, strategising involves simultaneous elements of co-operation, conflict, integration and separation in a company's relationships. Examples may include co-operation with a supplier in product development or with a competitor in joint logistics, competition between a supplier and a customer over which will develop a productive relationship with one of the supplier's own suppliers.[6]

    As long ago as 1967, Wroe Alderson noted the problems that were caused by over-emphasising the conflict in the relationships between companies: "Sometimes the element of conflict is so pronounced that an efficient channel can scarcely be said to exist."

---

[5] Despite what Michael Porter (1979) said: "The essence of strategy formulation is coping with competition."

[6] The idea of limits to an individual company's freedom of action is of course present in the strategy literature, but it is often expressed in terms of the constraints imposed by competitors. "Strategy deals not just with the unpredictable, but the unknowable, no analyst could predict the precise ways in which all impinging forces could interact with each other, be distorted by nature or human emotions, or be modified by the imaginations and purposeful counteractions *of intelligent opponents*" (Quinn 1988; our emphasis).

- *A company's "position" is based on its total set of relationships.* The traditional view of position is expressed in terms of products, services and markets. For example:

> "A firm's position consists of the products or services it provides, the market segments it sells to, and the degree to which it is isolated from direct competition. In general, the best positions involve supplying very uniquely valuable products to price insensitive buyers, whereas poor positions involve being one of many firms supplying marginally valuable products to very well informed, price sensitive buyers." Rumelt (1980: 59)

But a business company is unlikely to compete with similar companies supplying similar offerings along the same dimensions in a series of discrete transactions. Instead companies differ widely in their structure, in their offerings, in which elements of these offerings that they supply themselves, in their requirements from their own suppliers, in the problems that they aim to solve for their customers *and the relationships on which they depend.* For example: the offering of one supplier may include a standardised product supplied to all its customers. They may take responsibility for designing, producing and delivering most aspects of this offering themselves and rely on their suppliers only for a small number of standard components and service elements. This supplier is likely to address the problems of customers that understand how to use the product, but that need consistency in supply and low cost.

Another company may supply a similar product, but as part of an offering that includes extensive advice and adaptation for each customer. This company may source most or even all of its product from its own suppliers that also develop the offering. The company may also sub-contract to other companies the provision of customer advice and any adaptations to its offering. This supplier is likely to be addressing very different customer problems that involve the same type of product, but concern which type of product the customer should choose and how it should use it.

The first of these suppliers may have a staff of thousands, the second only of tens. The first will have considerable resources that it owns, the second will have few resources, but may be skilled in accessing the resources of others through its relationships. The offerings of the two suppliers differ even if they have similar products because they aim to solve different customer problems and have different relationships with their customers. These customer relationships will be closely intertwined with their other relationships with suppliers and vice versa. Both will be different from each other.

Hence we can only understand the *position* of the two companies within the network of relationships in which they operate. A company's network position consists of its set of relationships and the reputation, rights, limitations on behaviour and obligations which it has acquired through its interactions within those relationships.[7]

Each of the counterparts with which a company has relationships will have different expectations of it. Each will use it differently and will value their relationship with it in

---

[7] Later in this book we will discuss the processes by which companies seek to change their position in the network and manage this set of relationships. We will refer to this as the management of the company's relationship *portfolio*.

different ways. For example, the relationships of an IT consultancy with IT equipment suppliers will be different from its relationships with software houses and with customers that have strong or weak IT skills.

- *A company's network position changes and develops through interaction with other companies in different positions in the network.* In this way, a company's position is *created* partly by its counterparts, rather than solely being the outcome of its independent strategy. Each company's position is affected by changes in those around it, so that if one company has a problem, this might affect others around it. For example, if a large customer takes over a major rival, then it is likely to impose its network of suppliers on that customer to the exclusion of its previous suppliers.
- *Interdependence is multi-dimensional.* Interdependence has three dimensions: (a) The *links* between the *activities* of the company and those around it. This includes such things as integrated production scheduling to minimise logistics or co-ordination between architects and consulting engineers involved in a building project. (b) The *ties* between the *resources* of the companies. This includes such things as joint investment in maintenance or operations facilities by airlines or oil companies, or investment in joint product or service development by equipment and component producers. It also includes appointment of dedicated staff to work on an advertising account with a client. (c) The *bonds* between the individual *actors* in the companies. These relate to the ties of experience, friendship and trust that enable individuals to co-operate with each other and which increase efficiency.
- *Relationships are assets in strategy development.* A company's interdependence with others is not a restriction on its operations. Instead its relationships are a *resource* on which it can build. For example, an equipment manufacturer's relationship with some respected industrial users of its products could be a valuable resource in developing relationships with other users. Similarly, a retailer's relationship with a large group of consumers is a major factor in its interactions with its suppliers. Both companies would probably believe that their position gave them the right to be consulted by a supplier that was planning to change its product range, distribution or pricing structure. At the same time, these companies would perhaps feel that their position means that they are obliged to operate to the highest standards of safety and employee welfare and they would feel that they couldn't "get away" with the sort of practices carried out by less reputable companies.
- *Interdependence means that the management of customer–supplier relationships is essentially similar for both of the companies involved.* Purchasing is no longer considered to be responsible for just obtaining the right products at the right price at the right time, with what is "right" being largely determined by others in the company. Nowadays, the performance of purchasing is not judged solely by the negative criteria of minimising delays and reducing costs. Today, purchasing is seen as a function with a much stronger role in deciding which activities should be carried out inside the company and which should be carried out for it by others with which it has relationships. Both customer and supplier have to search for and assess potential relationship counterparts. Both have to decide on their aims for a relationship and whether these can be achieved at the expense of the other party or in co-operation with it. Both customer and supplier

bring their resources to a relationship and invest in it. Both have to decide how important the relationship is and how much to adapt their own offerings or operations to suit the requirements of the relationship.

We believe that is only possible to make sense of what happens in a relationship by simultaneously studying both of the companies involved. Similarly, it is only possible to manage a relationship by looking at it from the perspective of both of the companies, rather than simply by carrying out "supplier-assessment" or "customer-segmentation" alone.

The Myth of Completeness

This myth also has its roots in traditional ideas of strategy:

> "A well formulated strategy helps to marshal and allocate an *organisation*'s resources into a unique and viable posture based on *its* relative internal competencies and shortcomings, anticipated changes in the environment and contingent moves by intelligent opponents." (Quinn 1996: 3; authors' emphasis)

This definition emphasises the company's *own* resources and skills and its *internal* competencies and shortcomings. We believe that this approach has led to the myth that a company is a complete organisation able to operate on the basis of its own abilities and resources.

The IMP approach

The IMP approach is built on the fact that no company has sufficient resources to satisfy the requirements of any customer and therefore is dependent on the skills, resources and actions and intentions of suppliers, distributors, customers and even competitors to satisfy those requirements. Similarly, no company can exploit its own resources except in conjunction with those of others. Very frequently, even the *development* of those resources takes place in a relationship with others:

- *Strategy involves using a company's own resources and those with which it interacts and with which it is interdependent.* Companies work with, through, against and in spite of others to combine and take advantage of their own resources and those of their counterparts.
- *A large part of what a company sells is made up of what it buys.* The value of a company's purchases often accounts for 60–80% of its cost of goods sold. More importantly, a large proportion of the value of a supplier's offering is provided by the skills and resources of its suppliers, which are accessed through its relationships.
- *Companies are becoming less complete.* Each generation of new offerings is likely to involve more and different technologies. The development of each generation of new technologies is likely to cost more than previous ones. Because of this, companies are likely to become more dependent on the skills and resources of other companies to supplement their own narrower concentration on fewer skills.

- *Core competencies are based in the network.* A core competency for a company results from "the *creative bundling* of multiple technologies and customer knowledge and intuition, and managing them as a harmonious whole" (Prahalad 1993). But more and more, a company must bundle together the technologies of a company's suppliers, its customers and others, as well as its own. This process of bundling is *interactive* as each of the companies involved will have its own view of its technologies and those of others and of the network position it wishes to achieve through its interaction. Thus, a company's ability to bundle will depend on its overall network position and its skills in managing relationships to activate and combine technologies and to assess the problems and requirements of both customers and suppliers.
- *Technologies are developed interactively.* In one study, companies estimated that on average about 50% of all their development spending was on projects in which external counterparts played a significant role, although there was a wide variation between "isolated" companies that operate with few development relationships and little idea of what is happening in their customers and suppliers and "broad co-operating" companies that are well integrated into their networks (Håkansson 1989). Business relationships are also a critical part of the process through which technology can be transformed into something with economic potential. Relationships help to put technologies into a context where they can create value (Ford *et al.* 1998).

Conclusion

In this chapter we have outlined some of the ideas of the IMP Group about the nature of business networks and of how companies operate within them. We see business marketing and purchasing taking place through *interaction* between two active parties. Business sales and purchases do not occur in an anonymous market. Suppliers and customers tend to know each other well and to have worked with each other over time *in their relationship*. This relationship is not a matter of choice for either supplier or customer. Their relationship is both the outcome of their past interactions and affects each new interaction as it happens. Business customers and suppliers face a similar task i.e. to manage their portfolio of relationships.

We also emphasise the complexity of the world of business and the limitations on the freedom of companies to act independently. Business companies tend to be dependent on a limited number of counterparts for a large proportion of their purchases and sales. The offerings that are exchanged in a business relationship will very often have been developed within that relationship by the two companies involved. Each relationship between business companies will be affected by what happens in a wider network of relationships in which the two companies are not directly involved.

We can only understand a business sale or purchase within the context of the relationship in which it takes place and we can only understand a business relationship within the network of which it is part.

The outcome of an individual company's strategy will not just depend on its own actions, or even the reactions and re-reactions of a counterpart supplier or customer. It will also depend on the actions of specific competitors, co-developers and others that surround it. This means that the successful management of inter-company relationships depends on understanding the nature and dynamics of the wider networks. It is to this that we turn our attention in Chapter 2.

References

Alderson, W. (1967) "Factors governing the development of marketing channels", in Bruce Mallen (ed.) *The Marketing Channel: A Conceptual Viewpoint*, Chichester: John Wiley.

Ansoff, H.I. (1965) *Corporate Strategy: An Analytical Approach to Business Policy for Growth and Expansion*, New York: McGraw-Hill.

Araujo, L. and Easton, G. (1996) "Strategy, Where is the Pattern?" *Organisation*, 3(3), 361–383.

Ford, D. (2001) *Understanding Business Marketing and Purchasing*, 3rd edition, London: International Thomson.

Ford, D., Gadde, L-E., Håkansson, H., Lundgren, A., Snehota, I., Turnbull, P. and Wilson, D. (1998), *Managing Business Relationships*, Chichester: John Wiley.

Håkansson, H. (1989) *Corporate Technological Behaviour: Cooperation and Networks*, London: Routledge.

Kotler, P. (2002) *Marketing Management*, New York: Prentice Hall.

Mintzberg, H. (1985) "Of strategies, deliberate and emerging", *Strategic Management Journal*, 257–272.

Mintzberg, H. (1987) "Crafting Strategy", *Harvard Business Review*, July–August, 66–75.

Porter, M. (1980) *Competitive Strategy: Techniques for Analysing Industries and Competitors*, New York: Free Press.

Prahalad, C.K. (1993) "The Role of Core Competencies in the Corporation", *Research, Technology, Management*, November–December, 40–47.

Quinn, J.B. (1996) "Strategies for Change", in H. Mintzberg and J.B. Quinn (eds), *The Strategy Process*, 3rd edition, Upper Saddle River, NJ: Prentice Hall.

Rumelt, R.R. (1980) "The Evaluation of Business Strategy", in W.F. Gluek, *Strategic Management and Business Policy*, New York: McGraw-Hill.

THE MANAGER AND THE NETWORK

2

Aims of this Chapter

- To explain the nature and dynamics of business networks.
- To explain some of the changes that managers face in these networks.
- To highlight some of the questions that often concern managers about their operations and to interpret these in network terms.
- To describe some of the paradoxes of business networks that lie behind some of the questions and problems that managers face.
- To point to the opportunities and constraints for a manager caused by these paradoxes.

Introduction: Markets and Networks

The traditional view of the position of a business manager can be illustrated in Figure 2.1. In this view a company operates by taking products and services from a supply market. It then combines these inputs and directs them to its customer markets. It chooses between suppliers that compete with each other to offer it enhanced inputs such as components or services at the lowest price. Similarly, the company competes with its competitors to offer enhanced products and favourable prices to its customer market, probably targeting one or more segments of that market with a dedicated marketing mix.

However, for a realistic view of the world facing the manager, we need to modify this diagram, as shown in Figure 2.2. This takes into account the fact that these customer and supplier markets are not homogeneous. Some customers will be more important than others, both because they buy more or because their requirements are difficult to meet. Similarly, some suppliers will be much more important than others, either because they supply a large volume of the company's purchases or because what they supply is critical for the success of the company's own products. Finally, of course some competitors are larger or more effective than others.

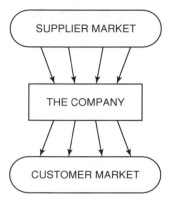

Figure 2.1   A Traditional View of the Company and its Markets.

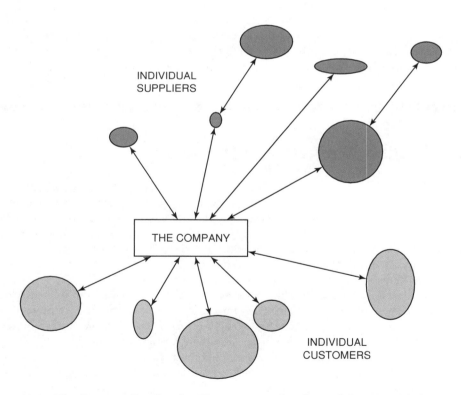

Figure 2.2   The Company Faced with a Heterogeneous Supplier and Customer Markets.

But this diagram *still* doesn't portray the reality of the position facing a manager and we have to modify it again as in Figure 2.3 to show how the relationships in a network are not simply the links in a linear chain centred on a single company and that all relationships are interconnected often in complex ways.

The manager operating in a network such as that illustrated in Figure 2.3 must deal with at least the following complications:

- Not only are a company's customers, suppliers and competitors different in their importance, but they are also likely to operate in quite different ways and have a wide range of relationships with other customers and suppliers.

Therefore, a supplier will face customers with access to very different resources and with different problems, not all of which it is able to solve. The supplier will have to specialise in a limited number of customer problems and ignore others. This can mean that a single customer may buy from a number of apparently similar suppliers, each of which actually solves a quite different problem for it. For example, a customer may buy

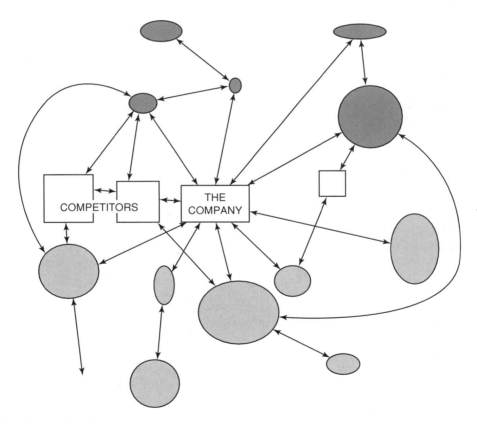

Figure 2.3   The Company in the Network.

electronic components to make up its own products directly from a manufacturer that offers low prices for high volumes. It may also buy the same components along with many others, in very small volumes for its development department, from a distributor that offers this wide range and also very quick delivery, but at a much higher price. The products are the same in both cases, but the problem is different and so is the solution.

- Similarly, a company is likely to face competitors that operate in a number of different ways. So it is dangerous to think of competitors just as members of a neat "industry" with the same type of products or services (Tunisini 1997; Stacey 1998). Because the solutions to a customer's problems are not usually provided by straightforward products or services, customers often choose from the offerings of a broad range of suppliers that operate in a variety of non-traditional ways. For example, a company can solve a data management problem by dealing directly with a hardware producer, a software house, a value-added reseller or by buying individual items at a discount from a "box-shifter" and assembling the solution itself.

    In fact, it is not possible to allocate companies into neat categories such as "manufacturer", "wholesaler" or "retailer". A large proportion of the offerings of many "manufacturers" is in fact purchased from other suppliers. For example, shoe "makers" such as Clarks and Nike buy most or all of the products that they sell from others. Many "wholesalers" are not simply distributors of the products of others, but distinctive value-added assemblers of the product and service offerings of numerous companies, while "retailers" often design and develop their own products which they then have produced by others.

- Despite the process of specialisation in business markets, companies are not subject simply to "five forces" (Porter 1980), but are affected by many and varied forces that arise from close to hand or from diverse technological or geographical locations in the surrounding network and which can affect a business with alarming speed. These diverse forces contribute to the increased dynamism and rate of change in the business world. This means that many analyses of business conditions based on an implicit stability are no longer viable (Porter 1980, 1987; Senge 1990). Volatility and dynamism are not simply abrupt, infrequent adaptive changes that can be dealt with in order to create longer periods of stability (Hedaa 1997). The many influences on a company from different sources and the multiple effects of any action by a single company mean that a narrow analysis of a linear "value chain" or "supply chain" will give at best a partial and most probably an erroneous picture of the world in which a company must operate.

- These forces increasingly limit a manager's *autonomy*. A manager's discretion to act independently and direct his own company is limited by the technological and resource dependencies between companies that are necessary to meet the requirements of final customers. This interdependence makes it difficult for the manager to think of individual actions that are isolated from the actions of others and from those that have occurred in the past and which form the basis of those in the future. The world that managers operate in consists of a complex pattern of relationships, whether close or distant and whether between customer and supplier or between development partners or competitors. These relationships are themselves inter-related into a network that forms the arena for managerial action and the basis for company activity (Easton and Håkansson 1996).

- Finally, the multiplicity of influences and the dynamism of the surrounding world mean that common views of strategy in the entrepreneurial firm are unrealistic. Strategy is less of an ordered process of analysing the environment, building and implementing strategy *against* the world, or to achieve *control* over some part of it (Hamel and Prahalad 1994). Strategy for the firm is a process of building, managing and exploiting relationships *with* others. Without relationships, business would be impossible and a company would be isolated in the network. Such a "lonely company" would be unable to exploit its own skills and resources to solve problems for customers and to sell its offerings. It would be unable to supply those offerings because it would not have access to the skills and resources of suppliers on which it depends. It would not have access to the knowledge and wisdom of others and would be unable to cope with the vagaries of the network. Without relationships, a company would be reduced to a collection of unusable equipment and real estate. Strategy is a process of reacting and re-reacting to the actions of other companies in its relationships (Wilkinson and Young 1997; Ford *et al.* 1998). A company is likely to be simultaneously working with, against, or in spite of these others, each of which may be vital to the company's well-being and which are in control of the technologies and resources on which it depends or which threaten it. In the short term, strategy is more likely to be about coping with situations than creating them. In the longer-term, the manager's strategy is likely to be concerned with situation-specific action within some view of overall direction (Goldstein 1994; Stacey 1992).

There have been a large number of empirical studies over the past 25 years that have examined the tangible relationships between companies that are connected together to form complex networks. Examples and useful collections include, Håkansson (1982), Henders (1992), Raesfeld-Meeijer (1997), Axelsson and Easton (1992), Gadde and Håkansson (1993), Halinen (1997), Iacobucci (1996), Laage-Hellman (1997), Wilkinson and Young (1997), Naudé and Turnbull (1998), Ford (2001), Ford *et al.* (2002). These relationships and the networks of which they form part exist as a kind of quasi-organisation. Relationships are the outcome of the changes that are occurring in the business world. It is through these relationships that companies cope with their increasingly widespread technological dependence on others and the need to develop and tailor offerings to more specific requirements. It is within relationships that technologies are not only exploited, but are also developed (Lundgren 1995; Ford and Saren 1996). What happens in these relationships influences what happens inside the companies involved and provides the means for and restrictions on the pattern of their external interactions. Inter-company networks are not simply the construction of researchers. They have a real existence as organised patterns of interaction, just like many other social organisations. Inter-company relationships and networks are useful explanatory tools for researchers. More importantly, interaction within relationships forms the basis for companies to buy and sell products and services, to learn, to invest and to exploit and acquire technology.

What is a Network?

In its most abstract, form a network is a structure where a number of nodes are related to each other by specific threads. A business market can be seen as part of a network where the nodes are business units, such as producers, customers, service companies and suppliers of finance, knowledge and influence. The threads are the relationships between the companies. Both the threads and the nodes have their own particular content in a business network. Both the threads and nodes are heavy with tangible and intangible resources: physical; financial and intellectual, in many different forms (Håkansson 1997). The business units or nodes consist of physical, technical and human resources bound together in a variety of different ways. Similarly, each relationship is a "quasi-organisation" that arises from the investment of physical and human resources by both companies. The network is not a world of individual and isolated transactions. It is the result of complex interactions within and between companies in relationships over time.

If we examine a simple situation of three companies, each of which interacts with each other, whether to buy or sell or co-operate in product or service development, then the way that each interacts with either of the other two parties will depend on what has happened between them in the past, on what each has learned in previous interactions with the third company, and also on what happens between the other two parties. It will also depend on what happens in the relationships between each of the companies and others outside the trio and finally, on what happens elsewhere in the network of relationships between other companies with which they are not directly involved. This network of relationships has a current effect on those companies and individuals within it, which in turn is the result of what has happened in the past and the expectations of those involved for the future.

This means that no single interaction can be understood without reference to the relationship of which it is a part and to what has contributed to that relationship. Similarly, no single relationship can be understood without reference to the network itself. Because each company is embedded in a network of relationships, it gains benefits and incurs costs from that network. Both the costs and the benefits are the result of the investments and actions of the company and of other parties.

An example of some of the things that can happen in a network is described in Box 2.1.

Box 2.1   An Example of a Network

Tape drives are used by many companies to make back-up copies of their data, to cope with loss or corruption of files. Tape drives store vast amounts of information on magnetic media. They are usually assembled into large systems called tape libraries.

Many companies produce equipment and media, but they only work together as long as each producer conforms to the same *format*, so compatibility is important for customers.

Technology development

Technology develops in two ways in this area:

- Format extensions are developments *within* a format, such as "longer play" and faster drives.
- Discontinuous introductions are completely new formats, such as DVD. New formats are only likely to succeed if they offer compelling benefits over established formats and if they are widely adopted. "Format wars" often break out in the early life of these developments as competing companies vie with each other to establish the "new standard".

Customer and supplier problems

IT managers face the problem of storing, managing and protecting growing amounts of data and therefore are always looking for faster and higher capacity storage systems. However, they also need cost-effective solutions, and discontinuous changes in suppliers' formats create problems and uncertainties for them. They either have to ignore the development and risk obsolescence and higher costs later, or buy partially into the new format and manage the incompatibility between new and old systems, or upgrade everything to the new format.

Format compatibility also causes problems for suppliers. Each generation of higher performance but compatible products is harder and more costly to achieve, until eventually the format cannot be sensibly extended any further.

Network structure

There are four main groups of companies in the network, in addition to end-users and these are illustrated in Figure 2.4. Three of the groups supply an offering based on equipment. The fourth is made up of suppliers of value-added services, who draw on a number of equipment producers. The three groups of equipment suppliers are as follows:

- Tape drive producers: tape drives conform to any one of ten formats. Some formats are supported by several drive manufacturers and some by only one. Tape drives are sometimes sold as stand-alone devices and sometimes sold integrated into a library. Tape drive producers have at least four types of customer relationships:
  - with library suppliers for integration into their libraries
  - with system suppliers who may build a single tape drive into a computer system
  - with end-users who might add a drive to their existing computer system or library
  - with value-added resellers that supply data storage along with other equipment as part of an integrated solution.

Tape drive producers also have relationships with suppliers of components and software for their drives:

- Library producers: these use standard tape drives as a sub-assembly. Library producers differentiate themselves on the basis of the speed, reliability, functionality and cost of their robotics and total system. Library producers will have customer relationships with end-users and intermediaries. They may recommend a particular

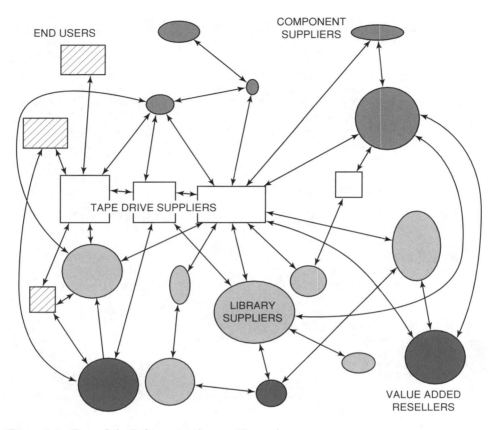

Figure 2.4   Part of the Information Storage Network.

drive, but will have relationships with several tape drive suppliers because they have to incorporate each customer's choice of drive.

- Tape drive component producers: these consist of suppliers of components that are unique to tape drives and suppliers of standard electronic and mechanical components that are also used by producers of many other types of equipment.

Company actions

Any supplier thinking of introducing a new format faces a choice:

- If the supplier co-operates with competitors and jointly introduces a new "standard", the standard will be adopted more quickly. But then each will have to fight for a share of sales.
- If they go it alone, they will "own" the new format, but run the risk that it will never become a "standard".

It is common for one group of companies to co-operate to extend an existing format, while another group co-operates to establish a "new standard" with which to attack the existing format. Different parts of the same large company may be in each camp!

Multiple relationships

The cost of developing a new component, drive or library is high and can only be justified by high volume sales. This means that companies must restrict the number of technologies in which they invest and try to maximise the exploitation of those technologies. This leads companies to sell to and buy from their competitors as well as more conventional customers and suppliers.

These different activities directly affect the relationships of each company. For example:

- HP could buy magnetic recording heads from a specialist head manufacturer or they could buy from their tape drive competitors: IBM, Seagate, SONY or STK.
- The IBM library division needs to offer a flexible range of tape drives, but it doesn't make all of the formats that their library customers might ask for. IBM has no choice but to purchase tape drives from other companies.
- Quantum wants to sell their drives and libraries to HP and IBM systems. Both HP and IBM might prefer that their customers buy their own drives and libraries, but they need to satisfy their customer requirements as fully as possible, so they have to buy drives and libraries from Quantum to meet particular customer requirements.
- Quantum had a proprietary format that dominated high-performance equipment sales, but HP, IBM and Seagate worked together to develop a higher performance format. This "open" approach accelerated the transition of customers from the old format because they believed that they were being offered a "new standard".
- This also meant that IBM, Seagate and HP were then competing with each other with the same drives, but all three companies believed this would be better than owning a niche that they had developed alone. If each had developed their own proprietary formats, customers would have had to choose between them. Faced with this uncertainty, they may have stayed with Quantum.

This simultaneous co-operation and competition between companies in a network is often referred to as "co-option".

Success in the network

Companies must cope with the complexities of the network, the incompleteness of their own technologies and the problems and abilities of those around them. This leads them to draw up a number of informal "rules" of behaviour. We can summarise some of these rules as follows:

- *Stay out of jail!* There are certain types of co-operation that are illegal, such as price and market fixing, monopolies, anti-trust, etc. A company needs to be clear about what is legal or acceptable in their relationships.
- *Professional self-interest is expected.* Each company needs to be aware that they are simultaneously co-operating in such things as establishing a new format and

fighting hard to achieve market share within that format. Claiming otherwise will be seen as naïve.

- *Relationship management skills.* Co-optitive relationships are easily broken due to the underlying tension of competition and differences in company culture. All the normal issues in relationship management are present, but often in an extreme form.
- *"Chinese walls".* These are needed to segregate information when co-operating with a competitor to avoid the risk that information will be used in other ways than for the subject of the co-operation. Formal non-disclosure agreements or dedicated teams in each company are often needed to ensure that information is kept on a "need to know basis".
- *Discipline and consistency of communication.* All levels of communication need to support the relationship and encourage mutual respect. For example, if R&D teams from the two companies are working together well, but the website of Company A is disparaging about Company B, then the relationship is likely to suffer.
- *Relationships are based on technology and position in the network.* Ultimately, companies only co-operate when they need to. Unnecessary companies just add complexity and slow everything up in multi-company co-operation. A company's technology and its relationships with others may attract or even force other companies to work with you.
- *Be a good company to work with.* Technology-intensive networks change rapidly and profits are likely only to be made early in the life of technology or format, before it becomes commoditised. A company with a reputation for openness and trust will attract ideas and proposals for working together from other companies. But at the same time it is important to be sure that the expectations of counterparts are realistic.

Source: This box was developed by Neville Pawsey, Blue Windmill Consultants.

Managerial Questions about Operating in Networks

Many of the questions that managers ask us and many of the issues in Box 2.1 relate to the networks that surround companies. Three of the most common questions asked can be outlined as follows:

- *How can we make sense of where we are in the complex and ever-changing world in which we operate?* What can we expect in our current situation? What have we got to offer to others and what should we seek from them?
- *How can we cope with the limitations of our knowledge and understanding of the surrounding world?* How can we capitalise on the opportunities that surround us? How can we gain the most from other companies and contribute to them most effectively? How can we work within the restrictions that the company faces when it tries to change its position? When and how can we act independently and how can we "strategise"?

- *How can we manage our interactions with other companies effectively?* When and how should we vary the company's interactions with others? How can the company deal with the *variety* of different opportunities and problems that it confronts? How are the company's dealings with each customer or supplier affected by its relationships with other companies and by what happens between these companies and others with which we have no contact? What about the effects on the company of changes and innovations that originate outside its normal operations?

We will now address these three questions in turn. In doing so we will explore the three network paradoxes, illustrated in Figure 2.5.

> *THE FIRST NETWORK PARADOX:*
> THE NETWORK SIMULTANEOUSLY ENABLES AND RESTRICTS A COMPANY
>
> *THE SECOND NETWORK PARADOX:*
> RELATIONSHIPS ARE DEVELOPED AND DEFINED BY COMPANIES, BUT COMPANIES ARE ALSO DEVELOPED AND DEFINED BY RELATIONSHIPS
>
> *THE THIRD NETWORK PARADOX:*
> COMPANIES TRY TO CONTROL THE NETWORK, BUT CONTROL IS DESTRUCTIVE

Figure 2.5   The Three Network Paradoxes.

How Can we Make Sense of Where we Are?

This question concerns the company's network position or how as a node it relates to other nodes through the relationships or threads between them. The question centres on what a company's important business relationships really mean for it. Answering it requires an understanding of both the nodes and the threads between them.

We can start by examining the "heaviness" of a network. Heaviness emphasises the intensity of the economic, technical and social dimensions of the network surrounding a company. It is a world that is much more full than empty and companies do not operate in isolation from others, nor in response to some generalised environment as "one against all". Instead, as we saw in the network example above, the actions of each company and the things that happen to them can only be fully understood within this structure of individually significant nodes and threads. The heaviness of the nodes and threads results from investments of resources that have been made over time through previous interactions. The history of a network is the process through which these resources have been designed, developed, allocated and combined in order to create a particular economic logic that has helped some of the participating companies to make a profit or at least to survive.

It is important to emphasise both the extent and variation of the resources in a network. These resources are based on investments of time and money to build, adapt, develop, understand, relate and combine different human and physical resources. These resources exist within companies and also to a large extent in the relationships between them (Dubois 1998). The resources influence the way that the companies operate both internally and in relation to each other. Relationships give each of the companies access to the resources of the other. No single company or relationship has been developed or operates independently of others. All are connected and are dependent on the resources of others, but each is unique. The network will not have been "designed" by any one of the participants, although some may believe that they have done so. Nor is the network controlled by any one person, although some may try to act as if they do control it!

All the participants will have some influence on the evolution of the network. All their decisions, all their actions and all the changes that take place are affected by the structure of the network and it influences both what can be done and the way in which it can be done (Anderson *et al.* 1995).

The first network paradox

The importance of the resources invested in the nodes and threads of a network lead us to the first network paradox:

> A company's relationships are the basis of its operations, growth and development and are at the heart of its survival. But these relationships may also tie it into its current ways of operating and restrict its ability to change. Thus the paradox facing managers is that a network is both the source of freedom for a company and the cage that imprisons it.

This paradox is illustrated in the example in Box 2.1. Each of the producers is dependent for future developments on the companies with which it works, in such things as developing new formats. But at the same time, each producer is constrained by the directions in which those companies wish to go and indeed whether they wish to make any changes at all to current formats or ways of working. A further illustration is provided by the network of companies and relationships involved in the Internet. Among these are software and hardware suppliers, fee-based Internet service providers, suppliers of access to the Internet, such as fixed-line telecomms companies, e-commerce traders, such as Amazon.com etc. and end-users of these services. Each has a network position, consisting of its relationships with others and its own resources and those that exist within and through its relationships. These resources – technical, economic and social – are the core of each company's strength and the basis for its growth and development in a rapidly growing and evolving market. For example, relationships between hardware and software suppliers and service providers enable them to offer innovative product and service features to end-users. But at the same time, each of these network positions represents an investment in current ways of working, current relationships and current ways of thinking. Thus they restrict the company's ability to develop new ways of operating or to react to new entrants with innovative ways of working that are not constrained by already established positions.

The existing structure of a network means that any change in a network involves costs, both for those involved in the change and perhaps for others elsewhere in the network. Some of these costs will be immediately apparent, such as those of hiring extra staff or establishing a local office to provide service for an important customer or changing the format of equipment. However, many costs are not readily observable, such as the unanticipated costs for a customer or supplier of modifying a product after delivery, or the effects of a change in a large company's inventory policy on the component manufacturers of a main supplier. The problem of accurately establishing costs makes it difficult for a company to assess the profits or value of a particular relationship.

Changing a company's network position always involves changes in its relationships, the companies with which it interacts and in itself. So a company seeking change will always be dependent on others to achieve that change, whether it is planning to introduce a new service, to alter logistical patterns or to develop a new product. A change that is seen to be positive by others might gain their support, so a company can mobilise part of the network in the direction it wishes, if that direction is in line with the aims of at least some other partners. The variety in the structure of a network means that there are always opportunities to enhance some part of its operations. Seizing these opportunities will be made easier if they benefit other companies as well, but made harder by the constraints of the existing structure.

Managerial implications of the first network paradox

There are several important consequences of this first paradox for any decision-maker within a company. These can be outlined as follows:

- *A company must analyse its position with respect to specific counterparts.* The paradox reinforces the need for a manager, when considering any change or development, to analyse his company's position in terms of its own resources, those of specific counterparts, including suppliers, customers and others, and the relationships that exist between them. This view of position is a more realistic basis for understanding constraints and opportunities than one based on the company's own set of products, its general market and its overall level of competition.
- *Change can only be achieved through the network.* The paradox indicates that every decision-maker is faced with myriad opportunities to act and is, at least *notionally* free to do whatever he wants, but his freedom to act and the effects of his actions will be constrained by the existing structure of the network. Change by companies and change within companies occur through changes to the structure of the network. The only way that a company can improve its position and achieve change is through the network. This requires persistence in interacting with others to convince them of the benefits of that change.
- *Companies in networks must manage the expectations of others.* Managing expectations is a particular problem for a company seeking change. Unless those expectations are or can be made realistic, then change will be difficult to achieve. The situation is made more complicated by the presence of many individuals with different information, needs and experience. A company seeking change in a network must both give others a picture of the intended direction of a change and find ways to relate changes in companies and relationships to the motivations and resources of others.

- *Change must often be achieved with existing counterparts.* Change in a network is initially dependent on the existing structure and existing resources of the network. This makes it difficult for a company to achieve change by changing its counterparts. Changing counterparts often takes a long time and involves considerable investment. The company must first find a suitable counterpart. Even if it can do this, the knowledge and understanding that exist in previous relationships will not be present. Therefore, both must be prepared to make the necessary investments, incur the costs and recognise and value the potential benefits of the new relationship and also accept its effects on each company's existing relationships. Because of this, managers in business networks have to accept that change must often be accomplished within *existing* relationships, where some of these investments have already been made and where the costs and benefits are more apparent. This is often the case with the development of new products or services. The key questions for both marketing and purchasing in business networks are thus more often how to interact more effectively with existing counterparts than how to choose new ones (Wynstra 1997).
- *A company's total set of relationships can only be changed slowly.* A major effect of the first paradox is that companies are likely to, and indeed will have to, change their set of relationships slowly over time, while continuing to work with existing ones, in the context of the evolution of the network. The paradox also emphasises that achieving change involves careful choice as well as the investment of resources and awareness of the differences in knowledge and understanding between new and existing relationships.
- *Technological change takes place between companies.* The first paradox should also affect the manager's view of the nature of technological change and its effect on the world around him. As we saw in the example above, much of technological development takes place *between* two or more companies and so technical knowledge is embedded both within companies *and* their relationships. Change and innovation do not occur because of a single new technology, but because of the development, synthesis and application of a "bundle" of different technologies, both new and existing across the network. The network provides this bundle (Ford and Saren 1996), but the existing structure of the network can act as a brake on innovation because of its investment in existing ways of working and the requirement for the innovator to enlist the co-operation of those with which it does not currently have a relationship (Håkansson 1989, 1994).

How Can we Cope with the Limitations of our Knowledge and Understanding of the Surrounding World?

This second managerial question builds on the first. It concerns how a company can use its existing relationships for its advantage, given the restrictions that they impose and how and when it can use new ones to change its position in the network, despite its limited understanding of the network. This is the process of bringing order to the value, costs and investments involved in making relationship choices. Insight into the question can be provided by examining the nature of the interface between the nodes and the threads in a business network. In other words, what are the interconnections between a company and its relationships?

There are two ways of looking at these interconnections. The obvious starting point would be that a company *creates* its own relationships. But an alternative view is that a company is the *outcome* of its relationships and that these define its characteristics and operations, so that it is rather like a cross-roads between relationships. Both views are equally valid and relevant to a manager.

The second network paradox

Companies operating in business networks have to live with both models of the link between a company and its relationships. This leads us to the second network paradox:

> A company's relationships are the outcomes of its own decisions and actions. But the paradox is that the company is itself the outcome of those relationships and of what has happened in them.
>
> Thus it is possible to analyse a company's position in a network from the premise that the company determines its relationships, or that it is determined by them. Both situations exist simultaneously and both premises are equally valid.

The example in Box 2.1 illustrates this paradox. Each of the producers may be seen to have established relationships with suppliers, customers and competitors, as part of its strategy. But analysis of the network also shows that the current position of those companies is the *outcome of their relationships* and the offerings that have been developed, marketed and purchased within them. Another interesting example of this paradox is provided by Ericsson, the Swedish telecomms company and Telia, the largest Swedish tele-operator. The two companies have had a close relationship for 100 years. They developed their first automatic exchanges together in the 1920s and it was in close co-operation with Telia that Ericsson developed the AXE-exchange that has had a major effect on its international success. Later, mobile phones were developed within this relationship. The relationship has had a profound effect on the evolution of both companies and on their current characteristics.

However, if we look at the relationship from a different perspective, then it is clear that each company has sought to operate the relationship in a way that suits each of them and each is mindful of their other relationships. For example, when designing a new release of the GSM system for mobile phones, Ericsson has to take into account a number of major users, of which Telia is only one. Ericsson also has to make the design suitable for users of other systems with which it has a relationship. Similarly, Telia has to make sure that the release is compatible with new releases from other important suppliers with which they have relationships, such as Nokia, so that all its customers can have the same service features, irrespective of the equipment they are using. In this way both companies have sought to develop the relationship in ways that suit themselves, their other relationships and their overall strategies.

Managerial implications of the second network paradox

The second network paradox has implications for both the overall management of business companies and for individual managers themselves. We will examine its implications for overall direction first:

- *Companies are conditioned by their relationships.* Relationships can provide access for each company to at least some of the knowledge of its counterparts and enable them to develop and exploit the resources of both companies. A network of relationships develops a commonality of knowledge and understanding between the parties about each other and about the substance of their relationships and the ways that they can and should deal with each other. In this way, companies become conditioned by their relationships (Håkansson and Johanson 1993). The knowledge, understanding, norms and values that the companies have acquired are a source of strength, efficiency and comfort for them, but they can also be an impediment to change. Thus a customer in the network example above may have a long-term relationship with a library supplier. This relationship provides security and efficiency but it may restrict that customer's willingness to consider a new format offered by a supplier with which it has no relationship.
- *Companies need to seek commonality in their relationships.* The costs and time involved in building relationships and in adjusting to different ways of behaving mean that it may be sensible for a company to develop those new relationships where the need for new knowledge is minimised, or where there would be some commonality with its existing relationships. This commonality is likely to occur if the new companies already have relationships with others that are similar to those of the first company.
- *Standardisation.* A company cannot afford to make all of the adaptations needed to satisfy the requirements of each of its relationship counterparts, nor can it manage all its relationships individually. So it will need to reduce its costs and enhance its benefits by seeking to standardise its relationships either by content, level of commitment or the requirements of either side. The example above provides a good example of the importance of standardisation.
- *Major choices concern relationship investment and adaptation.* The development of a relationship involves both of the companies in investment in their activities and resources and these must also be adapted to and linked with those of the counterpart over time (Håkansson and Snehota 1995). The substantive choices for a company centre on these processes of adaptation and investment. These choices need to be distinguished from the management of the company's sales force and in deciding on whom it should call or try to sell to (Turnbull and Zolkiewski 1997). Much of a sales force's time is likely to be spent with existing clients or with those with which the company already has a relationship, even if they are not currently buying. With new contacts, the sales force is engaged in developing bonds between themselves and individuals in the counterpart company and in information gathering. Similarly, questions of investment and adaptation in supply relationships are more significant than the detailed considerations of purchasing practice, such as whether to allocate junior or senior staff to purchases from different suppliers.

- *Strategy is inter-active.* A common view of business strategy is expressed in terms of a self-generated plan by which a company integrates its goals and actions into a cohesive whole. Strategy is seen as the way in which the company marshals its own resources in the light of its interpretation of the current and potential environment. But the second network paradox highlights the fact that a company's characteristics and its resources are dependent on its interactions and relationships. Similarly, its development and the outcomes of its strategy and its whole future are dependent on what happens in those relationships (Håkansson and Lundgren 1997).
- *Resource dependence.* No company has sufficient resources itself to satisfy the requirements of any customer and therefore it is dependent on the skills, technologies, resources, actions and intentions of suppliers, distributors, customers and sometimes even competitors to satisfy any new requirements. Similarly, no company can exploit its own resources in innovative ways except in conjunction with those of others. Very frequently, even the development of those resources is dependent on other companies.

The second paradox that a company both determines and is determined by its relationships also has implications for the process of relationship development, as follows:

- *Which party has most effect on relationship development?* On the one hand, it is possible that the company that is least committed to a relationship will control it at least negatively, by restricting its development. Conversely, the positive development of a relationship is likely to be driven by the party that is most committed to it. Clearly, a relationship is built on mutuality and its development is never determined unilaterally, even in those situations where one party appears overwhelmingly powerful or committed. However, despite the idea of mutuality, a relationship does not develop without effort and it is certainly important that someone believes in it and is prepared to work for it (Huemer 1998).
- *Nodes and threads are interdependent.* A network is composed of companies or nodes and the interactions, relationships or threads between them. The close connection between a node and a thread means that all actions in the two are interdependent. Everything that is done within a node can affect the thread and vice versa. The second network paradox emphasises that we can see a network as a collection of companies that define and develop the interactions between them. We can make equal sense by saying that a network is a collection of relationships and that these define the nodes between them. For a full picture the manager needs to take both views. If a manager just looks at a network of *companies*, then he will undoubtedly get a very restricted picture of activities and resources and of the reality he faces. If he looks at a network of *relationships*, then he will get a quite different picture that will highlight the fact that many of his problems may not be in his own company or his counterparts, but in the relationships between them.

Finally, the second network paradox has implications for individual managers themselves. The co-determination of nodes and threads in a network means that the more important a company's relationships are, then the more important the company will be. The development of each is critical to the development of the other. In turn, the more important the threads are, then the more important the actors who are involved in interaction in those threads will be. Threads are between nodes, relationships are between companies, but the interactions within those relationships are between individuals and are based on their self-knowledge and knowledge of each other. The more important a company's relationships are, the more important it is for each party to manage all of its interactions carefully and for each actor to interact self-consciously.

How can we Manage our Interactions with Other Companies Effectively?

The question of how a company should manage and vary its interactions with other companies brings to the forefront the importance of the place of a single relationship within a wider network.

Some relationships are easy to recognise as important to a company in their own right, perhaps because they are with a high-volume customer or a critical supplier. Others will be less important to the company individually, but they may be part of a group of similar relationships which together are significant. So it may be possible for the company to minimise its costs and maximise its effectiveness by developing a standardised way of dealing with each company in this group.

But whether individually important or not, each relationship cannot be considered in isolation. Not only is each one affected by all the other relationships of the two companies, but each relationship is a thread that is connected through the nodes or companies to other threads in the network. What happens in each relationship is affected by these interconnections to the rest of the network. Conversely, what happens in the relationship can be communicated through these interconnections and can have effects widely in the network. The total network structure is determined by how each thread is related to the others and the economic effects of any one relationship on the companies involved are affected by its interconnections with other relationships in the network. These interconnections can have a variety of effects:

- Interconnections can lead to the development of common *pictures* of the network, or of "what everyone knows". These can become norms or cultural patterns within a network and can strongly influence the reactions of companies to the actions or entry of others from outside their immediate experience. This has occurred in the case of strongly established formats in the network example above. In this way, the interconnections can be an impediment to change and innovation.
- The interconnections with the other relationships of a counterpart can mean that a manager in one node may have difficulty in anticipating the reactions of others to any action he may initiate.
- Interconnections can transmit knowledge and understanding across the network. In this way they can act as a vehicle of change, through which new ideas and ways of working can be transferred.

The third network paradox

Each company in a network will try, as far as it is able, to build and manage the threads between itself and its counterparts, in the direction that it wants them to go (Child and Faulkner 1998; Gulati 1998). It will also try to influence the threads between these counterparts and others in a direction that also suits its own requirements. In doing this it is seeking to determine its own position in the network by influencing the knowledge and understanding within other nodes and threads and also by influencing the pattern of co-evolution between them.

However, the more successful that the company is in imposing its thinking onto the network, the more that it is likely to restrict the initiative and change that could be generated by others in the network. This leads us to the third network paradox:

> Companies try to manage their relationships and control the network that surrounds them to achieve their own aims. This ambition is one of the key forces in developing networks. But the paradox is that the more that a company achieves this ambition of control, the less effective and innovative will be the network.

IBM provides an excellent illustration of this paradox. For a long time it tried to control its network, especially on the customer side. Through this control, IBM was able to develop a very efficient geographically based organisation for production and sales. The company also had very strict rules for those software companies who had the rights to sell IBM computers. IBM had no plans to change this organisation, until it became apparent that it had become static and that the networks of other companies had been developing much faster. IBM lost out because a controlled network cannot develop faster than the company that controls it.

Any such a company has little incentive to develop as long as it has control. The developments between advanced customers and other producers of hardware and software forced IBM to change its own internal organisation to become much flatter and much more diversified. In order to cope with the variety in the surrounding network, the organisation has had to become much more messy, with fewer strict rules and more freedom for individuals to take initiatives. Similarly, other companies with strong network control, such as Marks and Spencer in clothing or a number of Japanese companies in consumer electronics or car production have found that "their" network has become ossified and lacking in initiative. Marks and Spencer have sought to remedy this by substituting relationships with independent designers and new, more independent suppliers for their own design and previous highly controlled suppliers.

Managerial implications of the third network paradox

The third network paradox has strong implications for the effective management of a company's interactions, for the development of a company's strategy and for the ways in which a manager can understand the reality of networks:

- *There are dangers in a self-centred view of the network.* A single network will look very different from the perspective of different companies, each with their different motivations, resources and understandings. A company that sees the network in its own terms and only as a way of solving its own problems will fail to understand both the motivations and problems of others, the dynamics of the network and the interface between the well-being of others and itself. This approach will hamper the company's interactions with those around it.

Such a self-centred view of the network can often be seen in the approach that many companies take to their market research. This approach involves questions along the lines of, "What do you think of *my* offering and how does it compare to the offerings of those companies that *I* define as my competitors?" This implies that the company's offering and its position are of central importance to others. In fact, a customer will only consider the company when it has a particular problem and then only in terms of how effective its offering might be as a solution to that problem, not in terms of the company's idea of its own "quality". Similarly, it will see alternatives in terms of those problems and this may include radically different types of offering rather than those that the company recognises because they compete with it on similar terms.

- *There are dangers for a company in network control.* The third network paradox has strong implications for the conventional view of business strategy. All companies seek to manage their relationships for their own ends but, there is a danger in trying to achieve control over the network. If a company were ever to achieve such overall control, then the only source of wisdom and innovation in the network would be the company itself. Instead, each company must seek to manage *within* the network to gain advantage from the actions of others in seeking their own benefits and profiting from their initiatives. This requires the company to accept that conflict is both inevitable in a network and is a source of change.
- *There is no single strategic approach to managing in a network.* Managing in networks is not a linear process of achieving and maintaining control. Instead, strategy is about developing an interactive approach in *each* episode, relationship, network situation and strategic move. This approach is in line with Laurids Hedaa's (1997) comment that, "Everyone in a network is not the architect of his own fortune, but of each others."

Conclusion: the Manager and the Network

This chapter has emphasised that the complex networks in which business companies operate can dramatically affect the nature of their activities. In particular, managers must deal with a relatively small number of individually significant counterparts: major customers, critical suppliers and co-developers. As well as this, they must also find ways to deal with individually less significant, but collectively important counterparts. Because companies have to concentrate on a relatively narrow range of skills and technologies, they can address the problems of only a subset of the customers that buy products or services similar to theirs. Additionally, the need to rely on the technologies of suppliers means that they have to form high-involvement relationships with a subset of the supplier market. Despite the relative concentration of their customer and supplier relationships, they face competition from companies operating in a wide variety of styles throughout the network.

Business companies are constrained by the network that surrounds them. The variety of pressures on them from other companies, the dynamics of the network and the need to work through other companies in order to achieve their aims all mean that the company's scope for individual strategy making and implementation is constrained. These constraints exist despite the fact that a company's relationships are the basis for its growth and development. Companies also face the problem that although they try to manage their relationships and control the network that surrounds them, they face the paradox that the more that they achieve their ambition of control, the less effective and innovative will be the network and ultimately the less successful they will be.

The major conclusion of this chapter and at this point in the book is that the complexity of networks means that the company's interactions with others will always vary in different situations and over time. There are no standard solutions to network management. "Relationships require different mixes of co-operation and competition to be effective depending on the market(s) in which they operate, the pattern of their past interactions and/or the nature and goals of the firms participating in them" (Wilkinson and Young 1997, p. 90). But the chapter has also shown the value and importance for managers of thinking through what lies behind the things that they find themselves doing, behind the actions of others and the dynamics of the network itself.

Network variety means that the task of the manager is to be continuously clarifying and developing the way his company is embedded in the network that surrounds it. Network variety requires ever-new conceptualisations of situations, threads and nodes, to formulate new questions and not to look for optimal solutions. Further, the simultaneous opportunity and constraints of a company's network position and the interaction between the characteristics of nodes and threads mean that the management task is also to clarify how the network functions from the perspective of others. Network complexity means that each company is dependent on the skills and resources of those around it and so the task of the manager includes encouraging and helping others to continuously clarify their own understanding of the network.

Finally, the task facing the manager in a business network is to manage each of the relationships in which his company is embedded. It is to this task that we now turn in Chapter 3.

References

Anderson, J., Håkansson, H. and Johanson, J. (1995) "Dyadic Business Relationships within a Business Network Context", *Journal of Marketing*, 58 (October), 1–15.

Axelsson, B. and Easton, G. (1992) *Industrial Networks: A New View of Reality*, London: Routledge.

Child, J. and Faulkner, D. (1998) *Strategies of Cooperation: Managing Alliances, Networks and Joint Ventures*, Oxford: Oxford University Press.

Dubois, A. (1998) *Organising Industrial Activities Across Firm Boundaries*, London: Routledge.

Easton, G. and Håkansson, H. (1996) "Markets as Networks: Editorial Introduction", *International Journal of Research in Marketing*, 13(5), 407–413.

Ford, D. (ed.) (2001) *Understanding Business Marketing and Purchasing*, London: International Thomson.

Ford, D., Berthon, P., Brown, S., Gadde, L-E., Håkansson, H., Naudé, P., Ritter, T. and Snehota, I. (2002) *The Business Marketing Course*, Chichester: John Wiley.

Ford, D., Gadde, L-E., Håkansson, H., Lundgren, A., Snehota, I., Turnbull, P. and Wilson, D. (1998) *Managing Business Relationships*. Chichester: John Wiley.

Ford, D. and Saren, M. (1996) *Technology Strategy for Business*, London: International Thompson.

Gadde, L-E. and Håkansson, H. (1993) *Professional Purchasing*, London: Routledge (also published in Swedish).

Goldstein, J. (1994) *The Unshackled Organisation: Facing the Challenge of Unpredictability through Spontaneous Reorganisation*, Portland, OR: Productivity Press.

Gulati, R. (1998) "Alliances and Networks", *Strategic Management Journal*, 19, 293–317.

Håkansson, H. (ed.) (1982) *International Marketing and Purchasing of Industrial Goods*, New York: John Wiley.

Håkansson, H. (1989) *Corporate Technological Behaviour: Cooperation and Networks*, London: Routledge.

Håkansson, H. (1994) "Networks as a Mechanism to Develop Resources", in Beije *et al.* (eds) *Networking in Dutch Industries*, Amsterdam: Garant Uitgivers.

Håkansson, H. (1997) "Organization Networks", in A. Sorge and M. Warner (eds) *The IEBM Handbook of Organizational Behaviour*, London: International Thompson Business Press.

Håkansson, H. and Johanson, J. (1993) "Network as a Governance Structure", in G. Grabher, *The Embedded Firm: The Socio-Economics of Industrial Networks*, London: Routledge.

Håkansson, H. and Lundgren, A. (1997) "Paths in Time and Space – Path Dependence in Industrial Networks", in L. Magnusson and J. Ottosson (eds) *Evolutionary Economics and Path Dependence*, Cheltenham: Edward Elgar.

Håkansson, H. and Snehota, I. (1995) *Developing Relationships in Business Networks*, London: Routledge.

Halinen, A. (1997) *Relationship Marketing in Professional Services*, London: Routledge.

Hamel, G. and Prahalad, C.K. (1994) *Competing for the Future*, Boston: Harvard Business School Press.

Harrison, D. (1998) "Strategic Responses to Predicted Events: The Case of the Banning of CFCs", unpublished doctoral dissertation, University of Lancaster.

Hedaa, Laurids (1997) *Sat ud af spillet. Case: Tele Danmark Forlag*, paper published by the Personal Management Institute, Copenhagen: Samfundslitteratur.

Henders, B. (1992) "Positions in Industrial Networks", unpublished PhD dissertation, University of Uppsala, Sweden.

Huemer, L. (1998) *Trust*, Umeå: Borea Bokforlag.

Iacobucci, D. (ed.) (1996) *Networks in Marketing*, Thousand Oaks, CA: Sage.

Laage-Hellman, J. (1997) *Business Networks in Japan: Supplier–Customer Interaction in Product Development*, London: Routledge.

Lundgren, A. (1995) *Technological Innovation and Network Evolution*, London: Routledge.

Naudé, P. and Turnbull, P.W. (eds) (1998) *Network Dynamics in International Marketing*, Oxford: Pergamon Press.

Porter, M.E. (1980) *Competitive Strategy: Techniques for Analysing Industries and Competitors*, New York: Free Press.

Porter, M.E. (1987) "From Competitive Advantage to Corporate Strategy", *Harvard Business Review*, May–June, 43–59.

Raesfeld-Meeijer, A. (1997) "Technological Cooperation in Networks: A Socio-Cognitive Approach", PhD dissertation, University of Twente.

Senge, P.M. (1990) *The Fifth Discipline*, New York: Doubleday Currency.

Stacey, R. (1992) *Managing the Unknowable: The Strategic Boundaries between Order and Chaos*, San Francisco: Jossey-Bass.

Stacey, R. (1998) *Creativity in Organisations: The Importance of Mess*, Complexity Management Centre Working Paper, University of Hertfordshire, Hatfield, UK.

Tunisini, A-L. (1997) "The Dissolution of Channels and Hierarchies", PhD dissertation, Department of Business Studies, University of Uppsala, Sweden.

Turnbull, P. and Zolkiewski, J. (1997) "Profitability in Customer Portfolio Planning", in D. Ford (ed.) *Understanding Business Markets*, 2nd edition, London: Dryden Press, 305–325.

Wilkinson, I.F. and Young, L.C. (1997) "The Space Between: Towards a Typology of Interfirm Relations", *Journal of Business to Business Marketing*, 4(2), 53–97.

Wynstra, F. (1997) "Purchasing and the Role of Suppliers in Product Development", Lic, thesis, Department of Business Studies, University of Uppsala, Sweden.

THE MANAGER AND THE RELATIONSHIP

3

Aims of this Chapter

- To describe the substance of business relationships in terms of actor bonds, activity links and resource ties.
- To examine the three facets of relationships: (1) relationships as a device; (2) relationships as assets; (3) relationships as problems.
- To describe the development of business relationships over time.
- To examine the abilities, uncertainties and problems of companies and how these affect the behaviour of companies in relationships.

Introduction

Much of the argument throughout this book revolves around relationships, to show how important they are and how they affect the task of management. Some of the recent management literature, particularly that on marketing and strategy seems to converge on the notion that relationships matter (Sako 1992; Bleeke and Ernst 1993; Reicheld 1996; Dyer and Singh 1998; Johnson and Lawrence 1998; Johnson 1999; Lorenzoni and Lipparini 1999). Yet it is not easy to grasp what a relationship actually *is*, or to define the analytical concept of the relationship because the term is used so often with widely different meanings. Our starting point on relationships can be characterised in the following two statements:

1 It is not a matter of choice for a company whether or not it should have relationships. All companies have relationships now and all companies have always had them. We would go as far as to claim that a company cannot exist without relationships. But these relationships can vary in content, strength and duration.
2 Relationships are a mixed blessing. A company's relationships with its customers, suppliers and others are an asset to the company but are also a burden for it to carry.

All companies have relationships, but each can fail or succeed depending on how it copes with them.

We will therefore start this chapter by exploring the relationship concept more fully before we proceed with the question of how to manage them.

What is a Relationship?

Our idea of business relationships is not based on how two companies look at each other, or on whether they have positive or negative attitudes to each other. Instead, we are concerned with how they *behave* towards each other. We use the term "relationship" to describe the pattern of interactions and the mutual conditioning of behaviours *over time*, between a company and a customer, a supplier or another organisation. Time is the defining feature of a relationship. Both the past and the future affect current behaviour in a relationship and experiences, expectations and promises underlie the interaction within it. The time dimension of a relationship requires managers to shift their emphasis away from each single, discrete purchase or sale and towards tracking how things unfold in the relationship over time and changing these when appropriate.

There are several good reasons for adopting the behavioural concept of relationships. One is that attitudes are difficult to assess and handle analytically, especially for collective actors such as companies. Another is that attitudes are not easily related to their behavioural effects and it is these that we are primarily concerned with in business. Once we adopt the behavioural concept of relationship, it is easy to see why it is difficult to accept the idea that companies could exist "without relationships". Every company is a nexus of relationships with customers, suppliers and others with which it interacts and which actually define its business. It is in relationships that companies access, provide and exchange resources from, to, and with others. Once we adopt the behavioural concept of a relationship, then the issue for a company becomes how to cope with the relationships it has and how to make the best of them.

There is another consequence of defining relationships in behavioural terms. Claiming that a relationship exists between two parties does not mean that some particular type of interactions will *always* occur, or always *should* occur. Relationships exist in the whole array of forms that interaction can take. There is no such thing as a "standard relationship". Every relationship is unique in its content, its dynamics, in how it evolves, in how it affects the parties involved and in what it requires from them for success for each of them.

We argue that managing relationships is the critical task of business and the complexity of that management task reflects the complexity of the relationships themselves and the resulting network structures. Hence, we need a conceptual model that will help managers to assess what is happening in a relationship, what its effects are and how they should conduct themselves and develop that relationship. This is despite the fact that modelling interactive relationships is in many ways problematic.[1] An attempt to outline such a model is the subject of this chapter.

[1] See Håkansson and Snehota (1995).

The Substance of a Relationship

Many things happen in the relationship between two companies of even moderate complexity and what occurs will vary over time. In fact, any attempt to describe the substance of a relationship will inevitably be reductive and leave out some aspects that may be important for one or other purpose. However, it does help to understand the substance of a relationship if we look at three aspects of that substance and how they affect the way a new relationship develops over time. The three aspects are as follows:

- actor bonds
- activity links
- resource ties.

Actor bonds

A relationship usually starts with first contacts between individual actors from the two companies. At this point there will be considerable *distance* between them (Johanson and Wiedersheim-Paul 1975). This distance has a number of dimensions. *Social distance* measures the extent to which the actors are unfamiliar with each other's ways of thinking and working and are at ease with them. *Cultural distance* measures the degree to which the norms and values of the two companies differ. *Technological distance* refers to the differences between the product and production technologies of the two companies and hence the degree of "fit" between them. *Time distance* refers to the fact that the actors may be discussing business that will actually occur at some considerable time in the future. This may give a lack of urgency or unreality to their interactions.

The essence of the early interaction between the actors is two-way communication that enables the parties to become aware of each other and learn (and teach) each other about what they stand for, what they need from the relationship and what they can offer to it. They will also have to learn about more subtle and complex issues, such as what their counterparts mean by the things they say and the attitudes they show. Learning is the process by which companies reduce their uncertainties. But it is also the process of learning how to live with some uncertainties that cannot be reduced. Relationships will vary depending on the extent to which actors in the two companies feel that they need to learn, on their willingness to learn and on their ability to learn.

At some stage as the actors become acquainted with each other, their mutual knowledge will be sufficient for one or more of them to become committed to developing business between them. Sometimes actors in one of the companies will lack real commitment to the long-term future of a relationship and will try to take short-term advantage. For example, a customer may encourage a supplier to invest in a new relationship even when it knows that it will only need that supplier for a short time. Alternatively, a supplier may take advantage of a short-term product shortage by dramatically increasing its price. At other times, those in one or both of the companies will try to show commitment by seeking long-term mutual benefits. Each may be prepared to incur considerable costs so that both companies gain in the longer term. Commitment depends on trust between the actors, but the amount of trust in a relationship can also vary widely. Sometimes the actors will be entirely open in their dealings, sometimes they will behave with guile. On some occasions they will show genuine altruism, but other times they will simply cheat. The behaviour of those in the two companies will not always be predictable, or indeed make any sense when set against their stated aims, best interest or the good of the relationship. Every single relationship will develop a history of how the actors have treated each other and the degree of trust and commitment that has been built up.

This initial interaction is a prerequisite for any relationship to develop. It may be more or less complex or protracted in time. However, without communication, no substantial relationship can ever develop. The communication is interpersonal and thus cannot be separated from its social context. When it is effective, it results in the formation of actor bonds between the individuals involved, based on their mutual learning, trust and commitment.[2]

Activity links

If business between the companies is to develop from the interactions between individuals, then some *interlocking of behaviours* of the two companies will be necessary. For example, a first order will have to be processed, scheduled and fulfilled by the supplier and it will have to be specified, received and phased into the operations of the customer. Over time and with repeated transactions, this leads to the development of activity links between the companies. These links may encompass many aspects of the operations of the two companies, such as their design, production or logistics. Activity links involve costs, if only because co-ordination between any customer and supplier limits their ability to co-ordinate with others.

Resource ties

Suppose that both of the parties in a business relationship wish its development to continue. This development will require investment and this may include the time spent developing contacts with the counterpart, or developing the offering or introducing different equipment or working practices. Many of these investments will be normal and will be carried out by supplier or customer for each of their relationships. Others will be specific to a single relationship and these we refer to as *adaptations*. Adaptations are not always balanced between the two companies, but no relationship can evolve over time without at least some. Adaptations create mutual dependence and have opportunity costs because adaptations in any one relationship limit a company's possibility to adapt in others. Thus, the mutual adaptation of resources in the companies in a relationship form resource ties between them.

[2] For a full discussion of the connections between adaptation and trust, see Sako (1992).

The Facets of Relationships

The network is the arena in which business is conducted and each company's relationships are the means by which it deals with those around it and through which it employs its own abilities, gains from the abilities of others, develops its own operations and affects those of others. Business relationships are a major challenge for managers for a number of reasons, as follows.

First, most companies have to work with a few important customers that account for a major share of their sales. Failure in even one of these relationships can be critical to a company's operations. Even those companies that produce fast-moving non-durable goods for millions of consumers are likely to be dependent on their relationships with only a small number of major retail chains that sell most of their output.

Second, the supply side of many companies is dominated by a few suppliers that provide a large share of its purchases (and hence of the value of its sales), or provide offerings that are critical to the success of the company's offerings. Examples include the suppliers of aircraft engines to producers of commercial or military aircraft, or the independent actuaries whose advice is critical to the success of insurance companies.

Third, as well as these relatively few important relationships, companies are likely to have many more that are *individually* insignificant, but collectively important. These represent a particular challenge for the manager because he may have far less information about them, or they may not justify expensive resources in sales, purchase or management time or in modifying his operations to suit individual requirements. Nevertheless, taken together, the effect of these relationships on a company's financial and operating performance can be substantial.

Fourth, as we just have described, relationships are a challenge for managers as they are closely connected to time. A relationship connects episodes in different time periods to each other. What happens in them today is affected by what has happened in the past and will, in turn affect what happens in them in the future. The history of a business relationship will be full of earlier experiences – both good and bad – and these can be remembered and interpreted in different ways. At the same time relationships are also full of expectations of the future, many vague and diffuse for the long term, others very specific and clear for the short run for such things as delivery schedules and the detailed planning of short-term projects. Finally, of course, a relationship also represents the existing structure of activities and resources at the present time with all its current problems and contradictions.

Each of these aspects comes to life when a manager tries to handle, influence or control a relationship. The relationship may have been in existence for decades and a large number of people may be involved from both companies. There might be important development projects going on that will affect the future of this relationship or many others. The relationship may be in crisis for economic, technical or personal reasons, or it may be so important for the future of the company that it needs special attention either to develop it or to reduce dependence on it. Whatever the situation that he faces, the manager has to consider the full reality of a relationship and a close examination will reveal that each one has three clear and distinct facets, as follows:

- the relationship as a device
- the relationship as an asset
- the relationship as a problem.

We will now consider each of these three facets in turn.

The First Facet of Relationships: The Relationship as a Device

A relationship is a quasi-organisation that consists of people, routines and expectations. It has a real independent existence that is built up through an interaction process that affects the technical, administrative and social characteristics of both the companies involved. But a relationship can also be viewed as a useful device to enable a manager to handle other problems he might have in his company. For example:

- Relationships can increase the efficiency of a company's activities by the activity links between its internal structure and that of important counterparts.
- Relationships can assist innovation in the use of resources by the resource ties between its internally controlled resources and those of its counterparts.
- Relationships can also be used to influence the ways in which individuals in other companies operate or in their relationship with third parties, through the actor bonds between the two companies.

When relationships are looked at as a device, the need for effective *relationship management* becomes evident. Relationship management must deal with three important aspects of relationships as a device:

- as a device to achieve efficiency
- as a device to achieve innovation
- as a device to influence others.

Relationships as a device to achieve efficiency

Relationships connect what is happening in one company with what is going on in its important counterparts, such as customers, suppliers or complementary or competing companies. Relationships can increase a company's internal efficiency by systematically relating or linking its own activities across its formal boundaries to activities in other companies, whether suppliers or customers. This is shown in Figure 3.1.

A relationship that is used to create an efficient structure between two companies will actually be part of a much larger activity structure. Through such relationships a number of companies may systematically relate their activities to each other in order to achieve rationalisation based on the interdependencies between those activities. There are two main types of interdependencies. The first is based on the possibility of using similar

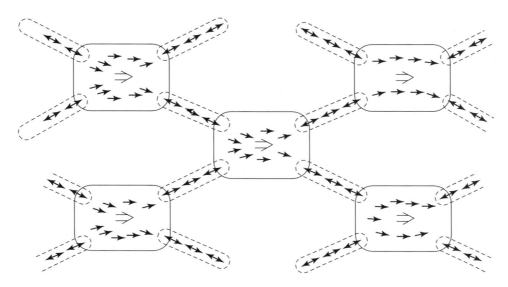

Figure 3.1   Activity Structures, Links and Patterns over Five Companies.

resources or activities in different companies. This may mean that scale advantages can be better captured by the existence of activity links between the companies.

The second is based on the fact that activities in different companies may be more or less complementary to each other, so that there are advantages in linking them together, more or less formally (Dubois 1998). Supply chain management is one example of how a number of relationships can be used to achieve these advantages.

The activity links in relationships make it possible to reduce the costs of operations, logistics, handling and other activities inside the companies. Deliveries can be made just-in-time and quality can be controlled. The operations in one company can be adjusted to the operations in others that supply it, receive from it or operate in parallel with it. These links are also closely related to all decisions about outsourcing and specialisation.

Relationships as a device to achieve innovation

No company has all of the resources internally that it needs in order to satisfy the requirements of its customers. All companies are dependent on the resources of their suppliers, co-developers and their customers. These resources of counterparts are of three types:

- operational resources, such as production, service or logistical facilities that may be complementary to its own
- technologies or know-how for the design and development of offerings and operations
- relationships of counterparts with other companies that in turn have valuable resources.

All these resources are accessed through a company's direct relationships.

Relationships also provide a device to combine a company's own resources and activities with those of others into a new resource constellation and thereby achieve innovation. Innovation is likely to be, "A coupling and matching process, where interaction is the critical element",[3] rather than being dependent on just a single new technology developed in one company. Further, innovation is not restricted just to change in the technical resources of a company, but occurs in and between other dimensions of both the companies. Table 3.1 illustrates the role of relationships in innovation on these other dimensions. Thus, a company's relationships have a key role in innovation in its own offerings and those of its counterparts. They also have a role in developing the operations for a new offering, in customising or adapting offerings and in the development of brands and in the creation of the identity of a business unit.

Table 3.1 **Relationships as a Device to Achieve Innovation.**

	Offerings	Operations facilities	Business units	Business relationships
Offerings	New offering development			
Operations facilities	Design for ease of fulfilment	Operations development		
Business units	Developing brands	Specialisation of facilities	Identity/position development	
Business relationships	Customised offerings	Fulfilment/ distribution arrangements	Connecting relationships/ managing portfolios	Networking

Source: Developed from Gadde and Håkansson (2001).

Relationships as a device to influence others

Relationships can be used as a device to influence customers and suppliers, as well as other types of counterparts such as regulating authorities, pressure groups, research institutes, opinion leaders, the media, or organisations that control infrastructure decisions.[4] This influence is based on the respective problems, uncertainties and abilities of the two counterparts.

[3] Tidd *et al.* (1997). See also Dosi (1988), Pinter and Edgerton (1996).

[4] An interesting example is the Nordic forest industry that has managed to develop much more productive relationships with environmental protection groups during the last decade. Previously, their dealings with each other were entirely antagonistic, but through developing a dialogue both sides have learnt much more about each other and their respective competences.

It is perhaps obvious that a business customer brings its problems and uncertainties to a supplier and the supplier brings its ability to provide a solution (Håkansson *et al.* 1976). But the supplier also has its own very similar problems and uncertainties and it also relies on the abilities of the customer.

A categorisation of the uncertainties and abilities of customers and suppliers is provided in Figure 3.2.

Customers' uncertainties and suppliers' influence tactics

Making a purchase to solve a customer problem is fairly straightforward when the customer knows exactly what it needs, when the type of offerings available is reasonably stable and when there are a number of reliable suppliers from which to choose. But the situation is not always so straightforward and customers may face at least three types of uncertainties, irrespective of their problem:

- *Need uncertainty*: A customer has need uncertainty when it has difficulty in specifying its requirements. This is particularly likely when those requirements are new or complicated, or when complex technologies are involved. Marketers at IBM have referred to this situation as the "FUD factor" (fear, uncertainty and doubt!). A customer with high need uncertainty is likely to "get into bed" with a company with which it already has a relationship, or one with strong abilities or reputation, even if these extend way beyond its immediate requirements. Business customers are likely to value suppliers with a strong brand that they feel they can trust. In this way, they are similar to consumers who have low self-confidence when making an unfamiliar, high-risk purchase such as a digital camera and who are likely to rely on a trusted brand.
- *Market uncertainty*: A customer may also be uncertain about the nature of the supply market it faces. There may be many different possible ways to meet its requirements. For example, a customer with a data-processing problem could perhaps choose between buying a new mainframe computer, or new software to network its existing personal computers, or having its data processed for it by an outside agency. Alternatively, the

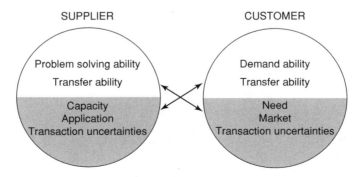

Figure 3.2 **The Uncertainties and Abilities of Buyers and Sellers.**

technologies on which the supply market is based may be changing rapidly and this makes the timing of any purchase decision difficult. In this case we say that the customer has "market uncertainty". Such a customer would be unlikely to "get into bed" with a single supplier as this would restrict its access to different types of offerings, or the supplier itself may become outdated in a rapidly changing market. A customer with market uncertainty will need to scan its supply markets widely and may use several suppliers and "keep its distance" from all of them. Again, there is a direct parallel between this situation and the experience of the consumer buyer of products in a rapidly changing market, who spends a lot of time scanning journals with titles such as *What Computer?* or *What Hi-Fi?* to check up on the continuous stream of new offerings.

- *Transaction uncertainty*: A business customer may be faced with suppliers it doesn't know or trust, or it may be concerned that it might not get what it thought it ordered, with the performance it expected or at the best price. In this situation the customer has "transaction uncertainty". A customer with transaction uncertainty will want to interact closely with a supplier to check its skills and resources and monitor such things as its deliveries, quality and price. The buying company with high transaction uncertainty can use a number of parallel suppliers and change between them quite frequently as the need arises, or it can concentrate on developing a single closer relationship in which it seeks to improve the offering of its counterpart.

The uncertainties of business customers will not remain constant. Need uncertainty and market uncertainty are likely to decrease as customers become more familiar with the technologies on which offerings are based, how they can be used and the different alternatives available. In contrast, transaction uncertainty may increase over time. For example, buyers making their first purchases of a personal computer were faced with many companies they had never heard of, with numerous different operating systems and requirements that they had no real idea about. In these circumstances, many were happy to rely on the reassurance of the IBM logo. However, after they had made a number of purchases they became more able to assess their requirements. A dominant design of operating system had emerged and many experienced customers now see personal computers as almost a commodity, with similar offerings from many suppliers with similar abilities. Buying a well-known brand is now less important.

Of course, changes in technology or customer requirements can reverse this process and both need and market uncertainty can increase. Also, as some customers have grown in experience, new ones have entered the market with similar uncertainties to those of their predecessors.

Suppliers' influence tactics

The business marketer has two available strategies to take advantage of the different uncertainties of the customer and to influence it in the direction it wishes. First, manipulate customer uncertainties, for example, the supplier could try to increase the customer's need uncertainty by emphasising that a purchase is more complex than it thought: "Buying a distributed production-control package is not as simple as you might think". Or it could seek to reduce the customer's market uncertainty: "All of these personal computers are made in the same factory in Taiwan." And at the same time the supplier could try to increase the customer's market uncertainty: "But the prices vary widely between different suppliers."

Secondly, apply its abilities. A supplier can try to influence a customer with particular uncertainties by applying either of two types of abilities in the relationship:

- *Problem-solving ability* enables a supplier to assess what solution a customer should use to solve its problem and to develop an offering that will provide that solution. Problem-solving ability is most likely to influence a customer when it has high need or market uncertainty. Use of this ability often means that the supplier can charge a higher price than when just supplying a product that the customer is able to choose for itself. The importance of problem-solving ability to customers with these uncertainties is indicated by the old saying, "No-one ever got fired for specifying IBM."
- *Transfer ability* enables a supplier to provide a solution to a customer's problem quickly, easily, consistently and at the promised cost. This ability is likely to influence customers with high transaction uncertainty, but that know what they need and what is available and so have low need and market uncertainties.

Strength in problem-solving may require heavy investment in sales and customer support and organisational flexibility. In contrast, transfer abilities may involve investment to reduce internal operations costs, with consequently lower flexibility, but higher consistency and much greater investment to ensure reliable and perhaps sophisticated logistics.

Suppliers' uncertainties and customers' influence tactics

A supplier's uncertainties have a number of similarities to those of a customer and these enable customers to influence their relationship with a supplier in the direction they wish it to take.

Life would be simpler for a supplier if it could be sure of how much of its offer it is likely to be able to sell in the future, if it knew how its offerings could best be used and for which problems or applications they would be most suitable and if its customers were reliable partners. But of course these conditions may not apply and the supplier may face the following uncertainties:

- *Capacity uncertainty*: This refers to uncertainty over the amount that a supplier is likely to be able to sell in the future. Capacity uncertainty is likely to be high for those suppliers with high fixed costs of operation or development, such as petro-chemicals manufacturers, shipping lines, or software companies, or those with relatively undifferentiated skills, or where the customers are large and concentrated. In this situation a supplier is likely to seek close relationships with at least some of its customers to ensure continuous order volumes, even if at a lower price.
- *Application uncertainty*: The way that an offering can best be used by customers may be difficult for a supplier to determine, or may change rapidly, often into quite different

directions. For example, a supplier of disc drives for computer data storage believed that the major application for its products was to provide a safety back-up storage for its customers' computing. It later became apparent that the disc drives were increasingly being used as archives for long-term data storage. This had major implications for how durable the hardware had to be and for the design of its operating software. A supplier that has high application uncertainty will need to be able to monitor its customer relationships and the changes that customers face, whether they are generated internally or in the surrounding network. It will also need to be skilled at communicating the results of this scanning to those inside its company who are responsible for its own development.

- *Transaction uncertainty*: A supplier may not trust a customer to actually take and pay for the volume it has ordered and it may also be uncertain that the customer actually needs what it says it wants. This transaction uncertainty is likely to be acute when the supplier is dealing with a single, large customer, or those with which it is unfamiliar, or those for which it has had to undertake considerable development work before payment. In a similar way to a customer with high transaction uncertainty, a supplier is likely to interact closely with a few customers to cope with this uncertainty, or try to limit its dependence by having low-involvement relationships with a larger number of customers.

Customers' influence tactics

Customers, just like suppliers, have two available strategies to take advantage of different uncertainties of a supplier and to influence their relationships in the direction they wish. First, manipulate supplier uncertainties, for example, a motor manufacturer wanting to encourage a component company to develop a dedicated offering to meet its requirements may try to reduce the supplier's capacity uncertainty by playing down the volatility of demand for the offerings: "The car market is remarkably stable and is affected by cyclical economic changes far less than people think."

Alternatively, the customer could try to influence a supplier in price negotiations by reducing the supplier's application uncertainty. It could argue that the type of offerings that it requires is likely to remain stable in the future: "The car industry is moving towards fewer model changes and so you would have ample volumes over which to recover your development expenditure."

At the same time the customer could try to increase its transaction uncertainty: "There are too many European car makers and a shake-out is long overdue. You need to concentrate on reliable future partners, even though prices may be lower."

Second, it can apply its abilities. A customer can also try to influence a supplier with particular uncertainties by applying either of two types of abilities in the relationship. These abilities can make the customer more sought after by suppliers and hence more willing to meet their requirements. However, the importance of these abilities will depend on the particular uncertainties of the supplier at that time.

- *Demand ability* enables a customer to advise a supplier of the type of offering that it should produce. This can be a very powerful influence on suppliers with application uncertainty and is a particularly important source of influence in the relationships between major retailers and small suppliers. Demand ability also enables a customer to offer the supplier both the quantity and the type of demand that meets its requirements. This is important as a way of influencing suppliers with capacity uncertainty.

- *Transfer ability* is the buyer's skill as a relationship counterpart. This includes its abilities and reliability in transferring information on volume and timing and its skills in logistics, and of course its ability to pay its bills. A customer's transfer ability is particularly important for suppliers with transaction uncertainty.

Over time the abilities of customers that are important to suppliers will change. A supplier that is just starting to develop or market a new offering will know little about the application of the offering or the likely volumes of sales that it can expect. Such a supplier is likely to seek out and be influenced by customers with strong demand ability, particularly if new technology or high investment are involved. The supplier will probably be willing to forgive the customer even if it is badly organised and has low transfer abilities. Later, the supplier may wish to devote less attention to a product or an application that has become routine and will not value a customer's demand ability. Instead, it is likely to favour those customers with strong transfer abilities that are "less trouble" to deal with.

The Second Facet of Relationships: Relationships as Assets

Relationships are a company's most important assets, because without them it cannot gain access to the resources of others, acquire the supplies it needs, or solve its customers' problems and thus generate revenue. Relationships are not simple mechanical constructions that can be turned on or off easily, or that will always produce the same benefits. Instead they are social entities where the possible benefits very much depend on the involvement of the two parties and the degree to which they are prepared to actively react, adapt, learn and invest. Relationships are in many ways the assets that bind together all of the other assets of a company and convert them into something of economic value. This facet of relationships highlights the need for sound asset management.

Managing relationship assets over time

We have already emphasised the time dimension of relationships and one of the most important aspects of relationships as assets is that they have to be built up over time through a process of incremental investment. These investments include sales calls and technical liaison, or slightly modifying the service or product elements of an offering to suit a customer's requirement, or introducing a new logistical arrangement to cope with a supplier's location. Because these investments are incremental and carried out by many people, they are often not identified and treated as just the general costs of the business, rather than being chargeable to a specific relationship.[5] Also, because it takes time to build a relationship, there are costs that arise before and sometimes exceed the revenues, especially during the initial periods. Some relationships never provide a positive return on the investment that has been made either in terms of sales revenue, profit, purchased volumes or technical benefits. This means that it is important to screen potential relationships before entering into them and to audit them on a continuing basis throughout their life.[6] A single relationship may be an important asset in its own right, but may also have a wider effect on the company's other supplier or customer relationships.

The task of managing relationship assets is essentially similar for both suppliers and customers, even though the relationships themselves can vary a great deal tremendously between each other:

Some relationships centre on just a single transaction, but it could take years before a deal is made or delivery is complete, such as when buying a complete electricity generating station. Other relationships involve many purchases or continuous delivery, such as in the case of insurance, security services, components delivered to a production line, or successive generations of capital equipment. Some relationships comprise a series of brief encounters by telephone, or electronic messages, each for a small order.

Some relationships may become very productive assets for both parties and the volume of business may grow rapidly. Others are unsatisfactory for one or both of those involved and become inert or a source of constant argument and recrimination.

A third group may stabilise at a low level of interaction so that the customer buys only a small proportion of its requirements from the supplier and being one of many customers for the supplier makes little effort to develop business. These variations are partially due to the different requirements, uncertainties and abilities of the companies in a relationship.

We can examine the process of relationship change and development and highlight the management tasks involved by considering the different "stages" that a relationship can be in and how it moves between these stages (Ford 1980). Before we start, it is important to emphasise that all relationships do not move into each of these stages in a pre-determined way. Many relationships fail to develop at all after an initial contact, others are short-lived either because their usefulness disappears or because either party is unable or unwilling to develop them. In contrast, many business relationships are long-lasting and pass through some of the situations that we will describe on a number of occasions. Managing relationship assets is not a linear process of moving them in one direction towards some ideal state. Instead, it is much more about coping with different circumstances at different times with varying aims, expectations and ways of dealing

---

[5] Many so-called CRM (customer relationship management) software packages will record the achieved price from each customer and assign average costs of production, but neglect the more significant investment costs in each customer relationship and hence give an unrealistic picture of true relationship costs and profit. Activity-based costing is a technique that enables companies to provide a more accurate idea of the real costs involved in particular relationships, see Kaplan and Cooper (1998).

[6] A "relationship audit" for assessing relationships is described in Ford *et al.* (2002) and discussed in Chapter 4.

with each other by both companies, some of which will be constructive and some which will only damage the relationship. Figure 3.3 outlines the development of business relationships and we can describe this by using a number of concepts that we have discussed earlier in this chapter.

Stages in relationship development

The pre-relationship stage

Every relationship arises from some pre-existing situation and so we must take that as a starting point for our analysis. Let us suppose for illustration that two companies are dealing with each other on a continuing basis. Perhaps the situation is one of sole-supply, or perhaps the buyer chooses from a number of suppliers, depending on its particular requirements at any one time. There is likely to be quite a lot of inertia in this situation for both the customer and the supplier. Looking for new suppliers or customers and evaluating them takes a great deal of time and effort. Business customers, just like individual consumers, do not have the resources to re-evaluate every purchase that they make. So unless a purchase is particularly important, it is unlikely that the customer will evaluate it, unless a particular problem arises.

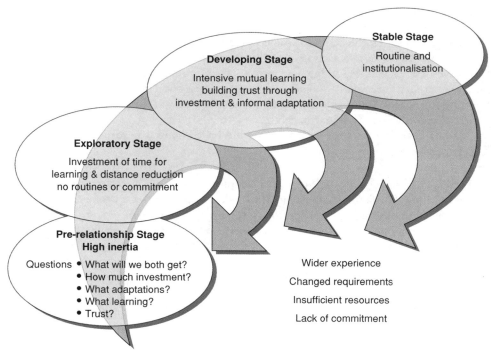

Figure 3.3   The Development of Buyer–Seller Relationships in Business Markets.

A customer may evaluate a new supplier, if it offers a lower price or a better solution to a current problem. But in making its evaluation, the customer will also be concerned that this may lead to unknown problems. At least it knows what is right and wrong with its current supplier!

A customer may also face considerable costs in modifying its own offerings or procedures or in getting to know a new supplier. This can mean that inertia, or "bias towards the incumbent" will be present even in the case of high-value items.

The costs of processing many small orders is often greater than the price of the offerings involved and so many non-critical or low-value items are now often bought from a distributor under a single blanket order. This means that the customer ceases to evaluate each individual item and relies on the distributor's choice, unless a major problem arises.

The situation is similar for a supplier. Although a business sales force is paid to gain new clients, salespeople often prefer to spend their time with existing customers, with which they have well-developed actor bonds, so-called "convivial-contacts."[7] Many new customers will have special or difficult-to-satisfy demands and the supplier will have high application uncertainty. It may be apprehensive about making major investments in a new risky relationship when compared to the relative safety of its existing customer relationships.

So what are the things that would make a customer look for a new supplier or a supplier look for a new customer? It could be as the result of a detailed evaluation of an existing partner or of an overall portfolio of suppliers or customers. But for the reasons we have mentioned above, detailed reviews of a counterpart are likely to take place in only a limited number of cases.

It could also be as the result of some overall policy. For example, a UK computer company saw its future mainly in the European market and thus, to emphasise its "Europeanness", it decided to buy components from European suppliers, except when it had no alternative. Similarly, a manufacturer of aviation systems faced with a decline in military orders took a decision to switch its emphasis to developing relationships with potential customers in civilian transport.

One of the companies in a relationship could have changed needs and requirements. This can arise in a number of ways:

- A company can change its view of a counterpart's place in its set or *portfolio* of relationships. The company might wish to widen its portfolio of customers or suppliers and reduce the share of purchases from a particular counterpart.
- A company might also change its requirements of a counterpart on the basis of what it has learned in a relationship elsewhere in its portfolio. For example, many car component manufacturers have come to expect more co-operation, information exchange and commitment from their European customers because of their experience in dealing with Japanese customers.
- A company itself can identify changes in its requirements, perhaps because of a decision to change technology.

[7] This is the reason why many companies have introduced Business Development Departments within their sales force with the task of acquiring and developing new customer relationships.

- It could be the efforts of an outsider that makes one of the companies change its requirements, such as if the attentions of a low-cost foreign supplier altered the customer's views of its existing suppliers.
- Perhaps most likely, a company may start to look for a new counterpart because some particular episode in an existing relationship has sparked dissatisfaction. The episode could be when a supplier changed its price or provided an offering that did not meet its requirements, perhaps because it was concentrating on another customer, or when a customer only sent along a junior member of staff to meet the supplier's directors at a new product launch. Such an episode might appear to be insignificant in itself, but may be symptomatic of a change in attitudes or a weakening of actor bonds, resource ties or activity links. Or it may simply be seen as "the straw that broke the camel's back". Although the customer or supplier may not immediately cease to deal with their counterpart, they may reduce their commitment, stop investing in the relationship and look more closely at other counterparts.

Whatever the reason for looking for a new supplier or customer, companies in the pre-relationship stage are faced with a number of questions that relate to the variables we have used to characterise relationships:

- What will we each get from this relationship and what do we each want to get?
- How much do we have to invest in order to make the relationship work and how much must the partner invest?
- How much will this mean that we have to adapt from our normal ways of working?
- How much do we have to learn in order to deal with this partner (or to reduce the distance between us) and how much can we learn from it?

The evaluation of a new counterpart in the pre-relationship stage will require considerable two-way communication, but there will be no actor bonds between individuals. So the conversation is likely to take place without *commitment*, rather like that between a couple meeting for the first time in a singles' bar. This leads to the further question: "How can we develop the needed trust between us to enable a relationship to develop?"

The answers to these questions will vary considerably. For example, one of the parties may be looking for a new relationship to solve a short-term requirement and without permanence, while the other might have a tentative idea that it could be of major long-term significance. All these aspects of a relationship are very difficult to judge in this pre-relationship state, because the "distance" between those involved reduces their understanding of each other. The rough estimates that can be made will probably mean that a number of potential partners can be quickly disqualified. It also means that companies will try to build their relationships slowly and will seek to minimise their commitment until potential outcomes become clearer.

The exploratory stage

This is the stage when the customer and supplier engage in discussion or negotiation about a possible purchase of a one-off business service, such as consultancy, or a piece of capital equipment, or during the time of prototype or sample delivery for a frequently purchased product or service. In this stage the amount of learning that it is required by the two companies is probably at its greatest. But the two parties in this stage may have little experience of working with each other, still have few actor bonds and little idea of what the other party can reasonably request of them, or even of what they hope to gain from the relationship themselves. Perhaps even more fundamentally, the two companies will need to learn about each other as people to reduce the considerable "distance" between them.

No routine procedures will have been developed to cope with issues as they arise and both parties are likely to have to invest considerable management thought and time to the relationship and they may have great uncertainties about any future benefits. In this stage the relationship will appear to be costly and the future benefits uncertain, particularly when compared with other, existing relationships.

There will also be a lack of trust and a concern about the other company's commitment. For example, the supplier may doubt that the customer will actually take the quantities it suggests, or it may believe that it is only being used to shake up an existing supplier. The customer may doubt that the seller will actually deliver what it is promising. In turn, the seller may feel quite comfortable in promising all kinds of high performance on the basis that it won't have to deliver this until a distant time in the future!

All this means that commitment by the two parties is vital if the relationship is to develop from the stage of exploration. Each party has to convince the other that they are seriously interested in the relationship and at the same time have to gain the interest of the other party. Demonstrating commitment is an important way to earn the trust of its partner so that it can come to expect similar commitment in return. But the exploratory stage mainly consists of discussion and negotiation and a company does not have many opportunities to demonstrate its commitment in a concrete way – perhaps neither money nor offerings have yet to change hands. Because of this, the way that it structures the interaction and invests its management time will be important.

The developing stage

A relationship is in this stage when the business between the two companies is growing in volume or changing in character in a positive way. In a new relationship, this could be when deliveries of continuously purchased services or components are building up, or after contracts have been signed for a major capital purchase. Older relationships could also be in the developing stage when volumes are being increased at the initiative of the buyer or when new requirements are being addressed or a new offering is being jointly developed.

The development stage is associated with growing actor bonds, resource ties and activity links. The uncertainties of the two companies about each other's ambitions and abilities will have been reduced by the development of actor bonds between them. In this stage, learning is likely to be more directed towards the specifics of the relationship and finding out about the investments and adaptations that the companies should make.

These adaptations may include major investment to develop a product or process or the pattern of interaction between the companies. A buyer or seller company might try to change the social behaviour of its personnel to fit with the other's expectations, or it might recruit a local representative to smooth out problems. In this way the investments themselves also contribute to learning by both of the companies.

However, improvements in social interaction and developing actor bonds alone are insufficient to build trust between the parties. Beyond a certain point, trust between business companies can only be built on actions, rather than promises. It is in this stage that adaptations by the two sides leading to activity links and resource ties become important. Adaptations are the way in which a company shows that it can be trusted to respond to a counterpart's requirements. More generally, it is a *willingness to adapt* that demonstrates the company's commitment to the development of the relationship. This is the case in relationships that are in the developing stage for the first time. It is also the case in those relationships that have re-entered the developing stage because of some change in requirements by one or other of the parties.

The formal adaptations that have been mandated on each party by a contract can only demonstrate commitment in the rather negative sense by not being broken (Sako 1992). Instead, it is *informal* adaptations that are a major indicator of commitment to the relationship. However, these informal adaptations can be costly, such as when the supplier agrees to a late product redesign, or when a customer accepts a price increase because of an unexpected cost change at the supplier. The correct decisions on the type and extent of informal adaptations are vital to ensure the successful and profitable development of relationships. But their informality makes them difficult for the company to control, such as when a salesperson agrees to a delivery change which may seem marginal to him, but which throws a production schedule into disorder.

As the relationship between companies develops, their mutual adaptations increase and their commitment to each other grows. But this development does not continue inevitably and either party can cause development to slow, whether consciously or not. Even in the development stage it is possible for one or both of the companies to revert to the pre-relationship stage with another counterpart for the reasons we have outlined. There are also a number of factors which are intrinsic to the relationship development process itself which can cause problems and these are likely to become more apparent as the relationship acquires the characteristics of the mature stage.

The mature stage

This stage occurs when the companies have reached a certain stability in their learning about each other and in their investments and commitment to the relationship. This could occur after the delivery of an offering has become routine, or after several purchases of capital products. It is not possible to put a time-scale on reaching this stage as some relationships may never achieve it and others will quickly become quite stable if only a little learning and investment are required. The mature stage in a relationship has positive advantages for the companies. It can lead to the establishment of standard operating procedures, norms of conduct and trust. This means that the uncertainty that each feels in its dealings with the other will be low and the companies will have low costs in handling the relationship.

However, the mature stage can also lead to problems. These occur because the routines that allow the relationship to operate with low costs and little managerial involvement may not be questioned, so that they increasingly relate less well to either company's evolving requirements. We refer to this process as *institutionalisation*. The effects of institutionalisation can be important both in the relationship itself and elsewhere in the wider network. For example, a relationship might have grown to the point at which the supplier delivers a wide range of products as part of its offering, even though the customer could well manage with far fewer. This might increase the supplier's production costs and reduce its profit from the relationship. Consequentially, the supplier might reduce its commitment to the relationship, with consequent adverse effects on its future. Additionally, the supplier's increased costs in this one relationship might have a knock-on effect on the company's ability to be successful in others. The pattern of deliveries between the companies might be based on the supplier's production schedules and might not meet the customer's requirements for lower inventory levels. This could cause the customer to evaluate alternative suppliers, even though the product's performance and quality levels still exceed its requirements. This evaluation might in turn cause these alternative suppliers to change their production scheduling which could also benefit the original customer's competitors. The supplier or the customer in a relationship might become over-dependent on its counterpart, leaving itself open to exploitation. For example, dependence on an accounting company to supply financial management may mean that the customer's own financial skills atrophy to a point at which it is no longer able to assess the service it is receiving.

In other cases, stability could give the impression that one or other of the companies is no longer committed to the relationship. Paradoxically, this can occur at a time when the importance of the two companies to each other is actually at its greatest.

Movement between different relationship stages

We have now come full circle in discussing the development of buyer–seller relationships. The decline into institutionalisation or the lack of apparent commitment by one party can mean that it no longer satisfies the changing requirements of the other. This can trigger the company to enter the pre-relationship stage with another company. Other relationships can switch into the developing stage if either party is able and willing to respond to new or different requirements. Alternatively, a company's experience in other relationships can highlight the value of an existing one and this can also move it back into the developing stage. Most well-established relationships will probably have gone through several periods of development and several periods of maturity. But it is also important to note that not all relationships will reach stability. Some will not develop, either because one or other party has insufficient resources or because one company has only a transitory need. Others will not develop, or wither or die because one of the parties simply does not appreciate the value of what it is getting from the other and allows the relationship to fail. Even when the companies realise the importance of their partner, they may allow the relationship to fade away through a lack of skill or simple inattention. Others will cease to develop because of the efforts of other companies.

In this section we have mainly concentrated on the development of one single relationship. However, one important attribute of relationships is that they are connected, i.e. they are related to each other. This certainly affects the way this asset functions and we will now look more closely at this aspect.

Relationship assets in a network structure

Each relationship as an asset and each investment in a relationship asset cannot be considered in isolation. Each of a company's relationships has to be examined in the context of all its others. This means that the key concepts of relationship investment – learning, adaptation, trust, commitment and distance – are all relative. The questions a company faces include: *who* should the company learn from?; *who* should it adapt to?; *who* should it trust and be committed to?; and *who* should it try to get closer to? Also, many relationships have similar requirements and a company may be able to combine relationships that can benefit from a single investment in facilities or knowledge. Thus, the outcome of investment in one relationship will often appear as decreased costs or increased revenues in some other relationship. The issues that a company faces in examining interconnections between investment in different relationships vary depending on the stage of the relationship, as follows.

Pre-relationship stage

The key question at this stage is how well a potential relationship will fit into the company's existing relationship structure. If it fits well, then it will not increase the costs of other relationships and will require few adaptations or special treatment. A more problematic case for the company is when a new relationship will affect others, perhaps strengthening some, but also threatening others. An example would be a relationship that involves major adaptations to develop a new offering. Perhaps this adaptation could be applied subsequently to benefit other relationships, but the costs involved may also reduce the company's ability to invest in different adaptations for some other relationships. New relationships of this type can never be evaluated directly, but must always be looked at strategically. They may lead to a major change in direction for the company away from an existing type of relationships and they are unlikely to be profitable in the short term. They are not only costly themselves, but may also increase the costs of other relationships. Also, the main benefit of investment in new relationships may actually come from their effect on other existing or new relationships.

Exploratory stage

It is important to examine connections between relationships in more detail during this stage. These connections may be technical, administrative, social or economic and usually a mix of each, both positive and negative. There may also be large potential connections depending on changes that can be made in the other relationships of both companies. For example, a customer's new relationship with a supplier of insurance services may be affected positively if the customer alters its relationship with its supplier of security services. Similarly, a supplier's relationship with a new customer may be affected negatively if it reduces its product range under pressure from an existing customer to lower prices.

The exploratory stage is an important time for finding and exploiting connections for two reasons: first, both sides in this stage are likely to be open to the idea of finding new solutions – the relationship will not be institutionalised and will still be receiving management attention. Second, the pattern of interaction that is established during this stage is likely to set the tone and structure of the relationship for the future.

Developing stage

The managerial task during this stage is to co-ordinate the adaptations made in the developing relationship with the characteristics of the company's existing relationships and adaptations made in them. This has to be carried out for both of the involved companies and the developing stage is characterised by *organising* the work carried out in different relationships. This may include the technical development of products or processes, logistic adaptations or changes in administrative routines. For example, it may be important for a customer to try to organise information flow with its immediate suppliers and their suppliers or for a supplier to manage technical development with its different customers or for a major retailer to co-ordinate international logistics with a number of its competitors.[8] The key role in this work is played by those individuals responsible for co-ordinating the companies' relationships with each other. But in most companies no-one is assigned to this task and so because it is often *ad hoc* and disorganised, it provides an opportunity for major improvements in efficiency and effectiveness.

Mature stage

A company faces the question of how any new relationships will fit with its existing stable ones. Stability in existing relationships is important to achieve efficiency, but a relationship in the stable stage may well restrict the development of new relationships. A key issue in this stage is to regularly examine new possibilities to connect existing ones in new ways and especially in relation to new ones. This is difficult to achieve for those involved in building the efficiency of existing relationships and often has to be assigned to special project or task groups. The stable relationships themselves must be analysed as a portfolio and we will examine this task in more detail in Chapter 4.

---

[8] This type of co-operation was recently advocated by Tesco, the increasingly international UK grocery retailer.

The Third Facet of Relationships: Relationships as Problems

Relationships are difficult to handle and always involve actual or potential problems. They make life difficult and cumbersome for all managers because they restrict the opportunities for action that is either independent or directed solely towards their own aims. Managers have to take care of the inevitable minor problems in a relationship, over such things as service delivery or cost movements. They also have to handle major problems that have to be lived with, even if they cannot be solved. These major problems may concern differences in expectations of the purpose of a relationship or the effects on one relationship of a counterpart's other relationships. Many problems arise because a relationship is an important source of change. It is also a place where changes converge as it is the interface between a company's own activities, resources and capabilities and those of its counterpart. This facet of relationships points to the need for effective *problem management*.

Many novels have been written about the problems in relationships between people. The same could be done for relationships between companies, because these are equally diverse. Some problems concern the development of a single relationship and others have to do with combining different relationships with each other. There are also problems to do with the third parties that influence or are influenced by a particular relationship and there are technical, administrative and human problems. We can point to five different aspects of a relationship that can lead to problems so that it becomes a "burden"[9] for the companies.

- *Relationships are unruly*: Developing a relationship with someone means giving up some freedom. So unruliness is a very basic aspect of any relationship, because it can never be fully controlled by one party. Developing a relationship involves reaction to the actions of a counterpart, rather than simply acting on one's own intentions. Reacting means coping with intentions that are not necessarily shared and not always fully understood. Each company must to some extent meet the expectations of the other and combine them with its own. Adaptations are a necessary ingredient of relationships and lead to dependence on the counterpart. The closer the relationship, the stronger the interdependence becomes. At one moment the relationship may be seen as a golden cage, because the loss of control seems worthwhile, but at another it may seem an ugly prison, when the company is dependent on a counterpart that controls many aspects of its operations and is unpredictable.
- *Relationships are undetermined*: Because relationships have a time dimension, they have a future that is uncertain and a history whose interpretation is both subjective and which can be changed. Their development depends on how the parties involved view each other's capabilities and motives and how they interpret their own actions and those of others. This interpretation can change over time with new experience.

[9] Håkansson and Snehota (1998).

- *Relationships are demanding*: Developing a relationship always demands time and effort. It is necessary to learn about each other, to define and implement adaptations and to systematically relate activities in the two companies to each other. All these actions demand resources and money and the costs usually precede the returns. The more involved is the relationship, the larger are the investments and the costs of making changes. High-involvement relationships can become a "black hole" of costs when mutual expectations are set free and neither of companies establish clear limitations.
- *Relationships are exclusive*: Developing a relationship means giving priority to a specific counterpart and this tends to exclude others. This is a limitation when other prospects are attractive and cannot be reconciled with the continuing relationship. The extent of this problem depends on the resource demands of each relationship and on how much the counterpart prioritises the company's own demands. Regardless of its causes, the exclusiveness of relationships can easily lead to conflicts in other relationships.
- *Relationships are sticky*: When a relationship is developed it is not just two parties that get closer, so do their friends. Thus, through developing a single relationship, a company can become related to a wider network of companies. This can be beneficial but it can also become a burden. The friends of your friend might not be those you would like to have as friends, but given the relationship, you might have to accept them anyhow.

It is important to recognise the negative dimension of relationship as it shows that a relationship is not a simple tool that can be used to solve all problems. Instead it is better to see relationships as a necessary tool that must be utilised with care and with due regard to their costs and problems.

Conclusions

This chapter has examined the nature and characteristics of business relationships. Any analysis of these most critical aspects of a company has to be multi-faceted. The first facet of relationships – as a device – indicates the potential of a relationship to achieve efficiency, innovation and to influence others, both immediately in the relationship and indirectly elsewhere in the network. The second facet of relationships – as assets – emphasises both the costs and the value of a relationship. A current relationship is the result of previous investments, both consciously and unconsciously made. It is unlikely that the extent of these investments and their costs are fully understood in many cases and it is even more unlikely that they are properly accounted for in any financial assessment of the company's position. The potential of a relationship measures the company's ability to achieve a rate of return on that investment. Again, it is rare for companies to fully consider either the potential of their relationships or to assess their success in achieving a return on those relationship investments. Because relationships are assets, it is vital to examine and manage them at least as carefully as other tangible, but more trivial physical assets. The final facet of relationships as problems is also important because there is a strong tendency both in the literature and among some managers to regard relationships in some general way as a "good thing". In other words, that all companies should work towards ever "closer", more "mutual" or trusting "partnerships". But all relationships involve costs, not only those of investment, but also the costs of disruption, loss of control and the negative as well as positive effects of any one relationship on others. It is important that managers regard their relationships as the unit of analysis in their activities, rather than simply concentrating on their sales, their offerings, their territories or their operations.

This chapter has strongly emphasised the time dimension of relationships. Relationships are never static and any understanding of them must include an idea of their dynamics. We have suggested that relationships can be examined according to the stage that they are in. This examination is not simple, because the stages of a relationship are neither pre-determined nor uni-directional. Also, examination of the stage of a relationship is of little value if it only produces a snapshot view. It is important that it relates the current situation to the activities that have led to it: investment, adaptation, commitment and learning, and considers how these factors are likely to project it into the future. This analysis is a necessary precursor to decisions on how to try to change that trajectory. These decisions are both more significant than detailed decisions of such things as offerings, price, sales and purchasing activities and, indeed, they should be the basis for them.

References

Bleeke, J. and Ernst, D. (1993) *Collaborating to Compete*, New York: John Wiley.

Dosi, G. (1988) "The Nature of the Innovation Process", in G. Dosi, C. Freeman, R. Nelson, G. Silverberg and L. Soete (eds) *Technical Change and Economic Theory*, London: Pinter.

Dubois, A. (1998) *Organising Industrial Activities Across Firm Boundaries*, London: Routledge.

Dyer, J.H. and Singh, H. (1998) "The Relational View: Cooperative Strategy and Sources of Interorganisational Competitive Advantage", *Academy of Management Review*, 23(4), 660–679.

Ford, D. (1980) "The Development of Buyer-Seller Relationships in Industrial Markets", *European Journal of Marketing*, 14(5/6), 339–354.

Ford, D., Brown, S., Gadde, L-E., Håkansson, H. Naudé, P., Ritter, T. and Snehota, I. (2002) *The Business Marketing Course*, Chichester: John Wiley.

Gadde, L-E. and Håkansson, H. (2001) *Supply Network Strategies*, Chichester: John Wiley.

Håkansson, H., Johanson, J. and Wootz, B., (1976) "Influence Tactics in Buyer-Seller Processes", *Industrial Marketing Management*, 4(6), 319–332.

Håkansson, H. and Ostberg, C. (1975) "Industrial Marketing: An Organisational Problem", *Industrial Marketing Management*, 4, 113–123.

Håkansson, H. and Snehota, I. (1995) *Developing Relationships in Business Networks*, London: Routledge.

Håkansson, H. and Snehota, I. (1998) "The Burden of Relationships or Who's Next?" in D. Ford (ed.) *Understanding Business Marketing and Purchasing*, London: Thomson Learning, 88–94.

Johanson, J. and Wiedersheim-Paul, F. (1975) "The Internationalisation Process of the Firm: Four Swedish Case Studies", *Journal of Management Studies*, October, 305–322.

Johnson, J.L. (1999) "Strategic Integration in Industrial Distribution Channels: Managing the Interfirm Relationships as Strategic Assets", *Journal of the Academy of Marketing Science*, 27(1), 4–18.

Johnson, R. and Lawrence, P.R. (1988) "Beyond Vertical Integration – The Rise of Value-Adding Partnerships", *Harvard Business Review*, 66 (July–August), 94–102.

Kaplan, R.S. and Cooper, R. (1998) *Cost and Effect: Using Integrated Cost Systems to Drive Profitability and Performance*. Boston: Harvard Business School Press.

Lorenzoni, G. and Lipparini, A. (1999) "The Leveraging of Interfirm Relationships as a Distinctive Organisational Capability: A Longitudinal Study", *Strategic Management Journal*, 19(5), 439–459.

Naudé, P. and Turnbull, P.W. (1998) *Network Dynamics in International Marketing*, Oxford: Elsevier Science.

Pinter, D. and Edgerton, D. (1996) "Science in the United Kingdom: A Case Study in the Nationalisation of Science", in J. Kriege and D. Pestre (eds) *Science in the Twentieth Century*, Boston, Harvard Academic Publishers.

Reicheld, F. (1996) *The Loyalty Effect: The Hidden Force Behind Growth, Profits and Lasting Value*, Boston: Harvard Business School Press.

Sako, M. (1992) *Prices, Quality and Trust: Interfirm Relationships in Britain and Japan*, Cambridge: Cambridge University Press.

Tidd, J., Bessant, J. and Pavitt, K. (1997) *Managing Innovation: Integrating Technological Markets and Organizational Change*, Chichester: John Wiley.

RELATIONSHIPS WITH CUSTOMERS

Aims of this Chapter

- To explore the concept of customer relationships and to examine the characteristics of those relationships.
- To explain what happens in a single customer relationship and how it may develop and the implications of this for the marketing manager.
- To develop the idea of the customer relationship portfolio and to examine the tasks involved in managing a relationship portfolio.

Introduction

Customer relationships are the most important relationships of any business. Their importance is highlighted in the quotation from Ted Levitt that is seen in the introductory chapter of many marketing textbooks: "The purpose of a business is to create and keep a customer" (Levitt, 1983). The criticality of customer relationships can be seen very clearly in so many start-up businesses that fail to get their first customer and never get off the ground.

A company's relationships with its suppliers, development partners and financial institutions all depend on its relationships with its customers and on solving their problems in those relationships. It is through the revenues from customers that every business, young and old, is sustained. These revenues reflect the extent to which a company's activities are useful to others and are valued by them.

Relationships with business customers are likely to be complex. Customers will be concerned about a supplier's performance in areas that extend far beyond the supplier's price or the superficial "quality" of its product or service. They may want to assess the supplier's willingness to develop or adapt its standard offering to their requirements, or the ways that *they* may have to adapt to cope with the supplier, what they can learn from the supplier and the long-term benefits and ease of working with it.

The Concept of Customer Relationships

The importance of customer relationships seems to have been accepted in the steady stream of books and articles dealing with so-called "relationship marketing".[1] However, acquiring a realistic concept of a business relationship is not simple. It is not helped by taking the stance that is implicit in some approaches, as follows:

> Companies didn't use to know about relationships with customers and didn't have them. But now we know that relationships are important and companies should develop them. Then everything will be fine!

There is a triple fallacy in such a stance:

- The first is the fallacy that companies did not have relationships in the past. Relationships exist and have done since individuals first traded with each other. It is not a matter of choice as to whether to have one or not (Blois 1998). In fact, a business relationship exists when:
  - What currently happens between companies is affected by what happened between them in the past.
    and
  - When what happens now is affected by their considerations of what might happen in the future.

  It is possible, but difficult, to list many situations between supplier and customer where a relationship *doesn't* exist.[2]
- The second fallacy is that having a relationship with a customer is automatically positive. This fallacy is related to the idea of "partnerships" in which the relationships between companies can and, it is suggested, *should* evolve to some sort of golden state of mutual respect and common interest. Yet we saw in Chapter 3 that relationships can be a problem for companies and involve costs and disadvantages that may outweigh any benefits. Also, relationships inevitably involve differences in aims and understanding between the companies and necessarily include conflict as well as co-operation. So it can make sense, depending on the circumstances to have either a high or low involvement relationship (Håkansson and Snehota, 1995).
- The third fallacy is related to the "Myth of Action" that we discussed in Chapter 1. Relationship marketing implies that a relationship is one-sided and consists of the actions of the supplier alone. But *both* the companies in a relationship will interact in an attempt to *manage* that relationship in the way that they think appropriate.[3]

---

[1] A most recent example is Christopher *et al.* (2002).

[2] A possible example, often quoted, is when a motorist on a trans-continental journey stops in a service station to fill up his car and then leaves, never to return. But even in such a situation, it is likely that the driver's willingness to call at that particular station will have been influenced by his relationship with the company or brand that supplies it.

[3] As well as the literature of relationship marketing where the idea that a relationship is managed unilaterally by the supplier is at least implicit, if not explicit, there is a similar literature on supply management that implies that a relationship is managed unilaterally by the customer.

The idea that relationships are the creation of the marketing company is based on a different concept of relationship from the one that we use in this book and we argue that it provides little reliable guidance for how companies should behave.[4]

The Characteristics of Customer Relationships

Customer relationships exist and marketing managers have to cope with their reality, rather than with some idealised form. We can outline the main characteristics of these relationships and what happens in them as follows.

1. *A sale is unlikely to be a one-off, easily identifiable event*: Each sale will probably be recorded by a supplier at a particular point in time. But it is often difficult to identify that sale as a single discrete event in the complex pattern of interaction that takes place between a supplier and a customer, over time. Contacts are established between people in a number of functional areas in both companies, information is exchanged and a complex *offering* may have to be discussed, specified, developed, ordered, delivered, modified, repeated, and so on.
2. *Offerings and payments between supplier and customer are likely to be complex*: An offering is not simply a physical product or service. Instead, it consists of a combination of five different *elements:*
   (i) product
   (ii) service
   (iii) advice
   (iv) logistics
   (v) adaptation from the normal elements of the supplier's offerings to other customers, or adaptations to its normal ways of working.
   Payments between customer and supplier are also likely to be complex. They may be made as follows:
   (i) initially after the offering has been developed
   (ii) after each delivery of one or more of the elements of product, service or advice elements
   (iii) before or after a particular adaptation has been made
   (iv) at fixed intervals over time or against a specified performance level of the offering
   (v) when a pre-determined improvement in the customer's operations is achieved, or on an annual basis or per person per day.
   The *costs* to a customer of making a purchase are also likely to extend beyond any of these payments that it makes to the supplier. Similarly, the supplier's costs will extend beyond those of the labour and materials used to provide its offering. Both will have to meet the costs of the complex interactions between them and the costs of developing

---

[4] For an outline of some of the problems with "relationship marketing", as conventionally defined, see Ford *et al.* (2002, 104–5).

and adapting their respective offerings and operations to cope with each other's requirements.

3. *The pattern of interaction in customer relationships can vary widely*: In the case of a single major purchase, such as an item of capital equipment or business operating software, then a "sale" will only occur after a considerable interaction between the companies. The offering that is exchanged is likely to involve extensive adaptation to a complex product, service, advice or logistics. After the sale has been formalised, delivery of all elements of the offering may take months or even years. This will involve such things as after-sales service and continuing advice or upgrades. The first sale might be the precursor of others in an irregular pattern over many years, some made by the original supplier and some by its competitors. Other types of sales, such as those involving business services, components, operating supplies or raw materials may occur frequently by one supplier, or by several suppliers simultaneously or in an irregular sequence. In some of these cases the interaction between the companies may be restricted to Electronic Data Interchange (EDI) or simply a phone call. In others, there may be complicated interaction to develop or fulfil an offering. Sometimes the characteristics of the product element will be very important, in others it will be much less so and service, logistics or advice may be critical. Sometimes the characteristics of the offering itself is of less importance to the customer than the supplier's ability to actually *fulfil* the offering speedily or reliably.

All this means that the business marketer's task is more than conventional "selling" of a product or service. Instead, it is about managing the company's continuing relationships with each of its customers as their problems and the solutions they seek evolve over time. Marketing is also concerned with allocating the limited and expensive physical and human resources of a supplier between different customers in a portfolio of relationships, adding new customers to the portfolio and deleting unsuitable ones from it.

4. *The nature and importance of a company's customers will vary widely*: It is unusual for a business company to have a large number of very similar customers. Most companies have a few customers that represent the bulk of their sales and possibly a large number of others, each with more limited sales volumes. The offering that is supplied to one customer may be of limited interest to others, because they face different problems. This can be the case, even if one or more of the elements of the offering that they buy are the same. Thus, some customers may buy the same product, but with a quite different service element or different logistics. Some customers may buy several different products and different types of services from the same supplier, while others buy few products of only one type and require a more limited service element. A supplier may have frequent and extensive personal contacts with some customers, involving a number of staff, while the contacts with others may be more tenuous or impersonal. Some of the relationships between a supplier and its customers may be mutually supportive, friendly and reassuring. Others may be distant, impersonal, or even hostile and confrontational. Some customers may not be the largest, but will be considered important for other reasons and given priority. Others may be viewed as individually insignificant, but part of an important group of customers for which it

may be worth developing a dedicated offering. What happens between a customer and its supplier is not fixed by the characteristics of the supplier's offering. Instead, it reflects the nature of the two companies that are involved. There are no two identical relationships in the same way that there are no two identical companies.

5. *Customers are involved in defining the content of a relationship*: Relationships are not the outcome of unilateral activity by the seller. Both supplier and customer will have an idea of what they expect from a relationship and of how important it is to them. These ideas will form the basis of their relationship, even though they may not be spelled out by either company to their counterparts or to themselves. Both companies will simultaneously be attempting to "manage" their relationship, although it is common that these attempts take place in isolation from each other. Successful management of a customer relationship not only involves assessment and action to suit the supplier's requirements. It also involves an awareness of the customer's attempts to manage the same supplier relationship. There are cases when a supplier will develop a standardised offering and sell it in exactly the same way to all of its customers, but such cases are rare. In many cases, even though the product or service element of the offering may be standardised, other elements will be adapted to meet the demands of each customer. In some cases the offering is specified jointly by both companies. In other cases the offering may be entirely determined or developed by the customer. Customers are also likely to adapt their own offerings and operations to suit the requirements of the supplier.

These adaptations may involve costs to the customer that far outweigh the price of the offering. They may also be a major reason for a supplier to seek a particular customer. Thus the flow of an offering between the companies is the result of the combined intentions and actions of *both* the supplier and the customer. A company's customer relationships will be affected by changes in the supply strategies of its customers. These changes include a trend towards reducing the number of suppliers and to rely on those suppliers for a range of activities previously carried out internally by the customer.

6. *The content of a customer relationship changes over time*: We emphasised in Chapter 3 that the evolution of business relationships is not a simple linear progression from an early stage to a single final stage, or "golden age". Relationships change as customers face new problems or require better solutions to their existing ones, or accept changes that are offered by a supplier, or learn of new solutions available elsewhere. Similarly, a supplier's attitude to customers and its skills in managing them are never fixed. They will experience problems and try to change the way that they deal with their customers. No relationship is likely to survive without change. It is the individuals involved in both companies who must face these changes and cope with them by modifying their ways of working and the arrangements between them.

7. *A customer relationship links a complex set of resources and activities*: A customer relationship is unlikely to involve only the sales and purchasing functions of the two companies. It is also likely to include those involved in the planning and allocation of operations facilities and service resources, those who develop offerings, those who fulfil offerings and who administer the exchange of finance between the companies.

The relationship between a supplier and a customer results from and may condition large portions of both organisations and their other relationships. The offering that is exchanged between the companies will depend on the resources and operations of *both* the companies and on their respective other suppliers and customers.

8. *A supplier's market is not defined by its products or services*: The product, service or other elements of an offering that are exchanged between companies are just part of the many variables in a relationship. The defining issues in the customer side of a company are the problems and uncertainties faced by its customers, for which they seek a solution within a relationship, based on their own abilities and those of a supplier. A supplier's offering is intended to provide a *solution to a particular problem*. Thus, the "quality" of an offering can only be assessed in terms of its suitability for a particular problem, rather than in terms of its intrinsic characteristics. In fact, the "quality" of a single offering varies between customers according to their problems.[5] Often, several very different offerings can provide competing solutions to a single problem. For example, it is common for customers to choose between an offering based largely on the product element or based on the service element. Often a customer has the choice to buy equipment and do a job for itself (product) or pay a supplier to do the job for it (service). Sometimes a similar offering can solve different problems for different customers. For example, a change in the logistics element of an offering can often bring it to a wide range of new customers. The way that a supplier operates, the offering it supplies, the abilities it uses, the competitors it faces will all depend on the problems, uncertainties and abilities of its customers. The way that a supplier operates will also depend on its own problems, uncertainties and the abilities that it seeks from its customers.

We can illustrate this if we compare a manufacturer of tyres that supplies car producers, with a manufacturer that supplies identical tyres to distributors that operate in the replacement after-market. Here we see immediate differences in the relationship between the different suppliers and customers, the offering that is supplied, the abilities, uncertainties and problems of the different customers, as well as the problems, uncertainties and abilities of the suppliers and the abilities of their customers that they are likely to value.

Therefore, a supplier's market is defined by the customer relationships in which it is involved and the problems that it solves in them. Hence the tasks of business marketing centre on assessing, developing and maintaining those relationships.

What Happens in a Customer Relationship?

Box 4.1 provides an illustration of some of the activities that may take place within a company's customer relationships at a particular point in time. This illustration also

---

[5] "Quality" actually has two dimensions. The first is the "quality" of the promise of an entire offering as a solution to a customer's specific problem. Thus this dimension extends beyond the more obvious product or service elements. The second dimension is the "quality" of the supplier's actual fulfilment of that promise (Ford *et al.* 2002).

shows that we cannot make sense of a single customer relationship without looking at how it is connected to the other relationships of both customer and supplier.

Box 4.1   Inside a Customer Relationship

Suppose we take the lid off a typical company that supplies offerings to business customers, whether those customers are manufacturers, distributors, or retailers. On any one day we might see some of the following things happen:

- Someone in the customer service department telephones a new customer to sort out details of delivery and service schedules. The customer is concerned about the delivery schedule because of pressure from one of its customers.
- A salesperson calls on a customer that is close to placing an order, after months of deliberation and negotiation. These negotiations have also included some of the customer's other suppliers whose offerings have to integrated by the customer.
- Another salesperson calls on a customer that has bought from the company for many years, but that has more recently been buying from a rival.
- Some of the company's development staff go with the operations manager from a customer to see how the company's offerings are used by another customer.
- The company takes delivery of components from a supplier for use in the offering for a particular customer. A buyer telephones the supplier to complain about a shortfall in the quantity received.
- Other buyers, together with development staff, discuss which piece of capital equipment to buy after long discussions with a number of potential suppliers and customers, some of which are well known to the company and others with which they have never dealt.
- A senior manager with a buyer and some research and development staff meet a scientist from a raw material supplier and the development manager from a component supplier. This meeting is to discuss the component supplier's new range of products and how they fit with the company's own developments. The manager is also anxious to find out from the other companies what his competitors are actually doing.
- Managers from the service, finance, and human resources departments meet with marketing staff from an independent service organisation to discuss contracting out some service work, previously done by the company itself. This will involve the service organisation recruiting some of the company's own service staff.

These easily observable activities are only a fraction of the thousands of interactions that the company takes part in on the same day, whether by phone, fax or mail, by electronic data interchange (EDI) or in person. These interactions are initiated by production staff, development workers, truck drivers and service engineers as well as by salespeople and buyers. All the interactions are deliberate, although an overall purpose may be difficult to discern. Behind the interactions and less easy to observe, are managers in the company who are trying to take an overview of these activities and to encourage them in a particular direction. They will also be trying to make and implement plans for particular staff to work within that overall direction in some or all of the following ways:

- The managers will be trying to change offerings, ways of working and the company itself. They will try to relate the company's offerings and operations to the emerging problems, uncertainties and abilities of its important customers and suppliers.
- They will try to assess which companies are their real competitors and take account of what they believe they are planning. They will try to enlist the help of the company's suppliers and customers to improve the performance and the fulfilment of their offerings.
- The managers will also read the trade press, listen to rumours from the sales force and pick up gossip at exhibitions to try to find out what is happening elsewhere in the surrounding network in companies, universities and other organisations with which they do not have direct contact.

All these individual interactions, problems and activities mean that the company's day appears to be hectic, for each interaction with another company changes something about the company, whether it is its current internal operations schedule, its future cash flow or its relationship with other customers. Despite this hectic appearance, there is an element of stability in the company's activities. Its marketing and purchasing strategies may change, but many of its customers and suppliers have probably been dealing with it for many years. Although new competitors will emerge and others disappear, many of the company's managers will be familiar with the styles, culture and even personalities of those with which it competes.

How a relationship develops

It may help to understand what happens in a customer relationship by thinking how a new one develops:[6]

- *Interaction*: A customer relationship starts with a first contact by either of the parties. This may lead to interaction, the essence of which is *two-way communication* through which the parties become aware of each other and learn (and teach) each other about what they stand for and what they could do for each other. At some point, the mutual knowledge of the parties is sufficient for each to assess whether the relationship is likely to develop. That development will depend on the *commitment* of the two companies and this, in turn requires at least some *trust* between them. The initial *uncertainties* of the two companies about their relationship do not necessarily disappear as it develops. Instead, these uncertainties may change through interaction, or be manipulated by counterparts and are important reasons for seeking the *abilities* of the counterpart. The initial interaction is a prerequisite for any relationship to develop. It may be more or less complex, both personal and impersonal or protracted in time, but, without it, trust cannot emerge and no substantial relationship can ever develop.

[6] This description follows from the analysis of relationship development in Chapter 3. For an examination of ideas on relationship development, see Halinen (1998).

- *Co-ordinating activities*: If the interaction between the two companies is to lead to some business, however limited, then it will be necessary to *co-ordinate activities* of the two companies. The supplier has to process a first order, schedule it for operations and fulfil it. The order itself must have been specified by the customer. It must receive it and phase it into its own operations. This co-ordination, to a large extent defines the nature of a relationship. Co-ordination between a customer and a supplier entails costs for both of them and limits their freedom to co-ordinate with others.
- *Adaptations*: Suppose that the initial business between the companies is considered to be satisfactory by both of them and that it continues. The pattern of interactions and activities that form the relationship is likely to require *adaptations* over time. The reasons for this may concern the relationship, the companies' other relationships, or the wider network. These adaptations may concern different elements of the supplier's offering or its facilities, equipment or operations. The customer may also adapt its offering to its customer or its operations or facilities (Hallen *et al.* 1993). No relationship can evolve without some adaptations, but they may not always be balanced between the two companies. Adaptations create mutual dependence and involve opportunity costs because they limit the ability of the companies to simultaneously make adaptations in different relationships (Brennan and Turnbull 1999).

Relationship development is seldom a uniform process of increasing business. Many relationships never really get going, others abort after only a short time. Few continue to develop, but some continue for a long period of time. Many slip into maturity or even inertia that may trigger either of the companies to develop alternatives or precede further development. Nor is it desirable that all the customer relationships of a company should always develop positively and marketers face difficult decisions about which relationships to try to develop, and which to allow, or "encourage" to die. Whatever the pattern of development of a relationship, we can examine it using the three critical processes that underlie the formation of all relationships (Håkansson and Snehota 1995):

- Interaction between individual actors, leading to the formation of *actor bonds* between them. An example of these bonds is the reliance and trust that may develop between service personnel from a supplier and the operations staff in a customer.
- Co-ordination of the activities of the two companies leading to the formation of *activity links*. An example of this occurs when a supplier to the fashion industry co-ordinates the colours it dyes garments to the pattern of daily sales in a customer's retail stores.
- The adaptation of resources of the two companies leading to formation of *resource ties*. An example of this would be if the supplier to the fashion industry and the retailer invested in a single software package to transmit real-time sales information and to control production and logistics.

Involvement in a relationship

These actor bonds, activity links and resource ties define the *involvement* of the two companies in a relationship, or the impact that it has on them. Examining bonds, links and ties is necessary in order to assess the importance and value of a relationship. Managing them is essential to the development of a customer relationship:

- Solid actor bonds in a relationship support extensive interaction, mutual knowledge and develop a high level of mutual trust with customers.
- Tight activity links closely co-ordinate different activities of the two companies.
- Strong resource ties dedicate different resource elements such as offerings, operations, facilities and organisation roles to a counterpart.

On the whole, the more and the stronger are the bonds, links and ties in a relationship, then the more involvement it represents.

The degree of involvement determines the impact that a relationship has on the two companies, because involvement both constrains and enables what each company in the relationship can do in that relationship and in its others. The degree of involvement in a relationship is not a unilateral choice by either of the companies, but something that emerges through the interaction between them. Thus, a supplier may wish to have a high-involvement relationship with a customer, often expressed in such terms as a "strategic alliance", but high involvement will only develop if that customer also wishes it to and the interaction between the companies leads to it.

A high-involvement relationship can have the following benefits:

- It can facilitate effective communication and flow of information.
- It can increase predictability, reduce problems of misunderstanding and enable both companies to cope with their uncertainties.
- It can enhance the efficiency of the two companies' combined operations and activities and facilitate a "division of labour" between them based on their respective abilities and resource investment.

But, on the other hand, high-involvement relationships with customers can have significant drawbacks (Macdonald 1995):

- A high-involvement relationship involves considerable investment by the supplier and customer and is likely to take a considerable time to achieve.
- It involves a significant element of risk that the potential of the relationship will not be achieved.
- A high-involvement relationship constrains the actions of the two companies within that relationship.
- It reduces the companies' abilities to change between relationships.

However, once achieved, a high-involvement relationship means that both customer and supplier are dependent on each other and this dependence may be the source of considerable future business between them.

There are limits to the number of high-involvement relationships that a company can handle. In contrast, low-involvement relationships are more likely to enable the supplier to standardise its offering for a number of customers, minimise the costs of adaptation and limit overall investment, but with the associated costs of greater unpredictability within each relationship and fewer opportunities for productive exchange of information.

The issue of relationship involvement emphasises two important elements of customer relationship management. The first is the need for a clear understanding of the economic value of relationships, and the second is the need to be able to assess a company's relationships with its customers. It is to these two elements that we now turn.

The Economic Value of Customer Relationships

What is a customer relationship worth? This is a sensible question when we think about how much effort and resources need to be put into working with a customer. The question is straightforward, but the answer isn't. Financially, the value of a customer relationship is the present value of the future profits that can be expected from it. But there are a number of problems with this view, as follows:

- Past and current business is unlikely to be a good predictor of the future of a relationship. The future will depend on the actions of both the companies and on what happens in their other relationships.
- An assessment of the value of a relationship will depend on accurately recording the revenues received and the costs incurred within it. Some costs are easy to attribute to a specific relationship, such as the labour and materials involved in producing a product or the time spent by service personnel. Yet others may be more difficult to estimate and measure, or to assign to a specific relationship, such as the cost of managing the relationship, or the appropriate share of investment in facilities, such as the company's information system that are used in a number of relationships. It is even difficult to record accurately the revenues for each relationship, as we would need to take into account a multiplicity of discounts and rebates in order to calculate the achieved price and to calculate the "profit" from that relationship (Ahlberg *et al.* 1995; Marn and Rosiello 1992).[7]
- Many of the costs and benefits of a relationship are intangible, or at least difficult to locate. For example, sales to one customer may lead to it becoming a "reference" for sales to others. Similarly, a relationship with a customer may lead to solutions to technical problems that can then be applied elsewhere. On the other hand, a relationship with one customer may "cost" a supplier dearly in lost revenue from sales to one of its competitors.
- Finally, the value of a relationship cannot be considered in isolation either from the value of alternative investments in other relationships or the aims and strategy of the company involved. For example, a particular customer relationship may be a valuable way to enter the Chinese market, or to develop the next generation of offerings, based on its unique competence in electronics or its special facilities. How much this relationship is worth will depend on how much the company wishes to enter the Chinese market or to develop into a particular area of offerings.

---

[7] Activity-based costing is increasingly used by companies in an attempt to more accurately assess the costs of different activities and has important application in relationship management. For an introduction, see Kaplan and Cooper (1998).

Despite the difficulties in assessing the value of a customer relationship, its economic consequences are real and are the dominant criteria which determine how to behave in a relationship. Analysing the economics of a business relationship *for both the participant companies* is a prerequisite to any attempt to manage it purposefully.

This brings us back to the question of whether only high-involvement relationships with customers make economic sense. The extensive interaction in high-involvement relationships is costly. It takes time and resources to visit customers, to answer their questions, to learn and keep up to date with their problems. Co-ordination is costly, it is resource-demanding and involves opportunity costs. Resource adaptation is even more costly because it involves resources being dedicated to a specific relationship. But we know that many companies do strive for high involvement relationships with their customers and there is some evidence that the pay-offs from them exceed their costs (Kalwani and Narakesari 1995).

There is one aspect of the economics of customer relationships that is conceptually simple yet causes problems in management practice. Because a relationship has a time dimension, benefits *follow* costs. Benefits materialise only after relationship bonds, links and ties have developed. But investments also decay if they are not sustained. Marginal savings may endanger a significant proportion of the benefits of a relationship and marginal investments may significantly enhance them.

Box 4.2 Variation in Customer Relationship Costs and Contribution

Any attempt to analyse the economics of a set of customer relationships is likely to highlight a considerable range in their costs and contribution. This is illustrated in Table 4.1.

The costs of its relationships with eight customers were examined for an industrial distributor in this study: two of the customers were construction companies; two were manufacturers and four were local government buying organisations. The relationship costs for both parties in the relationship were estimated through detailed interviews

Table 4.1   Relationship Costs and Contribution for a Distributor.

Relationship	Relationship costs as % of total sales volume	Approx. sales volume
Construction 1	38	£250k
Construction 2	21	£560k
Manufacturer 1	36	£77k
Manufacturer 2	31	£28k
Municipality 1	83	£30k
Municipality 2	81	£25k
Municipality 3	32	£44k
Municipality 4	46	£10k

covering all transactions over a three-month period. All "direct" costs were estimated for both sides and for the selling side the indirect costs of its infrastructure were also estimated and allocated. This was not possible on the customers' side because of the complexity of their purchases. The total costs are given in Table 4.1 for each relationship. They vary between 21% and 83% of the total volume of sales. This variation is particularly noteworthy in this case because the supplier was a distributor and thus was not involved in the potentially high costs of adapting or developing a physical product to meet the needs of individual customers.

Managing a Relationship with a Single Customer

Managing a relationship with a single customer has two aspects, as follows:

- To assess the relationship on a regular basis.
- To use this assessment for carrying out the major activities involved in relationship management: communication; defining and redefining the offering; fulfilling the offering and monitoring performance.

We will deal with these two aspects in turn.

Assessing a relationship

A business relationship involves interaction over time and this interaction is built on promises and expectations. Hence, the marketer should be less concerned about a snapshot taken of the relationship at a particular point in time and more concerned with assessing the processes and dynamics that are at work in it.

Regular assessment of a customer relationship is a prerequisite for conscious, purposeful intervention in it. Assessment is particularly valuable when any major change in the relationship is being considered, such as developing or adapting an offering or investing in operational capability for the relationship.

Assessing a relationship involves looking both backwards into its history and forwards to its potential. Even more importantly, it requires an assessment from the perspective of the supplier and of the customer. Figure 4.1 outlines a set of questions that summarise the issues involved in assessing a relationship.

History and current stage

The history of a business relationship is an important starting point in any assessment of it. Questions include which company started the relationship and why; what has happened in the relationship; what has gone right and wrong and why crises may have occurred? Customers have long memories of a supplier's good and bad performance which can strongly affect current and future business. An analysis of the views of each company

---

1   HISTORY AND CURRENT STAGE
- WHAT IS THE HISTORY OF THE RELATIONSHIP?
- WHAT IS THE CURRENT STAGE OF THE RELATIONSHIP: PRE-RELATIONSHIP; EXPLORATORY; DEVELOPMENT OR MATURITY?
- WHAT IS THE SCOPE OF THE RELATIONSHIP? WHAT IS THE VOLUME OF BUSINESS AND THE NATURE OF THE OFFERING?
- WHAT IS THE LEVEL OF INVOLVEMENT IN THE RELATIONSHIP? WHAT ARE THE ACTOR BONDS, ACTIVITY LINKS AND RESOURCE TIES?
- WHAT IS ITS FINANCIAL PERFORMANCE? WHAT IS ITS VALUE FOR BOTH COMPANIES?

2   POTENTIAL AND INVESTMENT
- WHAT DOES EACH COMPANY SEE AS THE POTENTIAL OF THE RELATIONSHIP FOR BOTH COMPANIES? WHAT SCOPE AND INVOLVEMENT DO EACH COMPANY WANT IN THE RELATIONSHIP?
- WHAT INVESTMENT IS REQUIRED FROM BOTH COMPANIES TO FULFIL THAT POTENTIAL?
- WHAT ARE THE THREATS TO THE RELATIONSHIP?

3   ATMOSPHERE OF THE RELATIONSHIP
- HOW COMMITTED IS EACH COMPANY TO THE CURRENT RELATIONSHIP AND TO INVESTMENT IN IT?
- WHAT IS THE DISTANCE BETWEEN THE TWO COMPANIES?
- HOW DEPENDENT ARE THE COMPANIES ON EACH OTHER?
- WHAT CONFLICT AND CO-OPERATION EXISTS BETWEEN THEM?

4   NETWORK
- WHAT IS THE NETWORK POSITION OF THE RELATIONSHIP FROM THE PERSPECTIVE OF BOTH COMPANIES?
- WHAT IS ITS ROLE IN THE SUPPLIER'S AND CUSTOMER'S PORTFOLIOS?

5   CURRENT OPERATIONS
- HOW DOES THE CURRENT MANAGEMENT OF THE RELATIONSHIP BY THE SUPPLIER AND BY THE CUSTOMER FIT IN LINE WITH THEIR OVERALL STRATEGIES?
- IS THE CURRENT PATTERN OF INTERACTION BETWEEN SUPPLIER AND CUSTOMER APPROPRIATE?

Source: This section was developed from Ford *et al.* (2002).

Figure 4.1   Assessing a Customer Relationship.

concerning the history of a relationship will explain much about the current stage of the relationship and its scope and involvement.

Each relationship will vary in its *scope*, in terms of the volume of business transacted and the content of its offering and in the degree of *involvement* it leads to for the participants. The customer relationships of a company are likely to be spread along both of these dimensions and assessment must reflect this.

It is not particularly difficult for a supplier to assess the scope of a relationship by recording the volume of business and exactly what is involved in its offering. But it is more difficult to assess the degree of involvement of the two companies. Assessing involvement requires examination of the pattern of interaction and the actor bonds, activity links and resource ties between the companies and also how both companies are affected by these.

It is likely that a supplier will be involved in relationships that represent a high percentage of its total sales and a high proportion of the purchases of a customer and also those that account for a much less significant portion of total sales or purchases. It is equally likely that the supplier will be involved in relationships whose importance differs markedly for customer and supplier and this relative importance is likely to vary over time. But when assessing a relationship it is important to appreciate that the volume of business is not necessarily related to the degree of involvement of the companies in the relationship or its impact on their respective businesses.

A customer and supplier are unlikely to have the same view of the scope and involvement that they would like in a relationship and hence will differ about its purpose. For example, the customer may wish the relationship to be narrowed in scope and only to be a source of basic items, while the supplier may wish to broaden the range of service or product or increase the complexity of the logistics or advice in its offering. Similarly, the customer may be unwilling to become very involved with the supplier or to incur any costs of adaptation, but the supplier may wish the relationship to include considerable technological development and learning between the companies. These differences in views will affect the marketer's assessment of the potential of the relationship and the tasks necessary to achieve his aims for it.

The financial performance of a relationship is an important indicator of the value of the relationship to the marketer. It is important that financial analysis for relationship assessment should extend beyond recording sales volume or superficial "profit" achieved from each customer. The analysis should show the return achieved in the relationship by relating sales volume to the direct costs of purchased items, internal operations, sales effort and logistics. Less direct costs should also be assigned to particular relationships, such as those of developing or adapting an offering or investing in production facilities or providing dedicated logistics. Less significant relationships will have to be analysed in aggregate form.

Potential and investment

Questions in this section must also examine the relationship from the perspective of both customer and supplier, as there are likely to be differences between their views. These views will affect their willingness to undertake the investments that are necessary to fulfil the potential of the relationship. The potential of a relationship may include "profit" – at various levels of cost allocation. It may include the possibility of acquiring new technology or accessing other relationships. But it is common for a supplier to fail to fulfil the potential of a relationship, either because it is unable to convince the customer of that potential, or the marketer is unable to secure the necessary investment from the customer or from his own company. This emphasises that skills of communication and influence are needed both *inside* the marketer's own company and in the customer.

Atmosphere

The questions in this section deal with the level of commitment of both companies to the relationship, which will be strongly affected by their previous experience and their assessment of its potential. An assessment of the distance between the companies and the levels of dependence and conflict is an important indicator of whether the supplier will be able to change the current state of the relationship. This may indicate that changes will be needed in the way that the supplier communicates with the customer or that it should seek to reduce its dependence on it.

Network

The current status and the potential of a relationship can never be assessed in isolation from the marketer's other relationships and the wider network position of both companies. By analysing the connected relationships of the customer, the marketer can find out where his offering fits with those of the customer's other suppliers (and its customers) to provide an offering to meet the needs of a final user. The problems, potential and investment prospects in any one relationship must be compared with the prospects of the other relationships in its portfolio. Also, each relationship within a portfolio must be complementary to the others. It is important that an assessment examines the position of a relationship within the network from the perspective of the customer. Although both companies are part of the same interconnected set of relationships, the role and importance of these connections may be radically different for the two companies.

Current operations

It is important for marketers to check that their current operations in a relationship are related to their overall strategy for that relationship. All too often the actions of individual marketers, or others in the company, are out of line with that strategy or with each other. For example, a development department may fail to respond to a modification request from a customer because it is concerned about the costs involved. This may jeopardise the future of a high-potential relationship. The pattern of interaction with a customer involves such issues as the frequency of sales calls on the customer and the seniority of those making the calls. Paradoxically, this is a relatively unimportant aspect of the overall management of a relationship, but in many companies it receives a disproportionate amount of attention. This is because these companies have failed to take a strategic approach to their relationships and instead are more concerned with short-term cost and revenue issues. An important marketing activity following the assessment of a relationship is to examine the implications of any differences between a customer's current operations within a relationship and their stated aims for it and its potential.[8]

---

[8] Of course, this process of assessing relationships is equally appropriate for both customers and suppliers.

Major activities in customer relationship management

Managing a company's customer relationships is very different from simply deciding what should be the features of its product, or its communication mix, its price or its distribution system. The continuity and interactivity of relationships mean that a set of activities must be performed by the marketer continuously and in parallel. It is these activities that build the bonds, links and ties that comprise the substance of a relationship and underlie its current value and potential. The activities are as follows:

- communication
- defining and redefining the offering
- fulfilling the offering
- monitoring performance.

Communication

This is the basis of interaction between supplier and customer. Communication in business relationships is usually intense, varied and two-way. Most communication is *interpersonal* and through this a relationship is assessed, commitment is demonstrated, trust is built, offerings are developed and fulfilled and problems are solved. The importance of the advice element in business offerings means that in many cases, communication is actually part of the offering. What is generally referred to as "sales" is the most obvious communication activity by a supplier. But communication in a customer relationship tends to be much broader than this. It usually involves several functions in both organisations, such as operations, R&D, administration and top management and can be initiated by either company. Research shows that we can categorise the roles of interpersonal communication in a relationship as in Box 4.3.

Box 4.3   The Roles of Interpersonal Communication in Business Relationships

- *Information exchange role*: Personal judgement as well as objective facts are involved in assessing a supplier's competence. Mutual trust and personal friendships allow confidential information to be exchanged, which provides market and technological feedback to the customer and supplier alike.
- *Negotiation and adaptation role*: Personal contacts provide a context in which negotiation can take place and a focus for co-ordinating adaptations in both companies.
- *Crisis insurance role*: Examination of inter-personal contact patterns between companies reveals that some appear to take place for no immediately obvious reasons. Such contacts are often deliberately established by companies as a form of crisis insurance. For example, suppliers often try to establish links between their own directors and high level personnel in a customer, which can be called upon in the event of a potential change of supplier by the customer.

- *Social role*: Not all interpersonal contacts serve clear organisational objectives and some exist purely for private social reasons. Social relationships can lead to actor bonds that can benefit the companies concerned. They can also work against the interests of companies, such as in the case of so-called "side-changing" when a salesperson identifies more closely with the interests of a customer than with those of his employer.
- *Ego-enhancement role*: This occurs when an individual tries to establish contact with senior people in a counterpart company as a way of enhancing his own status in his organisation. For example, a salesperson might spend considerable time trying to cultivate the purchasing director or even R&D director of a customer, even if they have no role in the relationship with his company.

Source: Adapted from Turnbull (1979).

A supplier that wishes to monitor and control the pattern of inter-personal communication faces a dilemma. Social contacts are an inevitable consequence of good functional contacts. If a supplier tries to restrict them, it may lose the benefits that come from the actor bonds that can be formed. Social contacts are particularly important in the early stages of a relationship when they can help to reduce the "distance" between the companies.

Another communication issue for the marketer is how to manage consistency in the complex flow of information with customers. Consistency in communication enables a coherent "message" to be delivered to each customer. But sometimes it may be necessary to be *inconsistent* and to communicate a different message at different times. This is often needed to "shake up" a relationship when the customer has become complacent or knows exactly what it can "get away with"! Sometimes it may also be appropriate for different parts of the supplier to transmit different messages to their counterparts. For example, development staff may be encouraged to be positive in talking to their counterparts about a particular project, but those discussing the financing of the project may take a more negative line (Ford *et al.* 1986). Even when the same message is planned to be communicated, this may be difficult to achieve and a major part of the marketer's job is to monitor the communications of his colleagues and to tell them exactly what is required from them in a particular relationship, based on his assessment of its value and potential.

Defining and re-defining the offering

The initial offering for a particular customer is likely to be defined interactively between the customer and the supplier. This offering will almost certainly have to change over time as the problems and abilities of the two companies evolve. New offerings must be identified, evaluated and fulfilled. Minor modifications to individual elements of the offering are likely to occur frequently, or even continuously. Managing the evolution of an offering is likely to be less problematic when a major part of it consists of a tangible product or logistics and be more complex when the value of the offering to the customer rests on less tangible advice or adaptation.

Fulfilling the offering

Value for a customer depends on the "promise" of a supplier's offering. It also depends on the supplier's ability to fulfil that promise. Fulfilment means that the offering *actually* solves the customer's problem on time, consistently and to the extent that was promised. The relative importance to the customer of the offering and its fulfilment can vary, as the following examples show:

- A supplier's offering may be based on a very innovative product or service, that it has developed to solve an important customer problem. In this case, the customer may be prepared to accept inadequate fulfilment such as late delivery, or even some unreliability, because it values the offering and the specification of the product or service so highly.
- Another offering may centre on a component used in mass production. Here, the supplier's ability to deliver that component consistently to specification and on time to several widely distributed locations may be more important than the specification of the component itself, as this specification may well be matched by other, less reliable suppliers.[9] A similar situation often exists for suppliers of software, where functionality may be similar between different offerings and the ability to fulfil on time with the necessary adaptation or "bespoking" is critical.

A broad range of activities will be needed in many relationships to fulfil all the elements of the supplier's offering. In many cases, the offering can only be fulfilled effectively when extensive activity links, resource ties and actor bonds have been developed.

Monitoring performance

Monitoring a customer relationship will involve assessing a large number of factors, but ultimately it is revenue and cost considerations that will determine what happens in it. Assessing even short-term costs and achieved revenues can be difficult and this causes problems when the marketer is negotiating or determining price. This problem is made worse when relationship investments are involved that may only have a potential return in the long-term future. When considering price and financial performance it is important for the marketer to distinguish between the value to his company and to the customer of their current transactions and the value to both of them of the relationship of which they are part. The activity links, resource ties and actor bonds in a relationship can provide value to both companies in a number of ways:

- Lower operational costs because the supplier or customer has modified their offering so that it "fits" more easily with that of the counterpart.
- Reduced development expenses for both companies based on information from each other about the capabilities or use of the offering.
- Improved material flow for both companies brought about by reduced inventories due to changes in delivery frequency and lot sizes.

[9] For a complete examination of issues of fulfilment in business marketing see Ford *et al.* (2002), Chapter 7.

- Quicker and cheaper problem-solving through familiarity with each other's ways of working and through trust in each other.
- Reduced administration costs through more integrated information systems and because of experience of each other's ways of working.
- Both customer and supplier may be able to apply what they have learned in any one relationship to other relationships.
- They may be able to gain access to other parts of a network through their relationship with particular customers and suppliers.

These values need to be assessed by the marketer *and communicated to the customer*. If the marketer does not consider relationship value when setting prices, then he may set a price that is too high and harm the relationship. If this happens, he will lose the benefits of previous investments in the relationship and fail to gain advantage of future benefits. Marketers' relationship management and pricing policy must reflect the fact that the costs of keeping a customer are far less than gaining a new one. This has a number of aspects:

- The supplier must be careful not to take its long-term relationships for granted. It must continue to invest in them at a level that relates to their potential and resist the temptation to "milk" them for short-term profit.
- It must also adjust its prices to give its customer a share of the benefits of its lower costs, especially because the relationship may have already solved some of the customer's most difficult problems and so the customer is likely to be less excited by the marketer's offering.
- On the other hand, the marketer must also bear in mind when pricing that the customer will also have lower costs of relationship management in established relationships and would have to incur "switching costs" in developing a relationship with a new supplier.

One way of managing price in established relationships is through so-called "open book" agreements where the supplier agrees to disclose its costs of supply and to price at an agreed margin on top of these. This transparency provides the customer with reassurance that the marketer is trying to achieve cost improvements, but is not taking advantage of the customer. Many marketers are apprehensive about these agreements. But they do provide marketers with an opportunity to be open about a relationship and its value to them and to demonstrate commitment to its future.

We can recognise some of these activities from marketing textbooks. However, in business relationships they acquire a new dimension. Rather than being based on unilateral decisions at a single point in time about offerings, communication, fulfilment and pricing, these activities are likely to evolve incrementally through interaction between the participants.

Managing a Portfolio of Relationships

A business company typically has a limited number of customer relationships, certainly when compared with the millions of customers of suppliers of fast-moving consumer goods or of large retailers. But even though total numbers are relatively small, there is likely to be a great variety in its relationships:

- Some of these relationships will be long established, others will be more recent.
- Some will represent a large proportion of its total sales, others will be of lower volume. Some will represent a large proportion of the purchases of its customers. Others will be only minor purchases for them.
- Some of its relationships may be high involvement for it and/or for its customers, others will be less so.
- Some will provide an opportunity to develop new technology, others may give access for the supplier to a wide range of end-users or to other parts of the network.

This variety leads to important but difficult choices for the business marketer. These choices centre on how she can prioritise her relationships so as to allocate her scarce development, adaptation and relationship management resources most effectively. The choices are complicated because a supplier's different customer relationships are interconnected. Together, the choices about individual relationships and the inter-connections between them are a problem of *relationship portfolio management*.

Underlying the portfolio concept is the idea that the different customer relationships of the company represent expensively acquired, valuable assets. The problem is how to balance the investment of time, money and resources in each relationship asset and maximise the return across the portfolio. This rate of return cannot be expressed in narrow financial terms and a company may seek many different types of contribution from its relationships, such as technological, operational or commercial learning or network access. A customer relationship portfolio has some similarities to, but also some differences from a financial portfolio, as follows:

- Both types of portfolio involve attempts to balance individual investments with different levels of risk and reward, to maximise the return across the whole portfolio. Some customer relationships might involve the risk that invoices won't be paid. Others might involve considerable investment in product or process modification with the risk that this might not be recouped if sales volumes are lower than expected. In contrast, some relationships may offer lower volumes or profit, but consistent sales and regular payment.
- A customer relationship portfolio involves a much wider range of types of investment than a financial portfolio. These can include investments of sales and management time, offering and operations development, physical resources as well as money. Both types of portfolios constitute major assets for their holders, but a relationship portfolio is often more perishable than a financial one. Although a financial portfolio can lose some of its value, it remains the property of its owner. But it would be unwise for a marketer to consider that he owned his customers!
- A customer relationship portfolio involves continuing investment to maintain each relationship.
- The potential returns from a relationship investment can be much wider than the narrow monetary return from a financial portfolio. It can include the benefits of joint

offering or operations development, transfer of technology or business methods, access to a customer's own network or improved credibility with other customers.

- Investments in a relationship portfolio are interconnected and what happens in one can affect what happens in others. On the one hand, skills and knowledge acquired in one can sometimes be applied to others. On the other hand, changes in the offering, operations, contact pattern, delivery schedule or terms of trade offered to one customer can alter the expectations of the company's other customers and hence its relationship with them.

A central issue in portfolio management is to find suitable criteria to deal with the resource allocation problem. Many suppliers allocate their resources across customer relationships according to criteria that are neither clear nor explicit. Many suppliers have customer portfolios that reflect the initiative of their customers rather than their own intended strategy. Thus, it is common for high-involvement relationships to be developed because of requests from customers that the supplier does not feel able to refuse. At the same time, similar relationships may not be developed with other customers where the potential pay-offs would be greater and more in line with the supplier's objectives. In this way, the resources of many suppliers are invested where the returns are doubtful.

The way to cope with this problem is to make explicit the criteria for resource allocation, assessing each relationship and prioritising them according to the extent that they contribute towards balance in the portfolio and the overall interests of the company. This requires a great deal of analysis beyond simply gathering figures on the current volume of business or "profitability".[10] Assessment must include the future potential of existing customer relationships and the estimated pay-offs from alternative levels of involvement in that and in other relationships. Much of this analysis will remain qualitative and judgemental. The aim is to produce criteria for priorities such as expected volume of business, expected profitability, potential developmental effects or wider network benefits. Research on customer portfolios has unveiled a number of analytical dimensions that could be used to evaluate alternative actions and a set of tools such as different portfolio matrixes to track the change in customer relationships of the company over time.[11] One example of these is illustrated in Figure 4.2 using relationship cost, net price achieved and relationship value.

In Figure 4.2, the two dimensions of relationship cost and net-price-achieved provide a picture of current relationship profitability. The dimension of relationship value is concerned with longer-term potential. This potential may be expressed in terms of volume, profitability, technological development or network access. Although a customer relationship may be marginal or unprofitable at a particular time, its strategic importance could mean that it should be retained and developed.

---

[10] Many software-based approaches to CRM (Customer Relationship Management) record "profit" as achieved price minus direct costs, thereby neglecting indirect relationship-handling costs, relationship investment and potential benefits, both financial and broader ones. For a review of the value and problems of this approach, see Ang and Buttle (2002).

[11] For a review, see Zolkiewski and Turnbull (2002).

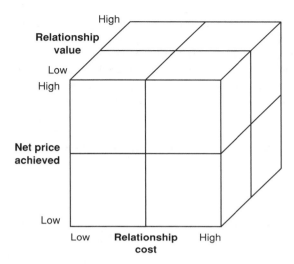

Figure 4.2   Three-dimensional Customer Classification Matrix.
Source: Developed from Turnbull and Zolkiewski (1997).

Managing a portfolio of customer relationships involves some truly strategic issues, as follows:

- *Structure of the customer base*: This refers to the number and type of customers of a supplier and this can vary enormously, from a small number of similar customers to thousands of very different ones. Typically, there tends to be some concentration in a customer base so that a few customers account for a major part of the business. The customer base is likely to be quite stable for most suppliers, except those that are newly started. New customers will account for only a small proportion of sales and the bulk will be within long-established relationships. A typical underlying problem is the tendency of the current customer base to decay. This means that in order to maintain or develop the volume of business, a supplier must identify alternative ways to grow the business. Broadening, maintaining or restricting the customer base are the options open for suppliers to consider, depending on their own resources, the nature of competition and the problems and resources of customers. There is no rule about what an ideal structure should be.
- *The scope of customer relationships*: This refers to the volume and characteristics of the supplier's relationships. Suppliers in business networks often have relationships with a range of scope. The scope of a supplier's relationships can vary even when its customers all buy an offering that includes an identical product, but where those customers have different problems. For example, a producer of electrical components such as switches may have the following relationships:
  - with manufacturers that produce equipment of which switches are part;
  - with systems integrators that purchase subsystems and components for their own offerings;

- with distributors of electrical components, that supply to a wide range of customers;
- with supply houses that deliver mainly to construction companies;
- with exporters that supply to the Asian market;
- with its own subsidiary that services customers in power transmission.

In each case, the volume and characteristics, or scope of the relationship, will be determined by these different problems. This could involve the supplier delivering no more than "naked" products to resellers or delivering a complex offering that requires the supplier to integrate its activities with other, related suppliers.

Attempts to change the scope of the relationships in a company's portfolio is likely to take a long time and to be expensive and will depend on the willingness of both supplier and customer. Changing the scope of any one of its customer relationships is likely to have a considerable impact on the supplier itself and the customer as well as on the rest of the portfolio. Thus it is important that any attempt to make a change in scope at either the individual or the general level is only taken after careful evaluation of the resource, cost, customer and revenue implications.

- *Relationship involvement*: It is likely that a customer portfolio will contain relationships with different levels of involvement, even if the company proclaims that its policy is to ensure "uniform treatment of customers". There are several reasons for this variation. One is that all customers will not have the same view of the benefits of a particular level of involvement. Nor, because of the costs involved in high involvement, is it always in the interest of a supplier. High-involvement relationships are likely to develop and continue only when there is some incentive for both parties.
- *Financial performance and profitability*: Profitability is likely to vary widely across a customer portfolio, whether that profitability is expressed narrowly at the level of direct costs, or with a more complex cost-allocation or whether only short-term or longer-term profit is considered. A significant proportion of the customers of many businesses will not produce acceptable profits at the level of direct costs and even more will be unsatisfactory or even loss-making at the level of a more complete analysis.

This invites concerns about "loss-making" customers and when these customers should be "dropped". The problem has several facets. The first is a concern about the quality of the data on which assessments are made and the level of costs that should be allocated to each relationship. Second, the supplier must question whether an apparently unprofitable customer relationship actually makes a contribution in some other non-financial way; whether it has a promising future and whether it is important for overall productivity, innovativeness or identification of opportunities. Only when such an analysis fails to provide any good reason for maintaining the customer can we deem it to be truly "loss-making".

Conclusion: Managing Relationships with Customers

Customer relationships are a way for a supplier to solve its problems by providing solutions to the problems of its customers. These solutions are developed through the interaction between customer and supplier and are highly heterogeneous and context-specific.

The way that a single relationship or a whole set of relationships evolves can never be fully controlled by the supplier (or customer) alone. Every supplier faces pressures from different customers that pull it in different directions and the supplier will be tempted to follow at least some of these. There is nothing intrinsically wrong about this. After all, marketing is supposed to be about customer satisfaction! But there is an obvious danger that by following too many conflicting interests, the supplier will confuse its identity and over-stretch its resources. The central issue in customer relationship management is how to limit the inevitable pressures towards differentiation, while acknowledging that there can be no "grand schemes" across a majority of the company's relationships. This issue is highlighted when a supplier attempts such things as a generalised price change, or an improvement to the specification of an offering or in its fulfilment for all customers. Indiscriminate actions like this may be administratively convenient and operationally efficient, but they may also damage some relationships or entail costs in others, without gaining corresponding improvements in revenues.

Many companies have embraced the idea of "account management" of individual relationships. Account management leads to questions such as: "What do we want from this particular customer relationship?"; "What do we want the customer to think of us?"; "What do we have to do in order to achieve this?"; "Who in our own and in this customer's company can contribute to this relationship?", etc. Account management counters the tendency to apply mechanical or generalised approaches to relationships. But it is important for suppliers to appreciate that account managers may not be aware of how "their" relationships relate to others of the company, or to the wider context of the investment and operations strategy. Account management is no substitute for a clear understanding of the long-term investment costs of particular relationships, their true potential, their operational implications and their place within the company's overall portfolio.

Even if it is difficult to prescribe universal rules of relationship management, it is easier to think of some rules of effective relationship *behaviour*. These set a "relationship etiquette" and include things like planning and talking of the future together, using "we" problem-solving, showing appreciation and candour in communication (Corey 1991). There is perhaps a natural tendency in relationships for sensitivity and attentiveness to decline. Maintaining and developing customer relationship requires a conscious and constant fight against this "entropy". Developing customer relationships is not a goal in itself. Customer relationships need to be developed because they are the primary assets on which the future of a company is built.

Finally, many managers share the view that managing customer relationships is simply about being "nice" to customers. In other words, that relationships are based solely on the actor bonds between those in the two companies. But this aspect of integration between companies will be insufficient to ensure the productive development of a relationship in the absence of investment in resource ties and activity links. Companies are unlikely to have sufficient resources to be equally "nice" to everyone. Indeed, if the same level of resources were applied to all customers, then many would find it insignificant. Many relationships are costly to establish and maintain. They require substantial investments and these need to be planned and managed in the same way as investments in capital plant and offerings, if a worthwhile return is to be achieved. This in turn requires changes in a company's information systems and this depends on an attitude change by its accounting staff. A shift from products being the unit of analysis for profit reporting to one where relationships are the unit of analysis enables a company to answer the key questions: "Do we know what each of our customers cost?"; "Which of these customers can we afford?"; "Which do we want and how can we build our relationship with them?"

References

Ahlberg, J., Hoover, W.E., de Mora, H. and Naucler, T. (1995) "Pricing Commodities: What You See is Not What You Get", *The McKinsey Quarterly*, 3, 67–77.

Ang, L. and Buttle, F.A. (2002) "ROI on CRM: A Customer Journey Approach", *Proceedings*, IMP Group, Asia Conference, Perth, Australia, December.

Blois, K. (1998) "Don't All Firms Have Relationships?" *Journal of Business and Industrial Marketing*, 13(3), 256–270.

Brennan, R. and Turnbull, P.W. (1999) "Adaptive Behaviour in Buyer-Supplier Relationships", *Industrial Marketing Management*, 28(5), 481–495.

Christopher, M., Payne, A. and Ballantyne, D. (2002) *Relationship Marketing*, 2nd edition, Oxford: Butterworth-Heinemann.

Corey, E.R. (1991) *Industrial Marketing: Cases and Concepts*, 4th edition, Upper Saddle River, NJ: Prentice Hall.

Ford, D., Berthon, P., Brown, S., Gadde, L.E., Håkansson, H., Naudé, P., Ritter, T. and Snehota, I. (2002) *The Business Marketing Course*, Chichester: John Wiley.

Ford, D., Håkansson, H. and Johanson, J. (1986) "How do Companies Interact?" *Industrial Marketing and Purchasing*, 1(1), 339–354.

Håkansson, H. and Snehota, I. (1995) "Analysing Business Relationships", in H. Håkanssson and I. Snehota (eds) *Developing Relationships in Business Networks*, London: Routledge, 24–49.

Håkansson, H. and Snehota, I. (2002) "The Burden of Relationships or Who's Next?" in D. Ford (ed.) *Understanding Business Marketing and Purchasing*, London: Thomson Learning, 88–94.

Halinen, A. (1998) "Time and Temporality in Research Design: A Review of Buyer-Seller Relationship Models", in P. Naudé and P.W. Turnbull, *Network Dynamics in International Marketing*, London: Elsevier Science, 211–232.

Hallen, L., Johanson, J. and Seyed-Mohamed, N. (1993) "Dyadic Business Relationships and Customer Technologies", *Journal of Business to Business Marketing*, 1(4), 63–90.

Kalwani, M.U. and Narakesari, N. (1995) "Long-term Manufacturer-Supplier Relationships: Do They Pay Off for Supplier Firms?", *Journal of Marketing*, 59, 1–16.

Kaplan, R.S. and Cooper, R. (1998) *Cost and Effect: Using Integrated Cost Systems to Drive Profitability and Performance*, Boston: Harvard Business School Press.

Levitt, T. (1983) *The Marketing Imagination*. New York: The Free Press.

Macdonald, S. (1995) "Too Close for Comfort?: The Strategic Implications of Getting Close to the Customer", *California Management Review*, (37)4, 8–27.

Marn, M. and Rosiello, R. (1992) "Managing Price, Gaining Profit", *Harvard Business Review*, September–October, 84–94.

Turnbull, P. (1979) "Roles of Personal Contacts in Industrial Export Marketing", *Scandinavian Journal of Management*, 325–337.

Turnbull, P. and Zolkiewski, J. (1997) "Profitability in Customer Portfolio Planning", in D. Ford (ed.) *Understanding Business Markets*, 2nd edition, London: Dryden.

Zolkieweski, J. and Turnbull, P.W. (2002) "Relationship Portfolios: Past, Present and Future", in D. Ford (ed.) *Understanding Business Marketing and Purchasing*, London: Thomson Learning, 289–304.

RELATIONSHIPS WITH SUPPLIERS

Introduction: The Significance of the Supply Side of Companies

The supply side of companies has become increasingly important during the last few decades (e.g. van Weele 2000). One reason is that the costs of purchased goods and services represent the dominant part of the total costs of most companies. For example, for the car makers Ford and Volvo, purchased items are around 70% of total costs and for main contractors in the construction industry they are usually around 75–80%. These figures are the outcome of the ambitions of companies to concentrate more of their efforts on a limited part of the total activity structure of the networks in which they operate and to rely on the resources of suppliers for the remainder. By *outsourcing* activities to their suppliers, companies have been able to specialise and this has improved their efficiency by providing economies of scale in their operations.

It is not only how much companies buy that is changing. More important are changes in *what* is being bought and in the problems that customers look to their suppliers to solve for them. For example, rather than just having suppliers that manufacture items that they previously produced for themselves, many companies now rely on their suppliers to design and develop, as well as produce large "modules" that make up their own products. Similarly, many companies that previously contracted out their advertising now rely on other companies to manage much of their total marketing activities, such as operating call-centres or a sales force for them. Others now rely on their accountants to operate their entire financial control systems. Increasingly, suppliers contribute to the technical development of a company and are the source of much of the knowledge and skills on which they depend. This change has been accentuated because companies need an increasing number of different technologies to provide their offerings and each subsequent generation of technology costs more to develop.[1]

A further reason for the supply side of a company to come more into focus is the greater significance of the interfaces between it and other firms. Interfaces with suppliers are not just crucial when it comes to technical development. Many companies now depend on suppliers not just to deliver a piece of equipment to them, but instead to be responsible for the operation of that equipment throughout its working life. Also, management concepts and techniques such as JIT (just-in-time), TQM (total quality management) and the "zero-defect principle" have a substantial impact on the way firms operate. Applying these techniques requires the active involvement of suppliers and also affects the costs and benefits of both buyer and supplier.

The increased importance of the supply side has considerably affected buying companies' views of suppliers and the roles they can play. One might believe that the increasing reliance on outsourcing would imply an extension of the supplier base of a company. But, generally, companies have reduced the number of their suppliers considerably. The main reason for this is that collaboration in technical development and greater dependence on suppliers requires close, long-term co-operation between customer and supplier. Collaboration is resource-demanding and so firms have to restrict the number of companies with which they are deeply involved. Developments on the supply side of companies have made individual suppliers more significant and relationships with them are important assets for customers. The main issue facing managers is no longer about "buying the right products at the right time and the right price", but of handling and developing relationships with key suppliers over long periods.

What Suppliers Can Do for a Company

Changes in the way that companies use their supply side have meant that the purchasing function has a strategic role to perform. Supplier relationships can contribute to two aspects of this strategic role: *rationalisation* to increase efficiency and *development* to improve effectiveness (Axelsson and Håkansson 1984). These are important aspects of the facet of relationships-as-a-device that we identified Chapter 3.

---

[1] We discuss the role of technology in business relationships more fully in Chapter 7.

The rationalisation role of purchasing

The rationalisation role of purchasing comprises numerous activities, many of which are carried out on a day-to-day basis to decrease costs and increase efficiency. These may include changes in the offering that is purchased and/or the way that it is fulfilled by the supplier, as follows:

Rationalisation and the offering

This aspect of rationalisation relates to identifying the most appropriate solution to solve a particular problem. This includes decisions of whether to purchase an offering or to produce in-house, as well as what should be the specification of the offering to be purchased. Purchasing can contribute to improving performance in these processes by co-operating with other functions such as design, development and operations, and interacting with suppliers to make use of their problem-solving abilities. Logistics are a critical part of many of the offerings bought by suppliers and purchasing has an important role in the rationalisation of these. The automotive industry is well known for efficient just-in-time deliveries. Less spectacular, but no less significant, examples of rationalisation of logistics have been reported elsewhere. For example, a manufacturer of electronics could only provide a three- to four-day delivery of spare parts to its customers, despite having 135 distribution centres all over the country. To improve the situation the manufacturer established a relationship with a specialised logistics provider that served a number of other manufacturers. This firm was able to reduce delivery times to 24 hours at the most and reduce the number of distribution centres from 135 to 7. Although transport costs increased because the number of warehouses was reduced, total costs were substantially reduced (Minahan 1995). Performing this role requires purchasing to be closely related to potential suppliers to learn about what they can offer and this, in turn, can reduce the customer's need and market uncertainty.

Rationalisation and fulfilment

This aspect of rationalisation concerns how purchasing can increase the reliability and efficiency of the fulfilment of suppliers' offerings on a continuing basis. Each business transaction within a relationship involves a number of administrative operations from preliminary inquiries, through checking of quality, quantity and timing to invoice and payment and inventory control. This is a particular issue in the case of low-value items where the costs of administering orders can far exceed their purchase price. For example, the costs of handling a single purchase order for uncomplicated items like Maintenance, Repair and Operating (MRO) supplies are at least 20 dollars. The costs for more complex items may be in the range of 75–150 dollars, and one construction company estimated that it receives an average of 1.5 million invoices per year. Efficiency in high-volume purchasing requires effective routines to deal with a huge number of transactions, rather than optimising each single purchase decision. By consolidating purchases from a few suppliers, it is possible for customer and supplier to develop routines to rationalise these operations by blanket orders, system contracting, and purchasing cards.[2] Purchasing can contribute to efficiency in the fulfilment by liaising with suppliers to reduce their company's transaction uncertainties and to capitalise on the transfer abilities of both companies.

Box 5.1 illustrates the rationalisation effects that Boeing Corporation obtained through the relationships with its suppliers.

Box 5.1   Rationalisation through Supplier Relationships

Replacing a pattern of spot competitive purchases of aluminium of varying alloys, our Portland plant has firmly committed to fixed purchases of precisely defined blocks over a two-year period from two suppliers based in the Los Angeles area.

They have also completely overhauled the transportation system linking the Oregon plant with three key California-based suppliers.

The payoff for Boeing: The people who are doing the final assembly of the 777 are now getting all the flap supports they want, exactly when they want them, and at a unit cost that is 30%–35% lower than it was just a year ago.

Source: Stundza (1999: 71).

The development role of purchasing

Development is the second strategic role of purchasing to which supplier relationships can contribute. This is where the problem-solving ability of the supplier is most important. Suppliers are an important resource for technological development for customers and this development role has been enhanced by the increasing specialisation of the companies in business networks and the increasing technological intensity of their offerings. Because it is increasingly difficult for a company to develop and maintain its own capability in each of the technologies on which it depends, companies rely more and more on the developmental resources of their suppliers (Wynstra 1998). This means that the internal R&D activities of the customer need to be co-ordinated with those of its suppliers. It is important for the purchasing function to become involved as early as possible in the development process to bring in suppliers and use their capabilities. This importance is indicated by estimates that up to 80% of the total costs of a new product are determined in the design phase. Furthermore, early supplier involvement can also shorten lead times in the development of new products. This is particularly important because of the short life of markets and hence the short time in which new offerings can be exploited.

Box 5.2 illustrates the development role of suppliers to the Boeing Corporation.

---

[2] For examples of the many companies that have made significant administrative savings through joint operations with suppliers by eliminating purchase requisitions, see, for example, Bechtel and Patterson (1997) and Le Sueur and Dale (1998).

Box 5.2   The Development Role of Suppliers

One of the suppliers suggested that high-speed machining could be greatly facilitated, even revolutionized, if the aluminium blocks were made in a new way that reduces residual stress – the theory being that blocks forged the old way had greatly complicated the machining process. In effect the machine operators were being forced to whittle away at the sides of the block rather than sculpting it.

Working closely with its suppliers, Boeing tested and confirmed the approach that the machine operators could carve straight into a new kind of block. It proved to be a key insight leading to a whole series of changes between our Portland plant and its suppliers.

Source: Stundza (1999: 71).

Economic Effects of Supplier Relationships

Supplier relationships are one of the most important assets of a company. As with all other assets, the value of a relationship is not absolute, but depends on how it is used. Some suppliers are important because of their immediate, direct monetary consequences. Others have benefits that will show up only over time. It is important to appreciate that the impact on a company of a particular supplier cannot be assessed just from what happens within the relationship itself. It can only be determined in relation to the following:

- What the customer is looking for from the relationship.
- The way that it is used by the company.
- How it relates to the company's other relationships with suppliers and customers.

Some of the effects of supplier relationships are easy to explore and measure, whereas others are more difficult to identify because they are qualitative and will only become apparent in the future. This is what makes that value difficult to assess. Irrespective of these difficulties, the analysis of the current and potential contribution of suppliers is a prerequisite for understanding the consequences of how these relationships should be handled and developed.

Customer–supplier relationships impose economic consequences for both companies and affect others as well. In Chapter 4 we explored some implications of this from the perspective of the supplier, while in this chapter we are mostly concerned with the economic effects on the buyer side. In the analysis we make a distinction between relationship costs and relationship benefits, see Table 5.1.

Relationship costs

Because external purchases usually represent the main part of a company's overall costs, supplier relationships directly affect the costs of the buying firm. Savings from and

Table 5.1   Relationship Costs and Benefits.

Relationship costs	Relationship benefits
Direct procurement costs	Cost benefits
Direct transaction costs	Revenue benefits
Relationship handling costs	
Supply handling costs	

Reprinted from Industrial Marketing Management, 29, Gadde and Snehota, Making the most of supplier relationships, p 308, Copyright (2000), with permission from Elsevier.

through supplier relationships can be very important, and have a profound impact on the cost efficiency of a buying company. The most obvious item on the cost side is what shows up on the invoice from the supplier – "the direct procurement costs". These costs are easy to identify and measure. Reducing direct procurement costs has always been at the top of the purchasing agenda and, as shown below, this is the prime target when relying on a low-involvement relationship approach, but there are a number of other costs that arise from supplier relationships as well. Each purchasing transaction is associated with other expenses such as costs of transportation, handling of goods, ordering processes, and so on. These "direct transaction costs" are generally more difficult to measure, but as a rule they can be traced both to a specific transaction and a specific supplier.

Other costs cannot be directly related to specific transactions but to an individual supplier. Some relationships require substantial investments in terms of adaptations of the buying company's internal operations to those of the supplier. Other relationships impose substantial costs for supplier training and development and problem-solving in the relationship. These costs are thus dependent on the extent of involvement with the supplier and are identified as "relationship handling costs". In high-involvement relationships these costs are considerable, but in most cases, their absolute amounts are unknown because they only partly show up in company accounts.

Finally, the customer may sustain substantial costs that cannot be directly attributed either to specific transactions or to individual suppliers. "Supply handling costs" are structural costs that are common for the purchasing organisation as a whole, including, for example, communication links and administrative systems, warehousing operations, and general process adaptations.

Relationship handling costs and supply handling costs are functions of the activities that are necessary to develop and maintain supplier relationships. These costs tend to be related to the number and content of the supplier relationships rather than to the number of transactions. Therefore they rise when the number of suppliers increases, but they also depend on the nature of the relationship. These costs reflect the content of the relationship rather than the offering being purchased, as they originate in the organisational practices and the arrangements that both parties make with each other.

Relationship benefits

The obvious benefits of supplier relationships are that they are the source of the offerings that the company needs. These offerings may include elements of product, service, advice, logistics and adaptation and provide the facilities, equipment, components and operations that a company needs. More generally, specific supplier relationships provide access for a company to a major source of both technical and commercial skills that are held by its suppliers. These external resources represent a major potential contribution to the development of a company. If properly used, supplier relationships can dramatically enhance the resources and capabilities that a company can use and hence improve its overall standing and market effectiveness. In Table 5.1 we make a distinction between two types of relationship benefits: cost benefits and revenue benefits.

"Cost benefits' " are economic gains to the company from reduction of costs in other areas of its operations than in the relationship with the particular supplier. There are many examples of cost benefits that can be achieved through relationships. For example:

- Lower operational costs when a supplier provides a service that substitutes for task previously carried out by the customer.
- Lower production costs when a supplier modifies a component so that it "fits" more easily into the company's own product.
- Reduced development expenses based on information from a supplier about the use of its offering in the customer's application.
- Improved material flow brought about by reduced inventories due to changes in delivery frequency and lot sizes.
- Reduced administration costs through more integrated information systems.

It is an understatement to suggest that these cost benefits are tricky to measure; they are often even difficult to identify. The reason is that changes in purchasing behaviour and supplier relationships have widespread effects. Take, for example, the effects of just-in-time deliveries. The changes of delivery frequencies and lot sizes that come from JIT have an immediate effect on storage costs and capital turnover, but the real benefits of just-in-time deliveries are related not only to the materials flow. They have more to do with changes in manufacturing operations, rather than simply from a new approach to purchasing and logistics (Lamming 1993).

"Revenue benefits" are the benefits from a supplier relationship that enhance the revenue-generating capacity of the customer. In the short term, a new supplier relationship can lead to improvements in the offering of a customer and thus increase its sales. In the longer term, innovation in an offering or improvements in consistency can be achieved by utilising a supplier's development resources or through improvements in the consistency of its service, materials, components or operations methods. In this way, the customer gains long-term access to the "external" product and process technologies of its suppliers. Quantitative assessment of the revenue benefits of supplier relationships is very difficult, but this fact does not mean that they should not be assessed.

Both types of relationship benefits are similar to relationship handling costs and supply handling costs as neither of them show up clearly in book-keeping records, but there are also some notable differences. Supply handling costs can often be traced to some total structural cost such as the investment a company makes in information technology or logistics equipment. These costs can sometimes be attributed to a particular supplier relationship as can relationship-handling costs such as supplier training. Relationship benefits are likely to be both more complicated and diffused and it is often difficult to allocate them to a specific supplier. One reason for this difficulty in quantifying benefits is that the individuals in a company sometimes find it difficult to accept that they have gained from the superior knowledge of a supplier – the well-known "not-invented-here" syndrome. Such individuals might well be concerned that such an acknowledgement means that some of their activities will be contracted out to a supplier.

Implications for the value of supplier relationships

Analysis of the value of a supplier relationship is difficult for a number of reasons:

- The value of a supplier relationship cannot be judged in isolation. It depends on the *context* of the relationship and not just what happens in it. The costs and benefits of a relationship often affect many areas of the business, such as operations, development, logistics or marketing.
- The costs and benefits of a relationship to a company will differ in importance depending on what the company is looking for from that relationship and how it relates to the company's portfolio of other suppliers. For example, if a company does not look to a supplier to develop innovative services, then it is less likely to value that development if it does occur, or be prepared to incur the costs of it.
- The value of a relationship cannot readily be assessed by its current costs and benefits at any one point in time. The costs and benefits of a relationship are cumulative over the life of that relationship. Many relationship costs are incurred in the hope of benefits at some considerable time in the future, such as when a company invests management time in supplier seminars or conferences to achieve greater understanding between the different companies. Similarly, a company may receive short-term benefits from a relationship by taking advantage of a supplier's weakness, but this may lead to future costs when the situation is reversed.
- It is difficult to estimate the extent to which individuals in each company learn both technically and commercially through their interactions with supplier personnel.
- We will see in Chapter 7 that the majority of technical developments in business markets originate *between* companies in relationships, rather than within a single company. Despite the importance of innovation between buyer and supplier, it is difficult to assess the effect on the innovation potential of a company of its mutual adaptations of resources and the adjustments in its offerings, processes and routines.
- Finally, the two participant companies in a relationship are likely to have quite different perceptions of the value of that relationship to themselves and each other. The achievement of that value for each company will depend on the actions of their counterpart as well as themselves.

Despite the difficulties of assessing the value of a relationship, the importance of understanding the different types of short- and long-term costs and benefits of a relationship cannot be overstated. This understanding provides the basis for developing appropriate relationships with suppliers. Obtaining benefits from suppliers may require substantial involvement with them, which in turn increases relationship costs. Therefore, it is a crucial issue for the buying company to balance the level of involvement with suppliers in relation to the benefits and costs accompanying increasing involvement.

Involvement in Supplier Relationships

Buying companies develop various types of relationships with their suppliers. In some relationships there are close interpersonal contacts, in others, suppliers are kept at "arm's length". Joint development projects are conducted with some suppliers, while others function as subcontractors relying on specifications from the customer. Customers rely on some suppliers to provide service directly to their own customers, other suppliers provide staff to work full-time on the customer's premises while others provide only simple, standardised or infrequent service. In some cases products are delivered by suppliers "just-in-time", while in other relationships buffers and inventories are at hand in the material flows.

Generally, it makes sense for a single company to have different types of supplier relationships, since different suppliers make different types of abilities and resources available to the customer. We can analyse the characteristics and consequences of these different types of relationships in terms of the categorisation of high- and low-involvement relationships that we introduced in previous chapters.

Low-involvement relationships

Historically, buying firms were strongly recommended to avoid too much involvement with individual suppliers. Close co-operation with a supplier imposes dependence, which was considered to be both dangerous and costly. The advocates of a low-involvement approach identified four relevant advantages of so-called "arm's length" relationships (Anderson and Narus 1999):

- They are cheap to operate because the *relationship-handling costs are low*.
- Using a number of alternative suppliers simultaneously can help overcome short-term *transaction uncertainty* about fulfilment, such as concerns about delivery failure, product or service "quality" or fluctuations in demand.
- Too much investment in a single relationship might mean that the customer is "locked in" to that supplier. This could lead to a loss of long-term *flexibility* in such things as technical development.
- High involvement with a single supplier makes it difficult to *encourage competition* among different suppliers to improve their offerings or reduce their prices.

The low-involvement approach to supplier relationships considers suppliers as more or less efficient producers of *identical* inputs. This view is implicit in purchases by competitive tendering, which is common in government buying and in the construction industry. Each project then tends to be evaluated in isolation and on the basis of each supplier's price for a fixed offering. This price orientation neglects the effects of the indirect costs and potential benefits of a purchase. It is also rather adversarial, so that a price reduction is considered a gain for the customer and a loss for the supplier and vice versa. In practice, a low-involvement approach can work when the customer's problem and the required solution are clear and unquestioned and there are a number of suitable suppliers available (low need and market uncertainty). Examples include contracts for waste removal or office cleaning. Although, even in these cases, differences between the way that each company fulfils its offering can cause problems and cost increases in other dimensions for the customer.

Low-involvement relationships are handled with limited co-ordination, adaptations and interaction. No specific product or service adaptations are made, thus minimising resource ties. Activity links are weak owing to standardised order processing and shipments from centralised inventories. In such cases the interaction between the individuals in the two companies can be restricted to sales and purchasing administration, implying few and limited actor bonds. Therefore, a low-involvement relationship is characterised by low relationship-handling costs. This approach may also reduce direct procurement costs because it may encourage price competition among suppliers and usually there are a number of interchangeable suppliers of the standardised offerings that are subject to this type of exchange. On the other hand, splitting orders among vendors may increase direct procurement costs. Also, switching from one supplier to another makes it difficult to routinise exchange activities, which probably increases the direct procurement costs. The low-involvement approach may also lead to substantial "hidden" costs in other activities of the company. There may be costs for adapting internal resources to fit with what suppliers have to offer. In the absence of tight co-ordination the buyer might be obliged to create a buffer against possible risks. Furthermore, in order to secure availability of supplies and reduce transaction uncertainty, the customer might use a number of suppliers. However, this in turn leads to increasing supply-handling costs.

When it comes to the relationship benefits, the low-involvement approach offers minimal opportunities for reaping cost benefits, and is not likely to contribute to revenue benefits. This is illustrated in Box 5.3 where a representative of IBM explains the previous characteristics of the supplier relationships of the company.

Box 5.3   Illustration of a Low-involvement Approach

There was also a feeling that everybody in the industry was trying to steal our technology and ideas, which was true 20 years ago. Everything at IBM was a secret. In procurement we were the guardians of confidential information, the guard at the door who didn't let suppliers know anything.

- You couldn't have effective collaboration with suppliers because IBM didn't want suppliers to know what product their parts were going to be used in.

- You couldn't develop volumes very well because the volumes planned were a secret.
- You couldn't say which plant would build the product that the part was going to be used in. Parts would be shipped to central locations like Kansas City or St. Louis and then we shipped it from there so suppliers wouldn't know what plant it was going to.

Source: Carbone (1999: 39).

High-involvement relationships

These relationships are the most important ones for a company. They are based on an alternative idea of purchasing efficiency, a different view of the role of suppliers and the nature of relationships. Companies increasingly have come to rely on the resources of outside suppliers and this means that many of the customer's activities must be co-ordinated with those of its suppliers. This need for co-ordination will require both companies to adapt some of their activities and invest dedicated resources in the relationship. These adaptations create interdependencies and when this happens, it is not possible for a customer to switch suppliers frequently.

A customer taking a high-involvement approach to a relationship will not try to optimise the price it achieves in each single transaction. Instead, it will aim at improving its operations in the long term by using its suppliers' resources more effectively. This involves attempts to reduce the total costs of the relationship by effective adaptations by both companies. Examples of this include building activity links to enable a data company to process a customer's data overnight in a low-cost location such as India, or introducing Electronic Data Interchange (EDI) to enable a textile supplier to reduce the in-store inventories of a fashion retailer.

This approach also involves a customer in using suppliers in the development role of purchasing, to enhance its own offerings for its customers. Examples of this include joint development of a system supplier's offering to improve the service level in the customer's call-centre, or changes in the product designs of a supplier to enable a customer to change its product to provide a higher performance offering to its customers. Joint development with suppliers has become increasingly common. Integrating resources with suppliers can reduce the lead-time in developing new offerings and decrease total development spending. It can also increase the profits of both companies by contributing to better relationships between the buyer and its customers. But a high-involvement approach is always resource-demanding. Achieving the benefits of integration requires adaptations of resources, co-ordination of activities and intense contacts between individuals.

The financial consequences of high-involvement relationships are very different from those accompanying low involvement. The main rationale for high involvement is associated with relationship benefits. Increased involvement may produce cost benefits in terms of reduced costs of operations, material flows and service. In some cases the most important economic effects appear in other relationships of the buying firm. Furthermore, it is possible for the customer to take advantage of supplier skills and capabilities to improve its own offerings which, in turn, leads to revenue benefits. However, high-involvement relationships are costly. The gains in terms of relationship benefits cannot be attained without substantial co-ordination, adaptation and interaction, which entail costs. In particular, high involvement increases relationship-handling costs. Therefore increased involvement only makes sense when the increased relationship costs are more than offset by relationship benefits. Reaping these benefits most often requires non-standardised solutions and customer-specific adaptations. Box 5.4 illustrates Sun Corporation's attitude to its suppliers.

Box 5.4   Illustration of a High-involvement Approach

John Shoemaker, Vice-President for Purchasing at Sun Corporation, has witnessed how supply management at Sun has evolved: "When I first got here, Sun had a highly tactical strategy with suppliers. We did not work with them. We had adversarial relationships with them." However, Sun began forging long-term relationships with suppliers and took a more strategic approach to supply management. It signed long-term agreements with suppliers who were travelling down the same technology path as Sun. It developed an "open kimono" approach to suppliers who became involved earlier in Sun's new product developments. "It's totally changed from the old days when you didn't want suppliers to know too much. Now it's the opposite. They know as much of our business as we do. That's how you maximize their value-added."

Source: Carbone (1996: 38).

Variety in high-involvement relationships

There is great diversity in activity links, resource ties and actor bonds in high-involvement relationships.[3]

Activity links

These are intended to create efficient activity structures by relating the supplier's operations to those of the customer (see, for example, Dubois 1998). This linking is strongly related to the procedures, routines and systems in the two companies. Relationships where the content is dominated by activity links will be directed towards successive improvements in these repetitive processes. Now and then, radical transformations may be undertaken, for example, in terms of business process re-engineering. But most changes will take place through day-to-day rationalisations. Depending on the frequency and volume of transactions and the offerings involved, these activity links may be directed mainly towards either the physical

---

[3] For further analysis of variation in high-involvement supplier relationships, see Gadde and Håkansson (2001).

flow of product or service or the information flow and administrative routines between the companies.

Resource ties

These are the outcome of the ways that the companies have combined their resources. It is from the successive combining and recombining of resources that innovative solutions spring. Therefore, every supplier is a potential source of innovation owing to its particular knowledge and skills. In order to take best advantage of this potential, the customer must find ways to bind these resources to its own. This might be done by adapting the customer's own offerings or operations or by developing the ability to make use of the supplier's resources. Matching of resources is crucial to the efficient utilisation of suppliers. In order to reap the potential benefits of this matching, the customer must become very knowledgeable both about its own resources and those of the supplier. Most joint activities take the form of development projects. Joint projects have to be carefully designed and conducted to reflect both the respective resources of the companies and their relationship. Learning and teaching are central tasks in these projects for both the customer and the supplier.

Actor bonds

These have to do with attitudes, trust and commitment. Many joint development projects encounter severe problems in the early stages because of mutual misunderstandings and many relationships fail because of them. Companies need to develop efficient and creative relationships in exactly the same way that they try to work internally. Building trust and commitment are time-consuming processes, in which the social relationships with the individuals in the supplier company are crucial. These personal contacts are important, in particular for interpreting exactly what is going on. Actor bonds mean that a relationship with a supplier can withstand substantial strain, as long as the underlying policy is believed by the participants to be sound. On the other hand, even small changes may impact greatly on the supplier relationship if they are interpreted as shifting the underlying philosophy.

Involvement and continuity

Table 5.2 is based on a longitudinal study of the suppliers to a vehicle producer. The suppliers represent components and systems which together account for about one-third of the total costs of purchased goods. Table 5.2 shows that out of the 51 suppliers used for these components, no less than eleven had delivered for more than 20 years. Five have supplied the vehicle manufacturer for more than 30 years and four of them were still being used at the time of the study. But we also find that 18 companies had supplied for a period shorter than four years. Some of these suppliers had been used in parallel with others for a few years. Others had been tested, but had not lived up to expectations.

Table 5.2 The Relationship Duration of 51 Suppliers of a Vehicle Manufacturer.

Number of years as a supplier	Number of suppliers
1–4	18
5–9	11
10–19	11
20–29	6
30–39	5

Reprinted from the Journal of Business Research, Dubois, Gadde and Mattsson, To switch or not to switch – on change and continuity in buyer–seller relationships, Copyright (2003), with permission from Elsevier.

Continuity and high-involvement relationships

None of these 18 short-term relationships were of the high-involvement type. It would be very unlikely for a high-involvement relationship to be characterised by a low degree of continuity in this type of activity structure. High-involvement relationships are time-consuming to develop, because they are concerned with investment. This implies that costs precede revenues and customers and suppliers are likely to incur considerable costs in building a relationship. For example, the Managing Director of Sun Corporation argues that, "Each time we change supplier, it's a minimum two year investment on our side to help a company understand what it is to be a Sun supplier." Hopefully over time, a high-involvement relationship will generate benefits that exceed relationship costs and the costs of managing the relationship are likely to be lower after initial investment and learning by the participants.

Therefore, once the adaptations have been made, both buyer and supplier have an interest in keeping the relationship going. A further reason for high-involvement relationships to be long-lasting is that buyer and seller need to know a lot about each other before entering into this type of relationship. For example, co-operation in R&D requires a common history, trust and commitment, that all take time to develop. Consequently, numerous examples of long-term buyer–seller relations in industrial networks have been reported (see, for example, Håkansson 1982; Gadde and Mattsson 1987).

Continuity and low-involvement relationships

When it comes to the low-involvement relationships the situation is less clear-cut and both short- and long-term low-involvement relationships can be argued for:

- The importance of achieving low price that was so important in the traditional view of efficient purchasing relies on low continuity, where lack of involvement makes it possible to change suppliers without problems, because switching costs are low. By shopping around, a customer may benefit by reduced direct procurement costs. This approach is seen in Table 5.2, where more than one-third of the low-involvement relationships lasted for less than four years.

- However, a customer company may also argue for long-term, low-involvement relationships as well. Even in the absence of specific adaptations towards a particular supplier, it might still be advantageous to stay with that one in the long term. It has been confirmed that "durable arm's-length relationships" do exist (Dyer *et al.* 1998). In comparison with high-involvement relationships, these relationships are characterised by "less face to face communication, less assistance, and fewer relationship-specific investments". The main advantage of this approach is that it reduces the buyer's cost of searching for suppliers. Customers in durable arm's-length relationships avoid involvement, either because the costs of involvement are higher than the corresponding benefits or to secure the option to change supplier. It is evident that some of the long-lasting relationships in Table 5.2 were characterised by a low-involvement approach.

The Need for Variation in Relationship Involvement

Involvement and relationship variety

There are good reasons for a customer to develop various types of relationships with its vendors, either short- or long-term and either high- or low-involvement. Figure 5.1 summarises the characteristics of supplier relationships on these two dimensions.

The main conclusion to draw is that there is no pre-determined relation between involvement and continuity. Mainstream textbooks tend to argue that "close" relationships are associated with continuity while "loose" relationships imply switching among suppliers.

	LOW INVOLVEMENT	HIGH INVOLVEMENT
HIGH CONTINUITY	**1. LONG-TERM, ARM'S-LENGTH RELATIONSHIPS** CONTINUITY ALLOWS ROUTINISATION. LOW INVOLVEMENT MAKES CHANGE OF SUPPLIER EASY	**2. LONG-TERM, INTENSE RELATIONSHIPS** EFFICIENCY IMPROVEMENT THROUGH ADAPTATIONS LEADS TO COST AND REVENUE BENEFITS OVER TIME
LOW CONTINUITY	**3. SHORT-TERM, ARM'S-LENGTH RELATIONSHIPS** INCREASING EFFICIENCY FROM PRICE PRESSURE, REQUIRING LOW CONTINUITY AND LOW INVOLVEMENT	**4. SHORT-TERM, INTENSE RELATIONSHIPS** APPROPRIATE FOR BUYING COMPLEX SYSTEMS AND EQUIPMENT BOUGHT INFREQUENTLY

Figure 5.1   Involvement and Continuity of Supplier Relationships.

As we have tried to show, each of the four combinations of involvement and continuity has its own merits and is thus useful for buying firms.

"Long-term, intense relationships" (Cell 2) are the entities that provide major opportunities for improvements over time through mutual adaptations leading to reduced costs and increasing revenue benefits and cost benefits. These relationships are clearly the main assets in the supply base of a company. To make the best use of these potential assets the buying firm has to invest considerable resources.

"Short-term, arm's-length relationships" (Cell 3) approximate to conventional market exchanges. Purchases are considered as isolated transactions, making it possible for the buyer to encourage price competition among suppliers. This approach builds on low involvement and leads to low continuity.

"Long-term, arm's-length relationships" (Cell 1) are also characterised by low involvement. But here, repeated transactions allow the buyer to avoid the costs of searching for and evaluating suppliers. Low involvement reduces relationship-handling costs and provides opportunities for switching to suppliers offering better conditions.

"Short-term, intense relationships" (Cell 4) are for the purchase of offerings that are bought irregularly and infrequently. These purchases are likely to be large-scale projects and represent huge amounts of capital and complexity, such as process plants, major equipment and machinery, and other facilities. To handle these purchases, companies develop temporary organisations that may consist of representatives of many firms. In most cases these projects are characterised by high involvement, particularly in terms of interaction among people. Because it might be a long time to the next purchase, these temporary organisations may be dissolved and thus the continuity is low.

Figure 5.1 illustrates the importance for the customer of appropriate resource input into its relationships. Low-involvement relationships must be handled with a minimum of effort. It is crucial for the buyer to reserve its supply-management resources for its complex long-term relationships. These relationships must always have the necessary resource investment and be monitored and developed in accordance with changing circumstances.

Involvement and relationship performance

Bensaou (1999) illustrates how buying companies make use of different relationships. The aim of this study of 447 purchasing managers in Japan and the USA was to analyse the performance of different types of relationships. One variable of particular interest to Bensaou was the extent to which buyer and supplier made specific investments in their relationship. Supplier-specific investments by customers included tangible ones such as buildings, tooling and equipment dedicated to a specific supplier or products and processes customised for the supplier. Intangible investments included time and effort spent on learning about the supplier's business practices and routines, exchange of information and development of knowledge for nurturing the relationship. On the supplier side, the specific investments took similar forms and included both tangible and intangible resources. The research design made it possible to analyse the relationship between the occurrence of specific investments and the performance of the relationship when the following scenarios took place:

- Both buyer and supplier made specific investments ("partnerships").
- Neither supplier nor customer made specific investments ("market exchange").
- The supplier alone made specific investments.
- The customer alone made specific investments.

The study showed some notable differences between the countries. Relationships in Japan seemed to be characterised by a larger share of supplier-specific investments, while the opposite situation prevailed in the USA. But there was also an unexpected similarity between the two samples. The occurrence of market exchange and strategic partnership was about the same in both countries. In fact, the US companies scored somewhat higher on partnerships and lower on market exchange, which was contradictory to popular beliefs. However, more interesting for our purposes is that buying firms in both countries showed a considerable variation in their supplier portfolios.

What is even more important are the findings concerning the performance of different types of relationships. According to Bensaou's (1999) observations, there were major performance differentials between the various relationships. But the differences in performance were not related to the actual combination of supplier- and customer-specific investments or what we would prefer to call the "level of involvement". Bensaou's main finding was:

"No one type of relationship, not even the strategic partnership, is inherently superior to the others. Each [combination of involvement] contained low and high performing relationships, suggesting that each type of relationship can be well or poorly managed."

(1999: 37)

Again, we are provided with evidence of the need to effectively handle a portfolio of different relationships with suppliers.

Relationship involvement and volume of business

It is generally suggested that high involvement is preferable in supplier relationships that represent a major volume of business for the buying company, and that low involvement can be practised in low-volume relationships. However, both low-involvement relationships with major suppliers and high involvement with minor suppliers might be viable and effective strategies in some circumstances. First, high involvement in relationships for low volumes of business is an appropriate approach when the supplier has particular skills and capabilities that are not widely available, or where their offerings can have a considerable impact on the buying company's own offerings. The supplier may also represent great development potential. This situation is well illustrated by large pharmaceutical companies that establish high-involvement relationships with small innovative companies in biotechnology. Second, a customer company can handle only a limited number of high-involvement relationships because they are resource-intensive. Therefore it might not be possible to be highly involved with all suppliers representing major business volumes. A customer is thus faced with the necessity of determining which of its major relationships should be of the high-involvement type and which must be handled in other ways.

Low involvement with major suppliers is appropriate when the direct costs of purchasing are the most significant ones and the potential gains from further involvement are limited. This is often the case where standardised offerings and solutions are involved. In fact, savings from reducing the level of involvement in a large volume relationship may be substantial in some cases. A low-involvement approach is also likely to make sense when the customer will find it difficult to induce the supplier to make reciprocal efforts to develop a closer relationship. Being highly involved may not suit a big supplier because of the relatively small scale of the buyer, or the perceived absence of benefits in technology development, or simply because its efforts are directed elsewhere.

Supplier Networks

So far in this chapter we have focused on a buying firm's relationships with its individual suppliers. But the network context of each relationship must also be considered if a company is to make the best use of its suppliers. Considerable benefits for a customer can be achieved by active attempts to co-ordinate what happens between different suppliers and adapting the company's internal operations to networks of embedded suppliers rather than simply to individual vendors. This section examines two crucial issues in a network view of the supply side. The first deals with the number of suppliers and the sourcing approach of the buying firm while the second concerns the nature of the connections between the customer and its suppliers.

Number of suppliers and sourcing approach

The past few decades have shown significant reductions in the supplier bases of companies. There are three main reasons for this development:

- *System sourcing*: When companies concentrate on fewer activities they become assemblers putting together a huge number of components delivered by specialised suppliers. These assemblers often appoint a small number of "systems suppliers" that are responsible for the combined activities of a number of sub-suppliers. For the buying firm this means substantial reductions in direct transaction costs and the total relationship handling costs, while the direct procurement cost and the costs in the relationship with the first-tier supplier increases.

- *Consolidation of purchasing*: Many companies have concentrated on fewer suppliers for the items that they buy. For example, in 1981 Motorola had 109 active suppliers of capacitors (Stork 1999). The central purchasing department then installed a simple supplier rating system so they could inform the decentralised business units which suppliers actually offered the best business conditions. After a few years three suppliers had won 95% of Motorola's capacitor business. Another example is that Harley

Davidson has cut its supply base in half since 1990 (Morgan 2000). They did this in a conscious effort to eliminate the suppliers who were not "up to meeting the new objectives of cost, quality and timing". In the area of original equipment purchases, Harley Davidson concentrates 80% of its purchases on a critical group of suppliers who willingly take part in the company's supply strategies. The company is on track to move from in excess of 3,000 MRO suppliers to concentrating 80–90% of its buying to only three suppliers.

- *High-involvement relationships*: These are associated with a switch to single sourcing. Historically, the main advantage of single sourcing was perceived to be increased bargaining power. However, over time the need to reduce the indirect costs of purchasing led to an emphasis on high-involvement relationships with suppliers. Because these are resource-demanding they led to pressures to reduce the companies' supply base. Once this is done and buyer and supplier begin to work more closely together, a number of opportunities to improve relationship performance might appear.

The increasing reliance on single sourcing contrasts with previous recommendations for multiple sourcing and arm's-length relationships. The main reason for these recommendations was that the buying firm, by applying single sourcing, would lose the benefits of reduced transaction uncertainty, enhanced flexibility and stimulation of price competition, which stem from having many suppliers. However, it is by no means clear that multiple sourcing is the only means to achieve these objectives. For example, single sourcing may reduce transaction uncertainty more than multiple sourcing does. Single sourcing in combination with a high-involvement approach makes it possible to jointly develop logistics systems, which might improve delivery reliability substantially more than any multiple sourcing approach. Correspondingly, sticking to one supplier does not necessarily increase the likelihood of becoming locked into a specific technology. On the contrary, close co-operation and mutual openness regarding technical development may reduce the risks of these negative effects. Implications of a single source approach are analysed in Larsson and Kulchitsky (1998).

When it comes to the opportunities to play suppliers off against each other, we have already mentioned that this is favourable only in terms of reduced direct procurement costs. In cases where these costs are less important than indirect costs, single sourcing may be a better way to deal with cost rationalisation. Furthermore, what is often forgotten is that there is a cost of competition. There are substantial costs associated with "playing the market", such as those of prospecting for potential suppliers, tendering procedures and supplier evaluation. In many cases the gains from price reductions achieved through competitive procedures are more than outweighed by the increasing administrative costs of the procedures themselves. In some cases the company may attain short-term benefits by playing the market. However, in the long run, this may lead to increasing costs, because it is difficult for the buying company to benefit from potential rationalisation in supply handling by continuously searching for the lowest price. It also imposes restrictions in price negotiations because bargaining power is to a large extent dependent on the total business volume with the supplier. Other implications of multiple sourcing are that the economies of scale of the supplier are negatively affected and that it becomes difficult to ask suppliers for solutions that are well adapted to the internal conditions of the buying firm.

Level of involvement and sourcing policy

Figure 5.2 shows in matrix form two independent dimensions of purchasing strategy: sourcing policy and level of relationship involvement. Most available texts on the management of supplier relationships focus on two of the cells in the matrix in Figure 5.2 and recommend that companies should move from Cell 1 – low-involvement, multiple sourcing to Cell 4 – high-involvement, single sourcing.

Although we have argued the benefits of high-involvement relationships throughout this book, it is important to avoid a one-sided recommendations of a *general* move from Cell 1 to 4, which we think is an over-simplification of a complex strategic issue. Reality shows that buying companies in certain situations rely on a low-involvement approach and apply multiple sourcing – and that they do so for good reasons. High-involvement relationships are costly and can be justified only when the relationship benefits outweigh costs. Furthermore, high involvement requires interested counterparts, that are not always available. Therefore, it is perfectly rational for a company to manage some of its relationships under the conditions in Cell 1. We also suggest that changing conditions might lead a buying company to move some of its transactions from Cell 4 to Cell 1. This occurs when the conditions that justified a high-involvement relationship no longer prevail.

The other combinations in the matrix are also not only possible, but common and desirable. A company may choose to be highly involved with multiple suppliers (Cell 2). In this case, the buying firm may prefer to use more than one supplier for a component because its own customers prescribe which supplier is to be used. This is often the case when airlines and truck operators specify the types of engines to be used in their purchases. It is also common for equipment manufacturers to offer different options in the sophistication of their control systems, so they need to deal with more than one supplier. The fact that a company uses two or more suppliers for the same component does not necessarily prevent it from being highly involved with both of them.

A low-involvement approach with a single-source supplier (Cell 3) is a seemingly contradictory combination. However, it can offer advantages similar to those of low-involvement relationships with important suppliers. When direct procurement costs

Sourcing policy	*Single*	3	4
	Multiple	1	2
		Low	*High*

Relationship involvement

Figure 5.2   Relationship Involvement and Sourcing Policy.
Reprinted from Industrial Marketing Management, 29, Gadde and Snehota, Making the most of supplier relationships, p 313, Copyright (2000), with permission from Elsevier.

account for the major part of the total costs, then such relationships might be preferred. Distribution businesses often practise this approach. If the customer is only a small buyer, it may try to make itself a more interesting business partner by allocating the whole of its business to one supplier. However, if it is concerned about the vulnerability that comes with its small size, it may avoid too much integration with that supplier so as to retain the option of switching to another supplier if a better alternative appears or the situation demands it.

The four combinations of involvement and sourcing policy provide very different opportunities for improving purchasing performance. Each of them has its specific advantages. Companies considering only the traditional dichotomy found in Cells 1 and 4 are unnecessarily limiting their strategic scope. Again, variation is prescribed as a powerful recipe for effective purchasing. A buying company needs a bundle of supplier relationships with different, complementary characteristics. One crucial issue is how these different relationships can be appropriately combined.

Handling relationships with many suppliers

We have argued that a company needs a policy on the extent of co-ordination, adaptation and interaction with each of its suppliers. In the same way, a company needs to think about the connections *between* these suppliers. The company could choose to handle each of these supplier relationships separately. But it may be able to achieve substantial cost and revenue benefits by actively fostering connections between them, in such things as joint logistics or information systems. Two examples will serve to illustrate this phenomenon:

- Many companies have broadened their scope of supplies and become assemblers. They put together a huge number of components arriving from many specialised suppliers, all of which need to be on time because inventories have been radically reduced. The assembly operations of an automotive customer would be impossible if each supplier delivered in its own way and there are obvious advantages to the assembler if the suppliers deliver in a co-ordinated manner. In such a situation the customer company can improve performance by organising the supply network. However, the buying company must be careful with forcing suppliers to one-sided adaptations. Since most suppliers have other customers, it would cause them problems if each customer asked the supplier to adapt to their specific requirements. Therefore, suppliers welcome joint customer initiatives in this respect. Similar requirements from a group of customers provide advantages for suppliers because they then can deliver to a number of customers in a similar way.
- Supermarkets "assemble" an ever-widening assortment of products from a large range of producers and directly from growers in many countries of the world. They would be unable to operate if each supplier delivered to them independently. Thousands of separate trucks would have to call on each store. To cope with this and to minimise their logistics costs, supermarkets have taken the responsibility for integrating the logistics of the vast majority of their suppliers, involving them in delivering to the store's central warehouse in accordance with pre-determined schedules.

These examples illustrate the need for a customer to integrate the processes of different suppliers with its own operations. It seems likely that even more advantages could be obtained if the buyer promotes an exchange of resources and knowledge *among* its suppliers. In this way it would establish what we have called activity links or resource ties among its suppliers, not just in its own relationships. This approach has been adopted by Nike, who requires its more advanced suppliers to provide technical assistance to others.

Buying firms must be aware of and take advantage of opportunities for *networking*.[4] Each company has access to a large resource base of related suppliers and this resource must be adequately used. Some examples of this are given below.

Developing activity patterns and resource constellations between a number of suppliers are important tasks in networking, with the ultimate aim of increasing efficiency or enhancing innovation. A customer needs to know about a wide range of different companies, in addition to those from which it currently buys. It also needs social capital in order to influence them. This capital is, to a large extent, developed through the customer's business relationships with its direct suppliers and with others, including their suppliers' suppliers. In this context, networking involves working on the connections between a number of relationships. It is important to observe that increasing attention to key-account management by customers and suppliers may lead to a focus on individual relationships, with the risk that network issues will be neglected.

Personal networks are perhaps the most significant basis for networking. It is a key task for all the people involved to develop an extensive and dense personal contact network with suppliers and suppliers' suppliers. Some companies use seminars with suppliers and joint training programmes to enhance these individual networks.

Another means of attaining the same objective is to work systematically with projects where suppliers and sub-suppliers are involved. These projects should always also include visits and meetings with other people within the companies in order to make it easier to develop such networks. These projects should preferably involve more than two parties. Box 5.5 illustrates the benefits ITT Automotive have experienced through joint development efforts.

Box 5.5   Benefits from Joint Development

Every time you have a team approach with a common objective, then you're highly focused. When you get a supplier, an engineer, and a purchasing person together, you can co-ordinate the interfaces of the applications of parts. You can review the cost parameters versus a target. If you have the suppliers in up-front, they understand where you are starting from and what the target is. By having them work as a team, by having all expectations set out with respect to quality, cost, timing for prototypes etc., it's just a much faster process.

Source:Purchasing (1997a: 32S15).

---

[4] We will examine networking as a key constituent of managing in networks in Chapter 8.

As well as informal contacts between individuals, formal means, such as alliances with suppliers, are ways of improving the conditions for networking. This is of particular interest in cases where extensive knowledge exchange is required, such as when two or more companies agree to make use of each other's technology.

A major issue is how supplier networks develop. It seems that many Japanese sub-contractors have been more or less forced into relationships involving extensive co-ordination by a customer, because of the considerable power of those customers. Those suppliers that achieve a first-tier position seem to benefit from the process, but those on other tiers have very little discretion over their activities and are very vulnerable to changes in customer requirements or attitudes. Some more powerful suppliers have entered these relationships on more mutually beneficent terms. It is likely to be very difficult for a small customer to involve large suppliers in these efforts. In this case, the customer's best approach is likely to involve building on the inevitable similarities in the problems and approaches of different suppliers and to relate their own activities to these existing networks of relationships.

Critical Issues in Managing Supplier Relationships

It is necessary for any company to actively try to manage its supplier relationships to make the best use of the resources of its suppliers. There are two different dimensions to this. The first is about using each individual supplier in the most appropriate way; the second is about effectively using the combined potential of all of the suppliers in the network. The core of our argument is that the contributions that a customer receives from its suppliers will depend on how they are handled. This involves at least three managerial issues.

Monitoring relationships and modifying involvement

The level of involvement is a crucial issue in any relationship. High-involvement relationships may provide substantial benefits, but they also entail substantial costs. Therefore, an important managerial issue is about assessing those costs and benefits. Evaluations of this type are rare. Many firms tend to enter high-involvement relationships and accordingly reduce the supplier base without analysing the prerequisites and consequences of these strategic changes. For example, one study revealed that most firms "appear to be pursuing supplier reductions without clear assessment of the costs and benefits involved" (Cousins 1999). Another study reports on a relationship that was characterised by the fact that the customer, "had been overpaying for services in the name of partnerships, the terms and benefits of which could not be identified, let alone quantified" (Kapour and Gupta 1997). Benefits from partnerships are thus not reaped automatically. Therefore, the level of involvement must be continuously monitored and adapted to changing conditions. Box 5.6 shows the criteria used by Kodak for continuous evaluation of their supplier partnerships.

> **Box 5.6   Kodak's Criteria for Evaluating Partnerships**
>
> - Amount of technical support
> - Number of innovative ideas
> - Supplier's ability to communicate effectively on important issues
> - Flexibility shown by supplier
> - Cycle time, responsiveness, and improvements shown
> - Supplier identification with Kodak goals; are our goals common?
> - Level of trust that exists in dealing with the supplier
> - Strength of the relationship at each plant
>
> *Source*: Ellram and Edis (1996: 25).

Modifying involvement in a relationship in line with what is justified is one of the critical issues in supply network strategies. In most relationships there are times when it becomes necessary to consider decreasing the level of involvement. In some cases substantial gains might be attained through a standardised low-involvement relationship. In other situations the movement may need to be in the opposite direction, because there may be potential benefits in increasing involvement.

When supplier performance is seen to be inadequate, the buying company has two options: change supplier or improve the relationship. Traditionally, companies changed suppliers in these situations. However, nowadays, the main effort seems directed towards assisting suppliers to enhance their performance. For example, a representative of Harley Davidson stated that if suppliers are not doing well, "we send resources to help them" (Milligan 2000). This shift in attitudes implies that making the most of supplier relationships has become a matter of using *existing* relationships in the best way rather than trying to find the "best" potential partner.

Customer intervention

The second issue in managing supplier relationships is the need to remember that buyer–seller relations are two-sided. It is customer–supplier interaction that determines the performance of a relationship. Therefore, any attempt by a customer to manage a relationship must also take the interests of the supplier into consideration. For example, a customer cannot decide in isolation about what level of involvement there should be, "It takes two to tango." Thus, an interesting relationship from the customer's perspective may be impossible to develop because of supplier reluctance. Despite this, many customer companies try to determine the role of their suppliers mainly from their own perspectives. This is often seen in so-called "supplier development programmes" that usually aim at directing supplier operations to fit better with those of the customer. There might be good reasons for a customer to wish to help suppliers develop in this way, but they are unlikely to be successful unless they relate equally closely to supplier requirements.

Quinn (1999) argues that the buying firm should avoid too detailed direction of suppliers. The reason for this recommendation is that the vendor has been chosen for its competence and, typically, has more knowledge about what it should do than has the customer. A crucial issue for the buying firm is to balance its control ambitions with the most appropriate use of the supplier's resources. For the customer, one important step in this process is to shift its approach to managing *what* result is desired, rather than managing *how* the result should be produced. If the buyer specifies how to do the job in too much detail "it will kill innovation and vitiate the supplier's real advantage" (1999: 19).

Mobilisation and motivation of suppliers

One underlying theme of this book is that high-involvement relationships entail considerable costs for buying companies because they require significant and continuing investments. But these relationships impose costs on suppliers as well. Therefore, buying firms have to encourage and motivate suppliers to be able to mobilise them in high-involvement relationships.

Ellram and Edis (1996) illustrate how Kodak figures out the incentives and improvements offered to suppliers involved in partnerships:

- The first benefit for Kodak's suppliers is that they have secured Kodak's long-term business, which makes them better able to plan for their future investments and use of resources. The supplier can thus sharpen its resource utilisation, and focus on meeting the particular needs of fewer, key customers.
- Understanding the directions and needs of a demanding supplier may, in turn, lead to new development opportunities. A supplier may, for example, be able to develop business with Kodak's OEM suppliers, since Kodak requires OEMs to work with the designated partner on new product development.
- The supplier also may reduce its administrative burden and improve its use of resources when it has lower bidding and quotation requirements.
- The supplier no longer has to "hard sell" at all Kodak's locations as Kodak's internal teams do the selling job for supplier partners.
- Finally, the dedicated Corporate Account Management System helps to build a strong international customer/supplier network among all of Kodak's facilities, supporting improved relationships.

Once suppliers have been mobilised, they must be continuously encouraged and motivated to continue the relationship and contribute to performance enhancement. Some interesting examples of motivational programmes can be found at Caterpillar and Cessna. Caterpillar uses three types of activities to strengthen relationships with suppliers (Millen-Porter 1997) One of them is a business simulation game where representatives of Caterpillar and suppliers learn to identify potential benefits from high-involvement relationships. This is the most significant activity in trying to develop the contact pattern between the parties and to establish a common perspective on business operations. The two other building blocks in the supplier programme are a system for quality assurance and a "supplier show" where suppliers are given the option to present what they can offer.

Cessna has two main activities to support suppliers and strengthen relationships (Morgan 2000). The first is supplier conferences, which are seen as strategic communication and learning vehicles and are run on an annual basis. Another part of the programme involves the setting up of a supplier advisory board, which makes it possible for suppliers to get their voices heard by the Cessna management.

Conclusion: Making the Most of Supplier Relationships

Supplier relationships are an integral part of any company's operations. Recent trends in outsourcing reflect a growing awareness of the potential contributions from supplier relationships for cost reduction and revenue enhancement. Making the most of this potential requires a variety of relationships characterised by different levels of involvement. Reaping the benefits of supplier-relationship assets is, of course, not automatic. Many success stories often do not document the fact that they have been based on a radical overhaul of supply strategy. In particular, attitudes to the purchasing task, as well as to suppliers, need to be reconsidered. Achieving the benefits of improved supply relationships often requires changes in how suppliers connect into the various facets of the company's business. Accessing supplier skills and resources requires the development of high-involvement relationships. These lead to increased dependence on the supplier and some loss of autonomy for the buying company. These relationships require investment and maintenance costs. High-involvement relationships become very tangible liabilities as well as assets. Critics can well point to the risks that these relationships entail, such as rising switching costs if suppliers perform badly; the possible loss of business secrets and costs of commitment to close relationships. While marriages with suppliers can undoubtedly be beneficial, they remain open to challenges from other partners of the supplier.

Attempts to develop supplier relationships are likely to be troublesome if the company does not have a thorough understanding of the logic of its own business processes. This involves an awareness of the connections between its own activities and those of its suppliers, as well as those between its key suppliers and their other customers. It is important also to reconsider generally held beliefs and attitudes concerning what are often called "close" relationships. There is a tendency to portray arm's-length relationships as full of conflict, while "close partnerships" are assumed to be more friendly and co-operative. In our experience, this is a misconception. All relationships are characterised by a mix of conflict and co-operation. In fact, high-involvement relationships usually involve more conflict than low-involvement ones. In low-involvement relationships there may be frequent discussions about price levels, quality and delivery terms, but on the whole there is not so much to argue about. In high-involvement relationships arguments can rage over the details of joint investments, product adaptations and other strategic issues, even if the customer and supplier agree on an overall approach. The higher the involvement between the companies, the greater the interdependence and the more pronounced the potential for conflict. This fact is illustrated by the way Sun deals with suppliers:

"While Sun works closely with suppliers, involving them in product development and bringing them in-house, it doesn't mean that the company isn't demanding. In fact, Sun has a reputation for being tough with suppliers: on cost, delivery, and quality."

(Carbone 1996: 44)

The main characteristic of the relationship atmosphere in high-involvement arrangements is thus the simultaneous occurrence of conflict and co-operation. Owing to the mutual interdependence of the companies, conflicts have to be solved one way or another before they escalate to confrontation. This does not mean that conflicts should be avoided. On the contrary, diversity of goals and convictions are prerequisites for innovation. Therefore, it is necessary for each company to continue to emphasise its own objectives and interests. At the same time it must be accepted that the counterpart has other interests and objectives that also need to be taken into consideration.

References

Anderson, J. and Narus, J. (1999) *Business Market Management*, Upper Saddle River, NJ: Prentice Hall.

Axelsson, B. and Håkansson, H. (1984) *Inköp för konkurrenskraft*. Stockholm: Liber.

Bechtel, C. and Patterson, J. (1997) "MRO-partnerships: A Case Study", *International Journal of Purchasing and Material Management*, Summer, 18–23.

Bensaou, M. (1999) "Portfolios of Buyer-Supplier Relationships", *Sloan Management Review*, Summer, 35–44.

Carbone, J. (1996) "Sun Shines by Taking out Time", *Purchasing*, 19 September, 34–45.

Carbone, J. (1999) "Reinventing Purchasing Wins the Medal for Big Blue", *Purchasing*, 16 September, 38–62.

Cousins, P. (1999) "Supplier Base Rationalization – Myth or Reality?" *European Journal of Purchasing and Supply Management*, 5, 143–155.

Dubois, A. (1998) *Organising Industrial Activities Across Firm Boundaries*, London: Routledge.

Dubois, A., Gadde, L-E. and Mattsson, L-G. (2003) "To Switch or Not to Switch – On Change and Continuity in Buyer-Seller Relationships", *Journal of Business Research* (forthcoming).

Dyer, J., Cho, D. and Chu, W. (1998) "Strategic Supplier Segmentation: The Next 'Best Practice' in Supply Chain Management". *California Management Review*, 40(2), 57–76.

Ellram, L. and Edis, O. (1996) "A Case Study of Successful Partnering Implementation", *International Journal of Purchasing and Materials Management*, Fall, 20–28.

Gadde, L-E and Håkansson, H. (2001) *Supply Network Strategies*. Chichester: John Wiley.

Gadde, L-E. and Mattsson, L-G. (1987) "Stability and Change in Network Relationships", *International Journal of Research in Marketing*, 4(1), 29–41.

Gadde, L-E. and Snehota, I. (2000) "Making the Most of Supplier Relationships", *Industrial Marketing Management*, 29, 305–316.

Håkansson, H. (ed.) (1982) *International Marketing and Purchasing of Industrial Goods: An Interaction Approach*, Chichester: John Wiley and Sons.

Kapour, V. and Gupta, A. (1997) "Aggressive Sourcing: A Free Market Approach", *Sloan Management Review*, Fall, 21–31.

Lamming, R. (1993) *Beyond Partnership: Strategies for Innovation and Lean Supply*, Hemel Hempstead: Prentice Hall.

Larsson, P.D. and Kulchitsky, J.D. (1998) "Single Sourcing and Supplier Certification – Performance and Relationship Implications", *Industrial Marketing Management*, 27(1), 73–81.

Le Sueur, M. and Dale, B.G. (1998) "The Procurement of Maintenance, Repair and Operating Supplies: A Study of the Key Problems", *European Journal of Purchasing and Supply Management*, 4, 247–255.

Millen-Porter, A. (1997) "At Cat They're Driving Supplier Integration into the Design Process", *Purchasing*, 7 March, 37–40.

Milligan, B. (2000) "Harley Davidson Wins by Getting Suppliers on Board", *Purchasing*, 21 September, 52–65.

Minahan, T. (1995) "Can't Get a Handle on Freight Costs? Give Up Trying", *Purchasing*, 23 November, 35–36.

Morgan, J. (2000) "Cessna Charts a Supply Chain Flight Strategy", *Purchasing*, 7 September, 42–61.

Purchasing (1997) "Suppliers: The Competitive Edge in Design", *Purchasing*, 1 May, 32S5–32S23.

Quinn, J. (1999) "Strategic Outsourcing: Leveraging Knowledge Capabilities", *Sloan Management Review*, Summer, 9–21.

Stork, K. (1999) "Single Sourcing Part II", *Purchasing*, 4 November, 32.

Stundza, T. (1999) "Aerospace Purchasing Gets Overhauled", *Purchasing*, 5 June, 66–73.

van Weele, A. (2000) *Purchasing and Supply Chain Management: Analysis, Planning and Practice*. London: Thomson Learning.

Wynstra, F. (1998) "Purchasing Involvement in Product Development", Dissertation, Eindhoven Center for Innovation Studies. Eindhoven University.

DISTRIBUTION IN BUSINESS NETWORKS

6

Aims of this Chapter

- To explain the meaning of distribution and to discuss its role and importance in business networks.
- To explore the characteristics and consequences of different types of distribution relationships.
- To examine distribution from the perspective of users.
- To analyse distribution relationships in terms of the three network dimensions of actors, activities and resources.
- To provide a discussion of change and stability in distribution networks.

Introduction

The theme of this book is management issues in inter-company relationships. So far, however, our discussions have largely focused on the tasks of managing these relationships in situations where the offering of a supplier company becomes a direct input for a customer. Examples of this are when a supplier performs a service directly for a customer, or a supplier delivers raw materials, components or a piece of capital equipment directly to the plant of another firm. But the relationships between companies in business markets take a wide variety of forms, in addition to those between a producer and an immediate user.

Many manufacturers have hardly any direct contact with the end-users of their offerings, but instead have major relationships with industrial distributor companies. These distributors hold stock and deliver products to users and provide them with information and after-sales service. In these ways they are responsible for fulfilling important elements of the supplier's offering. Most manufacturers have found that distributors are the most efficient means to serve the after-market for their products and their huge numbers of small end-users. It is not only from the perspective of a manufacturer that "intermediaries" of various kinds are perceived to improve distribution performance. Lots of end-users have no interest in direct contact with manufacturers. They use distributors as a means to enhance the operations on the supply side of their companies. Normally a distributor is a significant actor both in the customer networks of manufacturers and in the supplier networks of users.

In most cases distribution is analysed from the perspective of producers. In one respected textbook this is expressed as "the route taken by a product as it moves from the producer to user" and this process is seen "through the eyes of marketing management in producing and manufacturing firms" (Rosenbloom 1995: 5). In this chapter we take a complementary perspective and explore distribution from the users' side. We do this by analysing relationships in distribution in their network context.

Some Fundamentals of Distribution

There are at least three interpretations of the word "distribution":

- *Distribution as the activities that bridge the gap between producer and user*: At a general level, distribution is the activities that "bridge the gap between the producer of a product and the user of it" (Lewis 1968). When this view is emphasised, the so-called *distribution functions* come into focus. These distribution functions are the activities that are necessary for gap-bridging and include, among others, promotion, negotiation, physical distribution and risk-taking (Kotler 2000).
- *Distribution as physical delivery*: A more limited interpretation of distribution relates to just one of the distribution functions. It sees distribution as the physical delivery of the offering. This view of distribution is concerned with the actual fulfilment of a business transaction. Fulfilment involves two flows that are normally associated with distribution. First, a flow of information needs to be established between companies. Second, the flow of products and services must be organised. Handling these two flows in an efficient way is considered the main issue in *distribution management* (see, for example, Stock and Lambert 2001).
- *Distribution as a network*: The third interpretation of distribution, which we follow in this chapter, sees distribution as the "network" through which offerings are fulfilled. This distribution network consists of the companies involved in distribution, the relationships between them and the resource infrastructure that they use in their operations. The companies involved in distribution include *manufacturers* and independent *distributors*, such as wholesalers and retailers. The distribution infra-structure includes the roads, railways, trucks, material handling equipment, ware-houses, communication systems and all the other facilities that are necessary to fulfil the offerings of suppliers. The network links the companies that make the promise of an offering, the intermediaries involve in its fulfilment and the customers that hope to

receive that promise (see for example Stern and El-Ansary 1996).[1] In this way, a distribution network connects the wider networks of these suppliers and users.

Suppliers and customers bridge the gap between them by making the best use of the existing distribution resources and by developing them further. In this chapter we are concerned with distribution in a broad context – involving both activity and resource structures and how these are governed by the actors that are involved.

In some cases a manufacturer and a user are in direct contact with each other. In many cases, however, a supplier delivers to other companies, which in turn deal with the final user. It is not unusual for two or more intermediaries to be involved in distribution operations, as in the case of wholesalers and retailers. Many companies use a combination of both direct and indirect distribution. SKF, the world's largest manufacturer of rolling bearings, is one example. Around two-thirds of its turnover consists of direct sales to industrial users handled by its own sales force and subsidiaries. Primarily SKF is in direct contact with customers buying large volumes of bearings. Another group of direct customers are those where the exchange of technical information is important. Either it may be the customer that is in need of technical support or it may be the case that the customer provides SKF with technical know-how. Car and truck assemblers are examples of this group. These customers may require adapted bearings, which are developed in interaction with SKF technicians. Furthermore, they buy large volumes on a regular basis, which provide opportunities for establishing integrated logistics systems to make the physical deliveries more efficient.

Other customers buy only small volumes of bearings. If they mainly use standardised bearings it would be very expensive for them to buy directly, because SKF's sales organisation is designed to serve large accounts. Sales visits and physical delivery to small buyers would entail substantial costs if the salesperson and the lorries were used for the offerings of only SKF. On the other hand, the salesperson of a distributor represents a portfolio of offerings from different suppliers. This makes both a sales visit and a delivery economically feasible, even if purchases of an individual product are only small. Distributors also serve the after-market for spares of those products that are delivered directly to manufacturers. For example, roller bearings in cars need to be replaced, either at repair workshops or through do-it-yourself activities. It would be very difficult for SKF to organise an efficient distribution system serving these end-users. Instead they rely on local distributors, which together account for about one-third of SKF's total sales and represent an even greater proportion of its profits.

Normally, manufacturers' own distribution arrangements account for the majority of total sales, while distributors handle the majority of the customers. For example, in one of the business units within ABB the 100 largest customers account for 60% of total sales.

---

[1] Although we refer to "manufacturers" and "distributors", it is important to note that there is no absolute distinction between them. Manufacturers do not produce an offering that is then distributed *unchanged* by distributors. A manufacturer's offering will consist of elements that it has bought from others that it adds to and transforms. This offering is sold to distributors that also add to it and transform it and sell to others and so on to the final consumer. Distributors and manufacturers have a similar role in this process. Both are "intermediaries" in the process of producing a final offering for a consumer.

These customers are supplied by ABB's sales organisation. The remaining 40% of sales is divided among 39,000 users. It goes without saying that it would be extremely complex and costly for ABB to be in direct contact with all of them and consequently distributors handle these users.

The Importance of Distribution

Distribution and intermediaries have become increasingly significant over time. One reason is that the "gaps" that must be bridged between companies and between them and consumers have grown larger and more numerous. Companies that need to be connected have become increasingly separated through greater concentration, specialisation and geography. When companies are global, supplying a "local" company may actually involve deliveries to several continents. When businesses become more specialised, the number of transactions increases and so does the need for distribution.

Consequently, the costs of distribution have increased considerably. For example, in the car industry, the distribution network normally accounts for one-third of total cost of the final car. This is because of the widening physical gap between companies, the need to reduce lead-times, provide enhanced service and tailor offerings to the particular needs of individual consumers.

This example also highlights the importance of distribution as a source of revenue and profit. This is because the solutions required by customers involve ever more complex and changing offerings. Over time the earlier focus on the product element of offerings has shifted to an emphasis on the other elements: service; advice; adaptation and logistics. A supplier's opportunity to differentiate from its competitors is more likely to be in these other elements, as physical products become increasingly standardised. These other elements are all likely to involve direct contact with the customer and hence involve distribution, either directly by the supplier itself or indirectly by others:

- Distribution provides the logistics element of a supplier's offering. It enables a supplier to solve a customer's problems about where, when and how frequently it needs to receive the product, service or advice elements of an offering.
- Distribution provides adaptations to other elements of an offering in product, service, advice and logistics. Many suppliers are unable to provide these adaptations themselves and have to rely on independent distributors for them. This may lead to increased problems for suppliers as the importance of adaptations to individual requirements increases.

Efficient information exchange is important to improve distribution performance and the flow of offerings through the network. But it is also vital if suppliers are to be able to respond speedily and flexibly to changing customer requirements.

Altogether the requirements of distribution capacity and capability have increased substantially. Suppliers face a major challenge in their distribution operations. On the one hand, customers require improved service levels, but, on the other, they demand decreasing distribution costs. At first glance this equation may seem difficult to solve and it would not be possible if the resources in the distribution infrastructure remained the same. However, developments in information technology and transportation facilities provide new opportunities for distribution. We will return to this issue in the section on differentiated distribution.

Distribution from the User's Perspective

The traditional approach to distribution in marketing textbooks has been to see it from the perspective of a manufacturer. In this approach, it is the manufacturer's task to design an appropriate marketing "channel" to the end-user for its products. Depending on prevailing conditions, the manufacturer may perform this task either by direct distribution or indirectly by using intermediaries. In the latter case, an important decision is to select the most suitable intermediaries to "channel" the goods from the factory to the intended users efficiently and at low cost.

Instead of this one-sided marketing channel view of distribution, our approach is *relational* and each distribution relationship is analysed in a network context. This has a number of implications:

- Our analysis does not centre on a single fixed product for which a channel is assumed to exist. Instead, we start with a user (who may not be the end-user) and are concerned with the *problems* of this user. It is most unlikely that these problems can be solved by a single product or service that can be identified from its point of manufacture and remains unchanged in its flow through a "marketing channel". We argued in Chapter 5 that requirements from users have become more complex as dependence on suppliers has increased owing to outsourcing and the increasing attention paid to high-involvement relationships. This means that users require more complex offerings to solve their problems.
- A network perspective on distribution involves a multiplicity of different activities carried out in varying combinations by numerous companies:
  - Many companies in different locations will develop and/or produce offerings that are sold to others and merged by them in a number of plants. These may be made available in a variety of distant locations by those companies or by others as part of their offering. Yet other companies will take these offerings and install them for a user as their offering.
  - Some companies will carry out many different activities themselves. Others will use third-party vendors or independent contractors, for example, in transportation or after-sales services. For example, some companies may manufacture most of what they sell, or provide all of the service element. Others will buy products and services from others and sell them on. Some will provide all the logistics, advice and adaptation that their customers need. Some will use others for this. Some will supply designs to others or buy them for their own offerings.
- The network view of distribution contrasts with the marketing channel perspective by emphasising that superficially similar companies can have quite different relationships

with the firms around them.[2] The network view shows that we cannot make a neat separation of companies into those that manufacture, wholesale or retail. Many "manufacturers" buy in what they sell and many "distributors" specify and control the design and manufacturing methods of what they buy.

- Finally, the network is at any point in time the outcome of the choices made by all the companies involved, which makes the idea of a single "channel captain" obsolete. No network, including those centring on distribution is designed, controlled or managed by one company or type of companies. This means that efficiency in distribution networks is dependent on the activities of many firms and that efficiency cannot be solely defined in terms of optimising the output of a single producer's factory.

If we take the supply side of users as our starting point for discussing the role of distribution, then it is evident that different end-users, ranging from large businesses to individual consumers, have very different requirements from distribution. To illustrate this variety we will start our analysis of the role of distribution from the perspective of a home computer user. We then extend the analysis to companies of various sizes.

Our first end-user is a home computer user who needs to create and print text-documents, manipulate and analyse numbers and manage records. The problems of this user can be solved by an offering that combines product, service, logistics, advice and adaptation. The product element will consist of hardware (a PC and a printer) and software (word processing, spreadsheet and book-keeping packages), the service element consists of installation, the logistics element is delivery to her house and the advice consists of basic training. It is unlikely that this problem will require significant adaptation by a supplier from its normal offering. The user has a number of options open to her:

- She can find an expert to diagnose her problems and recommend which solutions are required. She can then rely on the expert to procure the products on her behalf, set them up, install them and provide her with the basic training. A variation of this alternative would be if she specified a manufacturer's brand that she trusts and then relied on the expert for the other elements.
- A second option would be to peruse the computer press and suppliers' catalogues and then obtain offers from various suppliers. She could set up and install the equipment herself and then read the user manuals to train herself.

The choice of solution that this end-user makes depends on the uncertainties she has; how comfortable she feels with the technology; her knowledge of suppliers and her ability to provide the service element for herself.

The choice will also determine where the user goes to obtain her solution. If she takes the first option, she will be looking for a single supplier to provide her with a complete solution to her problems. She may choose a local dealer that can deliver within an overall cost and time constraint. If she takes the second option, she is primarily looking for the product element of the offering only and will provide other elements for herself. She will probably shop around to find the lowest price on the models of printer and PC she has

---

[2] For example, variations in the distribution of similar computers has been demonstrated by Hulthén (2002).

decided to buy. Her needs are most likely to be met by a dealer or a mail order supplier, or she may buy the printer from one supplier and the PC from another.

A large user, on the other hand, may have the problem of linking numerous, stand-alone, computerised business processes across geographical boundaries. It may want to redesign some of its core processes to improve the satisfaction of its own customers. Although this is a more complex problem, the potential uncertainties the user faces are the same, as are the elements of the solution that is sought: product, service, logistics, advice and adaptation. The options facing the company are also the same: it can outsource the whole task; utilise its own skills and resources; or employ some combination of the two. However, there are some differences compared with the home user's situation. One is that the service element that the company requires is likely to be a relatively larger part of the total bundle. Furthermore, the products are likely to be adapted in some way rather than the standardised off-the-shelf offerings bought by an individual user or a small company.

A large end-user is likely to prefer a direct relationship with a computer manufacturer. In particular, this might be when dealing directly can bring significant price or logistical advantages or when the relationship requires major integration and adaptation related to the product, service or advice elements of the offering. In the absence of these conditions a user is likely to prefer to deal with a manufacturer indirectly via a distributor, particularly if it already has a relationship with that distributor. A large end-user is also likely to be more able than a small user to substitute its own activities or resources for those of a supplier. For example, the user may decide to develop its own computing skills instead of buying in service or advice. The organisational structure of the buying company will also affect the search for a solution. The local branch of a large firm may have to use suppliers decided by its central purchasing department. When it comes to buying computers a large user will almost certainly be familiar with a set of suppliers it already has a relationship with. The experience of previous transactions with these suppliers to solve similar problems will have significant implications for the outcome of this episode. The network position of the user also affects the search for solutions and suppliers. A large buyer obviously can put more pressure behind its requirements. However, it needs to be emphasised that no end-users are entirely in a position of free choice. The nature of their existing relationships and the characteristics of the wider network that surrounds them will limit their options.

Distribution from a Network Perspective

A network view of distribution highlights that it is not possible to make a clear distinction between what firms that we call manufacturers, distributors and users actually do in distribution operations in business markets. A business customer like BMW uses the design and production resources of a component supplier such as Bosch to manufacture components for it rather than make the components itself. Bosch also manages relationships with many of its suppliers. These suppliers provide inputs Bosch combines to produce an offering for BMW. Thus, Bosch is rather like any other distributor that assembles an assortment for its customers. Similarly, Bosch also uses BMW's design and production skills to transform its own and others' components and thus bring them to a larger set of end-users. Similarly, BMW can be seen as a distributor of Bosch's products to new car buyers. In these operations BMW is acting in a similar way to the wholesalers and dealers that distribute Bosch's offerings to the after-market of existing car owners. BMW is also similar to the new car dealers that distribute BMW's own cars and the components from which they are built.

A main characteristic of distribution networks is the occurrence of *indirect relationships*. Neither Bosch nor BMW are normally perceived as intermediaries but it is obvious that each is an intermediary between other companies. In fact, in a network, all actors are intermediaries because each is embedded in relationships and each of these relationships is embedded in others. Similarly all companies are customers and all are suppliers. We refer to the terms manufacturer and distributors because they are commonly used and understood, but we emphasise the need for care if we are to avoid artificial categorisations. More importantly, a network view of an intermediary like a distributor will be very different from that of a channel view.[3] In the channel view, an intermediary is seen as a way of connecting a large number of manufacturers with a large number of users. Thus an intermediary is a means of promoting economic efficiency by reducing the number of contacts that are necessary. However, to understand what is really going on in manufacturer–distributor–user relationships requires a more comprehensive analysis. A distributor does more than connect a specific manufacturer with a specific user. The networks of all the manufacturers and users are connected through the distributor and its network. For an illustration, see Figure 6.1.

Owing to this complexity it is sometimes difficult for a firm to understand the actions and attitudes of a counterpart within the context of that individual relationship. Therefore, relationships among all the actors involved must be taken into account when analysing these issues. In this wider perspective even apparently strange things may make sense. Suppose that a producer of domestic appliances tries to persuade a distributor to increase its stocks of a product that only sells slowly and is not very profitable for the distributor. The reasons for this might be difficult for the distributor to understand, but can be realised if we look outside the immediate relationship:

- The manufacturer might be pushing this product because it is readily available when compared to others that are in short supply owing to restricted deliveries of components from its own suppliers.
- The manufacturer might be interested to extend the sales of this product because its own suppliers are pressuring it to take more of the components on which it is based.
- The manufacturer might be trying to increase its share of the end-user market for this particular product by getting all its distributors to sell more.
- The manufacturer might want all of its distributors to sell more of this particular product. It might hope that by achieving dominance among distributors it will discourage another manufacturer that is thinking of launching a similar product.

---

[3] For studies of distribution relying on a network view, see Andersson (1992), Tunisini (1997), Rosenbröijer (1998) and Hulthén (2002).

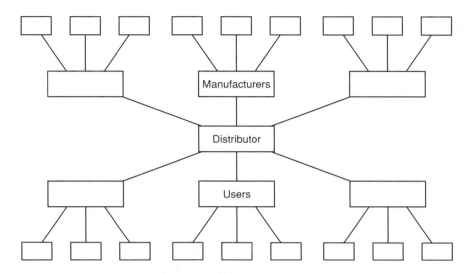

Figure 6.1   The Distributor as a Nexus of Relationships.

These examples are only a few of the potential effects on a relationship of the surrounding network. They arise from differences in motivations and ambitions, as well as from misconceptions of each other's intentions. It is not surprising that they can lead to conflict among the actors in distribution networks. We will come back to these issues later in the chapter.

Relationships in Distribution

From the above section and Chapter 5 on supplier relationships it is clear that buying firms have different requirements when it comes to the solutions of their distribution problems. Some users may favour advanced and costly distribution arrangements, such as just-in-time deliveries, because such solutions improve their performance in other respects. A continuous exchange with the same supplier makes these adaptations feasible. Other users prefer less advanced, less complex – and therefore less costly – solutions. They do so either because a complex solution would not make them better off or because they do not realise the advantages that could be gained from it. These users rely on transactional exchange. Thus one important characteristic of a distribution relationship is the level of complexity of the distribution solution that is applied. Different users perceive the value of advanced solutions differently. A supplier can choose to make different types of solutions available to be attractive to many types of users, or it can prefer to direct its ambitions towards specialised distribution arrangements.

The second important dimension of a distribution relationship concerns the level of involvement between supplier and customer. In Chapter 5 we concluded that users sometimes find it worthwhile to develop high-involvement relationships with suppliers, mainly to gain from solutions that are adapted to their specific needs and demands. On other occasions, however, they may prefer to avoid such involvement and rely on the type of freedom that characterises arm's-length relationships. In this case they make use of standardised solutions that entail low direct cost. We ended the chapter on supplier relationships by saying that both customer and supplier have to consider carefully what is an appropriate level of involvement.

To analyse the alternative situations further we turn to the matrix in Figure 6.2 where four combinations of the level of involvement and the complexity of the distribution solution are identified. We illustrate the differences between these combinations using a simple example of distribution relationships in the case of sheet steel.

Relationships in Cell 1 consist of low-cost distribution arrangements. This type of relationship is appropriate for users that would gain no advantages, or are unable to see the benefits, of a more advanced distribution solution, and/or an arrangement that is adapted to their specific situations. These buyers are not interested in high involvement, because they perceive these relationships too costly. Instead, they are more likely to appreciate the benefits of a simple and standardised solution, which also provides opportunities to switch suppliers easily. A supplier in this type of relationship must offer "sufficient" distribution value so that the sacrifices of the user are perceived to be less than the benefits. As long as these conditions prevail, it is likely that the relationship will continue, leading to a long-term relationship even in the absence of high involvement and adaptations. The main concern of the supplier is to bring down the users' cost as much as possible through cost-effective systems for exchange of information and physical delivery. A manufacturer of steel is likely to be able to provide economies of scale to users by serving its large customers for standardised products by delivering full truckloads. Small buyers, on the other hand, probably are better-off by purchasing from a distributor. In both cases the logistics operations can be undertaken either by the supplier of the steel or by an independent transportation company. Exchange of technical information usually is not a major concern for these standardised products. Order processing and other elements of administrative information play an important role, especially when the purchases occur frequently. Various types of information technology solutions can be applied to this task. In particular, the Internet has provided suppliers and users with entirely new tools for the exchange of information. Less complex arrangements at lower cost may be to use specialised call-centres.

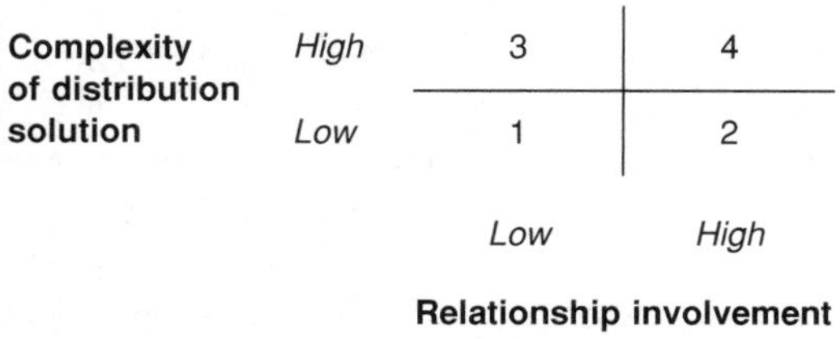

		Low	High
Complexity of distribution solution	*High*	3	4
	Low	1	2
		Low	*High*

Relationship involvement

Figure 6.2   Four Types of Distribution Relationships.

Relationships in Cell 2 also consist of low-complexity distribution arrangements. However, here, the distribution arrangements are adapted to the specific requirements of the user within a high-involvement relationship. This relates to the point made in Chapter 5, that there is a tendency for users to reduce the number of their suppliers and increase the responsibilities of the remainder. These wider, tailored services can take a number of forms. Some relate to the flow of products and services. For example, the customer may appoint its steel supplier to take responsibility for its inventories or to become a "total vendor" supplying the buyer with all its requirements for steel products, services and steel handling equipment. Others concern transport operations. For example, a supplier of bars and beams might develop specific container solutions that make unloading and handling on site more efficient for a building contractor. Others involve the administration of the information exchange between the companies. For example, some suppliers develop catalogues that are tailor-made for specific customers, including only that part of its product range with which they are concerned. The catalogue may be available electronically, or adapted to the ERP system of the user. In some cases the costs of these administrative operations are higher than the total amount paid for the products and services exchanged. Adaptations of this type may be undertaken either by a manufacturer, a distributor or a company specialising in logistics. For an example of a buying company using this strategy see Dubois (2003). When these adaptations occur, a user is likely to stay with this supplier rather than shopping around.

In Cell 3, the distribution solution is complex, but not adapted to the specific problems of individual users. The services provided are advanced and thus costly, but they pay off for customers through improvements in their internal operations. The flow of products and services may be handled through advanced warehousing and transportation equipment. The warehousing services of the steel supplier may include facilities for cutting, bending, blasting and other value-adding activities. In contrast to relationships in Cell 2, these suppliers undertake the operations on a large scale, mainly dealing with standardised solutions. Again, various firms may conduct these activities. The steel service centre may be operated by a steel manufacturer or a metal distributor. But it might also be run by a specialised firm buying sheets from a manufacturer or a distributor and then selling the cut and blasted sheet either through its own sales organisation or through some intermediary.

Developments in information technology provide opportunities for efficient exchange of information (see, for example, Evans and Wurster 1999; Lee and Whang 2001). The Internet provides a cost-efficient solution with certain benefits. But there are also IT systems that are more complex and can provide further advantages. One example is the different types of EDI (electronic data interchange) solutions that have been developed for use in various industries. One of the problems with this technique is that it requires considerable investment. Thus, many companies so far have resisted making use of these advanced systems for communication, instead relying on telephone and fax.

In Cell 3 relationships, suppliers do not adapt their distribution arrangements to individual users. Instead, the users themselves are willing to adapt their own systems to fit with the solutions offered by these suppliers, because the cost of doing this is less than the perceived benefits. Owing to the standardisation of the solution, the supplier is able to reap the economies of scale that are required for the development of these high-performing distribution systems. Suppliers taking this route generally invest more in developing advanced solutions for communication and transportation than they invest in specific relationships.

Cell 4 relationships are where considerable adaptations are made in the relationship and the distribution solution is also complex. A typical example of this type of distribution relationship is the just-in-time deliveries from component and system suppliers to car manufacturers. When car manufacturers re-organised their production systems, the demands for reliability in supply increased considerably. A crucial prerequisite for JIT deliveries is an efficient system for information exchange. These communication systems link the transportation and production systems of supplier and customer with one another and this, among other things, reduces the need for inventories (see, for example, Evans and Berman 2001; Lambert and Cooper 2001). For this type of integration to be effective, there must be substantial coordination of activities and communication on both sides and substantial investment. Once these investments have been made, they increase the level of involvement in the relationships. The types of adaptations to individual users discussed for Cell 2 relationships also occur in this cell as do the complex distribution arrangements present in Cell 3.

Suppliers of sheet steel have to identify those buyers of steel that find it worthwhile to make the necessary investments for just-in-time deliveries. Possible types of users would be large-scale producers of ventilation ducting, metal cans, etc. In this case the supplier has to develop distribution offerings that are considered valuable by the users, in spite of their costs. Suppliers involved in these relationships need the resources and skills to develop complex, high-performance solutions as well as the ability to deal with the complexity of high-involvement relationships.

Differentiated Distribution Networks

Analysis of the distribution demands of users and the different types of distribution relationships reveals a great variety in the complexity of the distribution solutions and the extent of supplier–customer involvement.[4] Coping with this diversity would place very heavy requirements on the resources and skills of suppliers. Because of this, many suppliers choose to focus on one of the four types of relationships, thus addressing only a few of the distribution problems of users. However, customers are keen to reduce their supplier bases and to increase the responsibility of each supplier. This could lead to problems for a supplier with narrowly defined distribution ability. Also, the problems and demands of users are dynamic, as is the surrounding network. Therefore, it is likely that many suppliers will try to operate in all four cells of the matrix and offer each alternative in different situations. To do this, they will either have to develop the resources and skills for each type of relationship themselves or develop relationships with others that can provide them on their behalf, see below. The alternative of a single "average" capability aimed at all four cells will not be able to compete successfully against distribution

---

[4] Hence leading to a wide variety in offerings and relationships for the same 'product' or 'service'.

solutions that more precisely meet the requirements of the relationships in each cell. A supplier providing an average solution will not be able to reach the cost level of suppliers focusing on the requirements of relationships in Cell 1, because it will also be trying to satisfy more demanding customers as well. Nor is it likely that average solutions will satisfy the demands for the advanced solutions required by relationships in Cells 3 and 4, because the supplier must be careful to keep its costs low.

The conclusion of this analysis is that an average solution will tend to be "stuck in the middle" and that distribution solutions must be differentiated according to different users' problems and their consequent requirements. Traditionally, distribution services have hardly been differentiated, even though customers' needs may have varied. The main reason is that the prevailing view was of a channel from a manufacturer to a user and this view focused on the output operations of manufacturers rather than the input side of users. But the demand for differentiation has increased substantially over the past decade. One reason is that purchasing activities in customers are now more important financially and more professionally carried out. Another driving force is technical development that makes new distribution arrangements possible.

Few suppliers can afford the multiple skills and resources to operate in all four cells of the matrix and therefore must develop relationships with other companies, each providing specific capabilities and resources.[5] Some of these companies contribute with low-cost arrangements, while others may provide more advanced solutions. Together these actors form constellations, which are more network-like than channel-like. Figure 6.3 illustrates these in the distribution network connecting users of computers and a PC-manufacturer.

The actual complexity of the networks in which these operations take place is considerably reduced in this figure. Each of the component suppliers will also have their own suppliers and although some of the end-users are households, others will be companies having their own customers. Each of the other actors will also have many relationships that are not illustrated. We can describe the network starting from company X which is primarily a manufacturer of computer hardware. This company has an offering consisting of product (hardware and software) and services. Some of the elements of the offering have been developed by X itself and some by a range of other companies. The offering will finally reach the end-users in the diagram as part of the offering of several other companies. Some of these, such as the independent distributors, may transport and stock the offering provided by X and make it available to other companies along with similar offerings from other companies. Other actors in the network such as the "value added resellers" (VARs) or "value added distributors" (VADs) will use their own expertise and resources to add to this offering, combine it with the offerings of others and provide a transformed offering to their customers.

The end-users in the network are likely to have a range of different requirements. Some will find very cost-efficient solutions useful. They are the skilled and experienced buyers of these types of offering (with low need uncertainty) that will not be willing to pay for advice or additional service that they do not consider useful. These end-users will

---

[5] This process is an example of "intermediarisation" and we will discuss this fully in Chapter 8.

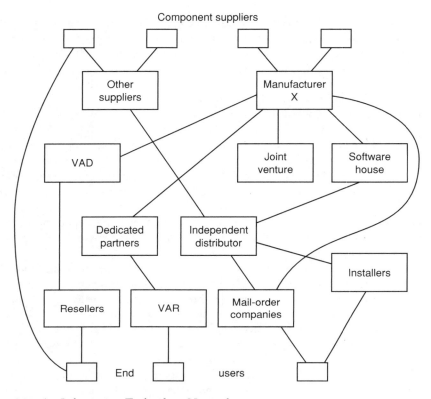

Figure 6.3 An Information Technology Network.

probably choose to buy individual items of hardware and software through mail order or from a low-service distributor, as is commonly the case for many purchases of personal computers. Other end-users might see the advantages in more advanced distribution solutions. They might wish to compare the offerings of various manufacturers, or receive advice and therefore they are more likely to use a high-service reseller. If their problems are complex, they might approach a VAR to take advantage of its skills. The VAR might also be interested in the end-user, if it offers an opportunity profitably to use or enhance its resources. Other end-users with large-scale or complex problems may use the services of a dedicated partner to which they contract out all aspects of the purchase and installation of hardware and software. Even maintenance and operations of the computer system can be outsourced to specialised companies.

Manufacturer X deals directly with some of the companies in the network, but most of its relationships are indirect. The intermediaries that are involved take various shapes. Some of these are general distributors serving a number of manufacturers, while others might be the exclusive business partners of manufacturer X, or deal only with a few VARs serving particular types of end-users. Where it comes to competitors, manufacturer X will not just face competition from other companies that are similar to itself (i.e. hardware manufacturers). Its toughest competitor for sales to an end-user might be a software company that offers a package including the hardware manufactured by X. On other occasions manufacturer X's own offering may include a computer developed and manufactured by someone else, because a particular customer required that (for an illustration, see Box 6.1).

Box 6.1   IBM's CSP Department

IBM has developed a Customer Solutions Procurement (CSP) department. CSP supports IBM Global Services which provides "one-stop shopping" for large companies buying information technology. The customer may need thousands of PCs, software, hundreds of printers, installation and computer programs. In some cases the customer prefers IBM's PC, but wants printers from another manufacturer. In these situations CSP becomes involved and the manager of the CSP-operations explains the way of working:

"If Lucent wants HP-printers, we are going to give them HP-printers. We'd rather give them our own but if they want HP, my guys will go out and buy them. The value that the customer sees is that he doesn't have to go out and buy it and make sure it is going to be compatible with their applications. They say: 'IBM, you put the whole together. We want you to do it all'."

Source: Carbone (1999: 40).

The analysis of the distribution network around manufacturer X illuminates the need for differentiation. Users' problems and requirements of solutions are different. Suppliers therefore must offer differentiated arrangements. The business partners of manufacturer X each provide their skills and capabilities and make it possible for X to apply various strategies for distribution. Any supplier in a similar situation must take as its point of departure the users' problems. Depending on the nature of these problems, the supplier must develop its ability to solve them. Analysing requirements calls for a network perspective on distribution. Because of this we will now examine distribution issues related to each of the three network dimensions: resources, activities and actors.

Distribution and the Resource Structure

A distribution network comprises numerous different resources. Some of these resources are collective in nature, such as roads, railways, etc. while others are within the boundaries of individual firms. These resources are connected and this affects both their value and their combined features. Companies are constantly trying to improve the utilisation of these resources and to combine them in innovative ways. The business relationships of a company play an important role in these efforts. They are established so that each of the companies can take advantage of the skills and resources of their counterpart. Distribution relationships are like other business relationships in that each company transfers some activities to the other party that it would otherwise have to do for itself. This other party then uses its particular resources to carry out these activities.

When examining distribution, we are mainly concerned with resource utilisation within *indirect* relationships, provided by intermediaries. In some networks, the role of intermediaries is profound while in others relationships are mainly direct, between supplier and user. But generally, we find diverse approaches in the same network, depending on the problems and abilities of different companies. In theory, it would be possible for either a supplier or a user to undertake any of the activities of an intermediary. In practice, this is often not possible because some of the necessary resources to do that are only possessed by a distributor and can only be acquired through long experience. Examples include being able to manage credit for a large number of small customers, or knowing how to assemble a viable assortment of products from a wide range of overseas suppliers. Other resources are unlikely to be economic for either a user or a supplier to develop because, unlike an intermediary, they are unable to spread the costs of them over many different relationships or offerings. Examples of these include the costs for a supplier of making sales calls on every final user, or for a user of maintaining a buying office in each different country from which it buys.

The role of intermediaries in distribution in business markets rests on the resources they provide for connecting different networks of actors. These resources are primarily of two kinds: *positional resources* and *technological resources:*

- Positional resources of a distributor consist of its relationships with many users and suppliers. These relationships provide access for the distributor's clients to the networks of these companies. Thus, positional resources allow a distributor to find, assess and assemble the assortment of offerings required by its customers from a widely scattered range of diverse suppliers. They also mean that the distributor has access to a similarly diverse and scattered network of customers for its suppliers.
- Technological resources of a distributor consist mainly of its abilities to effectively operate relationships in both supply and customer markets. This involves skill in managing inventories for both supplier and user, negotiating and handling orders, managing buying and selling relationships with many users and suppliers, providing credit to users and finance to suppliers, as well as skills in physical logistics. We refer to these skills as the *market technologies* of the distributors.[6] However, distributors increasingly have other technological resources as well. Many retailers have developed their skills in designing products and production methods so that they are able to specify these to their suppliers. This means that the resulting offerings will be unique to the retailer. The VARs in the computer industry exemplify such retailers.

Distribution efficiency can often be increased by moving activities from one actor to another, thus changing the utilisation of the resources in the distribution network. A common example is when responsibility for stocking, logistics or advertising is transferred

[6] For a discussion of market technologies, see Ford and Saren (2002).

from a supplier to a distributor or vice versa. This shifting of activities may also involve other users as well. For example, the furniture retailer, IKEA, switched the activities of assembly and transportation to consumers, thus imposing burdens on them. Consumers were willing to accept these burdens in return for low prices. This change also was dependent on the distribution infrastructure, because it required that consumers had cars to visit out-of-town show rooms and to transport the furniture home. This is an extreme example of the low-cost distribution relationships in Cell 1 of the matrix in Figure 6.2.

In spite of the heterogeneity of distribution arrangements, it has been possible historically to identify a fairly clear structure of roles for manufacturers, wholesalers, retailers and consumers, together forming a "channel". In particular, the need to keep inventories was one main determinant of these structures. Inventories were essential for the availability of products because lead-times in both production and distribution were considerable. In many cases two levels of intermediaries were needed for this task. In consumer marketing wholesalers and retailers filled this function, while in business marketing a nation-wide wholesaler together with local dealers did the same, although sometimes only one intermediate level of distributor was used.

Over time, however, these narrow channel-like structures have changed towards more complex network-like constellations. The type of distribution network that includes the computer manufacturer in Figure 6.3 is increasingly common. It shows the way that customers are able to obtain different solutions when suppliers mobilise the resources of a network of actors. This network is an illustration of the characteristics of forward-looking companies identified in a US study. These firms experimented with new distribution arrangements to improve flexibility and responsiveness to the problems of users. The managers of the firms introducing these innovations were found:

> "[to] view their distribution channels as webs of capabilities embedded in an extended enterprise. They have realised that by sharing their resources and capabilities in novel ways and new situations they can take advantage of profit-making opportunities that they could not exploit on their own."
>
> (Narus and Anderson 1996: 112)

One of the main reasons behind this development is an increasing reliance on specialised resources. Traditional intermediaries tended to be involved in all the main distribution functions. Even in the 1990s the typical American industrial distributor appeared to be a "full service intermediary" performing a broad range of functions. According to one study, "the distributor contacts customers and makes the product available by providing necessary supporting services such as delivery, credit, technical advice, repair service, assembly and promotion" (Herbig and O'Hara 1994: 199). It goes without saying that it is difficult for an individual firm to continuously develop the necessary resources in all of these diverse areas, particularly with the rapid development of transportation and communication. Therefore, in many situations it is more likely that specialised firms can take advantage of these opportunities. Examples of this trend in the network in Figure 6.3 include distributors dedicated to supplying modularised offerings at low cost or those that specialise in solving the particular problems of certain types of end-users, such as utilities or suppliers of advanced or client specific solutions.

Technical development also changes the relative importance of various resource elements. Inventories used to be a necessary ingredient in the "marketing channel" era and these were mainly in the control of intermediaries. Handling these inventories required the broad spectrum of activities typical of traditional distributors. When inventories become less important as improved systems and modularisation provided for "make-to-order", the value of the skills and capabilities of handling them is reduced. Instead abilities to deal with flows rather than stocks have become more important. This explains why specialised information and transportation companies have strengthened their positions in distribution.

Suppliers therefore need to adjust the capabilities and skills they have to changes in the network and in their end-users (see Box 6.2). It is the *combined* resources to which they have access that determine what value they can create for these end-users. Therefore, a supplier must constantly reconsider what counterparts it should be involved with and the nature of its resource ties with them.

Box 6.2   The Importance to Caterpillar Inc. of Resource Ties with its Distributors

---

Around 1990 Caterpillar Inc. was in major trouble due to increasing competition from the Japanese manufacturer Komatsu and was suffering heavy losses. During the mid-1990s it responded to this challenge and recovered financially to achieve record profits. According to the chief executive officer of the company, Donald Fites, a number of factors played a role in this recovery: long-term competitive value in terms of brand name and product quality contributed. Changes in the organisational structure were also important, as were huge investment to streamline manufacturing, increased attention to customers' problems and changes in exchange rates. However, the chief executive argued that: "The biggest reason for Caterpillar's success has been our system of distribution and product support and the close customer relationships it fosters." Furthermore, he was convinced that, "our single greatest advantage over our competition was, and still is, our system of distribution". This distribution system consisted of 186 independent dealers around the world. Caterpillar's view of the benefits provided by high-involvement relationships is as follows:

"Local dealers who are long established members of their communities can get closer to customers than a global company can on its own; *but to tap the full potential of such dealers, a company must forge extremely close ties with them and integrate them into its critical business systems*. When treated in this way, dealers can serve as sources of market information and intelligence, as proxies for customers, as consultants, and as problem solvers. Indeed, our dealers play a vital role in almost every aspect of our business, including product design and delivery service and field support and the management of replacement-part inventories. Dealers can be much more than a channel to customers."

Source: Fites (1996: 85; emphasis added).

Caterpillar Inc. is a good example of how the development of resource ties can enable a company to take advantage of the most appropriate combination of the resources of their counterparts. The company also illustrates the level of investment that is needed to establish and develop these resource ties.

Distribution and the Activity Structure

The development towards more specialised resources and actors in the distribution network is strongly related to changes in the division of labour in the activity structure. To an increasing extent the flow of materials has become separated from the flow of information. IT development provides means for rationalisation of information exchange, which in turn opens up the distribution field for new actors. Computer firms like IBM identified a potential role for a wholesaler of information, connecting the information systems of customers and suppliers. More software-oriented suppliers have also been able to establish positions as "information brokers" to exploit these conditions. Developments in information technology not only increase the range of potential collaborators, they also enhance the opportunity for a supplier and a user to deal directly because the costs of information exchange are substantially reduced. Transportation specialists also now play an increasing role in distribution networks. Freight forwarders, truck fleet operators and warehousing businesses have strengthened their positions by establishing efficient large-scale transportation systems as well as local timetable-based delivery services and efficient storage using advanced equipment.

Changes in the activity structure in networks can also mean that activities that were previously carried out by individual companies working alone are now carried out by groups of companies working together. For example, Caterpillar involves both dealers and their customers in programmes dealing with product quality, cost reduction and other manufacturing issues. Officials of Caterpillar make it clear that they do not view the distribution network as a one-way channel from the factory to the customers. On the contrary, dealers are involved in driving the development of the offering. Attaining these benefits requires support from Caterpillar. These support activities take the form of financial assistance and programmes for inventory management as well as technical material and training of dealers' personnel. Similarly, alliances between suppliers, users and transportation companies in the form of third-party logistics are common (Bagchi and Virum 1998; Murphy and Poist 2000).

Specialised actors emerge in a network because they can undertake each individual activity at its optimum scale and because they can develop greater skills and capabilities within a narrow scope of activities. Owing to prevailing developments it becomes less and less likely that one and the same company would be the most effective actor to undertake the whole bundle of distribution activities. An example of this phenomenon is seen in the continuing restructuring of the distribution system for passenger cars. Traditionally, there has been full integration of functions within a single dealership. Franchised dealers have been involved in sales of new and used cars, spare parts and in repairs and servicing. Despite the diverse natures of these operations, full integration was possible because each function could be made profitable at the scale of an individual dealer. Although fully integrated dealerships still exist, they are increasingly complemented by a large number of de-bundled enterprises, focusing on new or used-car sales, service or repair. Mail order and Internet business have also grown in importance as channels for spare parts. By specialising on a limited part of the activity structure, various intermediaries can acquire the most adequate resources for their tasks.

Postponement and speculation

Bucklin (1965) argued that the gap between the producer of an offering and the user of it can be bridged in two fundamentally different ways. The producer can rely on either "postponement" or "speculation". Postponement means that the producer delays the final completion of its offering until as close as possible to the time of the purchase. Often this means that the producer only produces the offering after an order is received and the customer has to wait for fulfilment of its order. This approach reduces the supplier's demand uncertainty (Chapter 3). It also means that the supplier is less likely to achieve economies of scale in production. However, it does mean that the supplier is more likely to be able to adapt its offering to meet individual requirements. Speculation involves the supplier in producing in anticipation of demand in the optimum quantities for economies of scale. Speculation provides for delivery from stock, but it is associated with large inventories between producer and user, both as a buffer to cope with fluctuations in demand and as the outcome of production in large batches. Speculation also restricts the ability of a supplier to adapt its offering to individual customer requirements.

Speculation was the dominant mode of distribution for a long time, because the manufacturing system required large-scale production. However, over time the opportunities for postponement have increased. Lead-times in distribution have been substantially reduced through the development of new infrastructure in terms of both transport and information systems. Production lead-times have decreased through more flexible manufacturing systems. Also modularisation in the design of offerings has simplified ranges, reduced inventory problems, speeded up deliveries and made it easier to cope with both variety and variation in customer requirements. When inventory buffers are reduced or no longer exist, the interdependencies between activities increase and call for other means of co-ordination. JIT deliveries and other types of integration that are common today require adaptations in terms of equipment, logistics, information systems and joint operations of various kinds. It is not only in the car industry that firms have been able to improve performance in delivering products and services rapidly from distant locations to final users. Benetton is a well-known example of an IT-controlled global logistic operation linking some 180 suppliers of raw materials, more than 400 manufacturing units and 6,000 retailers to customers in more than 80 countries. The sales results from the shops are updated more or less continuously and its information system makes it possible for Benetton's manufacturing to adapt to changes in demand in styles, colours and sizes. Their flexibility in manufacturing relies on computer-aided design of garments along with computerised garment cutting and assembly. The link to customers is a highly automated distribution centre from which products are delivered directly to the shops around the world.

Reorganisation of the activity structure in a distribution network can lead to substantial benefits, as illustrated by a strategic change in Atlas Copco, a Swedish manufacturer of hand-held tools. This company used to rely on two central warehouses in Sweden and huge inventories at its European sales companies. The costs related to this way of making products available to customers were substantial; capital tied up in inventories amounted to 55% of the company's yearly sales. In spite of this, customers were dissatisfied with the service level they received and almost a third of all orders were delivered incomplete. The major reason was the very wide product range, which made it impossible to stock the whole assortment at each of the sales companies. Atlas Copco's management was particularly concerned with the situation because they expected customers' service requirements to increase even further. However, it was obvious that to improve the service level with even larger inventories would eventually drive the company out of business. The response from Atlas Copco was to rearrange the activity structure and change from an approach of speculation toward one of postponement. They withdrew inventories from the sales companies, closed down the two warehouses in Sweden and established a new one in Central Europe. By investing in an advanced EDI system and establishing efficient logistic operations with a freight forwarder, it became possible for them to respond better to customers' orders than when stocks were held at the local subsidiaries. The company's delivery service improved considerably. At the same time, inventories as a proportion of sales were reduced by two-thirds, which in turn decreased capital costs substantially. Associated with these moves, Atlas Copco reduced the number of its production plants from seven, in three different countries, to only one. The improvements achieved by the company over two decades are summarised in Table 6.1.

The example shows that changing the links among activities can enhance distribution efficiency and effectiveness. Advanced information systems in combination with flexible manufacturing make it possible to postpone production operations. For example, suppliers to Marks and Spencer manufacture long, economic runs of some garments in a uniform un-dyed state. They are only dyed in the appropriate colour on the basis of information on which colours are in most demand on a particular day and shipped the following day.

Postponement has two major advantages over speculation. The first is that offerings can be adapted or "customised" to a much greater extent to each customer's requirements. The second is that inventories can be reduced to the advantage of both customer and supplier.

Table 6.1 Improvements in Distribution Performance of Atlas Copco through Reorganisation of Activity Links.

	Before the change	After the change
Number of factories	7	1
Number of central warehouses	2 (Sweden)	1 (Belgium)
Inventories as a proportion of yearly sales	55%	18%
Total lead-time	16–20 weeks	2–3 weeks
Service level (% of order lines as requested)	70	95

All of this points to the importance of not analysing distribution activities in terms of physical delivery of standardised, finished products. It is necessary to apply a wider perspective including the company's operations activities and its relationships with its suppliers as well. In fact, the major performance improvements seem to arise when the interface between the traditionally separate areas of operations and distribution is changed. Postponement assists customisation. However, speculation also produces advantages through standardisation. Therefore, the most appropriate strategy for a supplier is to try to combine the benefits of both standardisation and customisation. This provides a continuum as

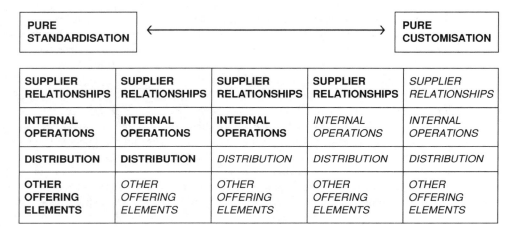

Figure 6.4   A Continuum of Customisation/Standardisation Strategies.
Note: **STANDARDISED IN BOLD**   *CUSTOMISED IN ITALICS.*
Source: Developed from Lampel and Mintzberg (1996: 24).

illustrated in Figure 6.4. Adaptation to customer requirements can involve both distribution methods and/or other elements of the offering: advice, adaptation, product and service. In many cases, adaptations in these other offering elements will require changes in the logistic element, either internally or using independent distributors. Similarly, adaptation in distribution may allow an otherwise identical offering to solve the problems of new customers. Adaptations in offering elements often require changes in operations and in the supplier's relationships with its suppliers. Also, these operations and supplier changes may be made independently of the offering to provide variation in scheduling to suit an individual customer.

This continuum provides a good illustration of what we mean by differentiation. Customers' problems are diverse and so are their perceptions of potential solutions. The different combinations of postponement, speculation, customisation and standardisation provide suppliers with numerous opportunities for differentiation. According to Lampel and Mintzberg (1996), customisation begins with downstream activities closest to the marketplace, while standardisation starts upstream and begins with fundamental design.

Distribution and the Actor Structure

The developments of the resource and activity structures in distribution networks lead to two main conclusions:

- Suppliers increasingly rely on a network of differentiated counterparts rather than a single marketing channel. These counterparts contribute a variety of resources that have to be appropriately combined in order to become effective solutions to users' problems.
- Activities in distribution have become increasingly interdependent owing to the shift towards postponement. Activity specialisation has led to a situation where activities increasingly are distributed among a number of actors.

Both these changes call for co-ordination of activities and resources to a greater extent than has usually been needed before and bring the relationship between the actors involved in distribution into sharp focus.

The relationship between a manufacturer and a distributor requires a great deal of co-operative efforts. But beyond this co-operation the relationship is also an arena for considerable conflict over such things as the division of work and profits. For example, Buzzel and Ortmeyer (1996) found that manufacturers' objectives "to move the greatest possible value of goods at the highest price" was difficult to combine with the retailers' goal "to negotiate the lowest price for these goods" (1996: 86). Conflict also arises because each company often fails to see their common situation from the perspective of the other company.[7] There is no necessary reason why the wishes and requirements of users and different suppliers involved in distribution should coincide. For example, a supplier might want to have a direct relationship with an end-user either because that user buys a large proportion of the supplier's total sales or because the supplier wants to learn from the user, or simply because it wants to get highly involved with that customer. This might run counter to the preferences of the user, for whom the supplier is not sufficiently important. Similarly, a distributor might wish to develop a relationship with a particular supplier as this would enhance its relationships with its own customers, but both the manufacturer and the users might prefer to deal directly with each other.

Conflict and co-operation co-exist because the relationships between the actors in a distribution network are characterised by both competitive and joint efforts. Conflict can occur between different companies of the same basic type, such as between similar computer hardware manufacturers in our earlier example or between similar retail supermarkets, centring on such things as obtaining new sites, price competition, adding new services, etc. Conflict can also occur between companies that superficially perform similar activities for others, but in ways that effectively comprise an entirely different offering. An example is that between a full-service computer distributor and a low-price "box-shifter", or between conventional supermarkets and discounters. A common case of this is when a so-called "category-killer" retailer enters a network with a radically

---

[7] We emphasised the importance of this wider perspective in all business relationships in Chapter 3.

different method of operation from traditional companies of which IKEA is but one example. Stores such as Toys-Я-Us and Wal-Mart are also representative cases. Both these companies have forced many incumbents out of the market, by the combination of their dramatically superior operating systems, cost structure, product range and the price they offer. Finally, as we have referred to above, conflict can also occur between companies carrying out different basic operations in the network, such as manufacturers and different types of distributors.

Managing distribution relationships is thus about handling co-operative as well conflicting issues. For a long time the latter seems to have been more prevalent. Alderson (1965) considered it a major problem that the conflicting aspects received the most attention. He even argued that "sometimes the element of conflict is so pronounced that an efficient channel can scarcely be said to exist". Producer–distributor relationships continued to be "market-like", similar to the arm's-length type of relationships discussed in Chapter 5. This caused no major problem as long as the interdependencies among the activities were low and the need for resource integration was limited. However, in today's evolving distribution networks, these conditions become problematic. We need therefore to discuss what kind of co-ordination mechanisms can be used to ensure that the activities and resources of different actors function well together.

Historically, co-ordination in distribution relationships was supposed to be achieved through two different modes. The first is through ownership and vertical integration, the second by the use of power. It has been argued that a common ownership of a manufacturer and a distributor would solve some of the problems identified. One way of doing this would be that either the producer or the distributor integrated vertically by acquiring the counterpart. However, it has been shown to be the case that a common ownership of the two organisations will not necessarily provide a solution for the underlying problems between them. Complex integrated companies might find that different manufacturing units are competing for the attention of their wholly owned sales and distribution operations. In the same vein, a manufacturer selling through a distributor might be reluctant to continue to do so if a competing manufacturer acquires the distributor. It might even end up in the situation where the distributor becomes solely a sales organisation of the acquiring manufacturer, which means that the positional resources of the distributor have deteriorated substantially. The conclusion is that increasing the bonds of ownership is only rarely an adequate way of handling co-ordination issues.

The second way to manage counterparts in distribution relationships has been to establish a power base to rely on. Power comes from dependence and some distribution networks typically have been dominated by one company or by a group of companies of similar types, such as wholesalers or manufacturers. Dominance stems from the resources the actors possess. These resources can be financial, technological or positional and include the company's relationships with other actors in the network. Traditionally, in many networks wholesalers exercised power based on their financial resources, which enabled them to provide credit to both manufacturers and users. Further, their positional resources gave access to distant manufacturers and retailers. Subsequently, many distribution networks were dominated by suppliers that developed strong indirect relationships with end-consumers, based on their ability to design and manufacture unique products (product and process technologies), but more importantly on their ability to build brands (market technologies[8]). More recently, many networks have been dominated by single types of retailers whose access to a large share of the end-market gives them strong influence over manufacturers (positional resources). These retailers have further increased their domination through developing their own brands (market technology) to reinforce their relationships with their customers at the expense of the manufacturers' relationships, such as in the case of Marks and Spencer. It goes without saying that a powerful actor can influence the rest of the network. However, influence based on others' dependence may not be the best way to make use of relationships, if co-ordination of activities and resources is crucial.

It should come as no surprise therefore that over time, collaborative relationships among suppliers and distributors have become increasingly important (Kumar 1996; McQuistion 2001). Rather than relying on manipulation and confrontation, these relationships take motivation and co-action as the basic points of departure. Also, instead of power, which tends to impose tension, they build on trust and commitment between the parties involved implying changing actor bonds.[9] These new bonds and the trust from which they spring are prerequisites for improving distribution performance. They form the basis for more efficient co-ordination of activities and a more effective combining of resources. The distribution relationships in the fast-moving non-durable goods industry described in Box 6.4 illustrate this evolution.

Box 6.4   Unilever: Evolution in the Relationships between Actors in Distribution Networks

Until recently the relationships between the actors in this network were rooted in the methods of consumer marketing that had developed at a time when retailers were relatively small and weak, especially when compared with major international actors like Unilever and Procter & Gamble. These companies saw their many brands as their core assets and media advertising as their most critical activity. Wholesale and retail distributors were looked at collectively as the means to achieve the necessary coverage of these markets to maximise the company's return on its brand and advertising investment. The main task of each brand manager was to maintain and enhance brand-values in the minds of consumers. Success was measured by the national market-share they achieved on their penetration of particular segments. The critical relationships were with its advertising agency and its final consumers.

In recent years, the growth of major supermarket chains has meant that manufacturers have to deal directly with a smaller number of individually important retailers each with well-developed negotiating strength and management skills. Retail buyers are also no longer just concerned with beating down prices from suppliers, but with their own customer segmentation and the launch strategies for new brands.

[8] Ford and Saren (2002).

[9] In Chapter 8 we will examine the strategic choices open to companies in networks in terms of, among others, coercing others or conceding to their wishes and initiatives.

Without the active co-operation of these retailers, a supplier's market share would suffer, irrespective of the strength of its brands. This led companies like Unilever to recognise the importance of tailoring elements of the company's offering to consumers, to the requirements of individual retailers. The sales force of Unilever was based on "key account selling" and sales results were expressed for each key account customer rather than for each product line on a national basis. However, suspicion between manufacturers and retailers meant that little information was exchanged between them and retailers still regarded manufacturers' sales activities as attempts to "stuff the trade with stock".

A new type of relationship was established when Unilever launched a pilot "category management" programme in the deodorants product area, with co-operation from seven major retailers. Both manufacturer and retailers together tried to manage the whole category of products together, rather than promoting each brand individually. Previously, Unilever had found that a sales gain from promoting a single brand or from a retailer promoting one of its brands, was often at the expense of the profitability of the category as a whole. Category management encouraged both companies to discuss the contribution of each brand to the revenue and profitability of the whole category.[10]

This example illustrates a number of common characteristics of supplier–distributor relationships, irrespective of industry. Changes in the positional resources of the actors involved imply that the relationships between them will change over time. In this case, retailers' positional resources have increased because of their access to a larger share of the consumer market and more accurate information about consumers. Furthermore, their role has changed to encompass previously supplier-dominated areas such as product development and retail promotion. Retailers have also achieved a greater professionalism in their activities. These factors together have made manufacturing giants with strong brands like Unilever and Procter & Gamble eager to change their relationships with retailers and enhance the bonds between them.

This leads to the conclusion that effective distribution arrangements are unlikely to be built in the adversarial atmosphere that was previously so common. In a study of successful distribution partnerships, Buzzel and Ortmeyer (1996) concluded that the role of relationship management has been very critical for the performance of these partnerships. They found inter-functional teamwork and new forms of incentives and compensation schemes to be crucial issues. The most important task for management was to change the basic culture between the parties, because in most cases these relationships had been characterised as conflict. The main issue therefore was to establish more trustworthy relationships "since trust is the critical issue in building and maintaining partnerships". We find it appropriate to conclude this section with a quotation from the CEO of Caterpillar, one of the examples we have been using. In an interview in the *Harvard Business Review*, he expressed thoughts that can be summarised as a kind of

---

[10] For a discussion of category management, see Mouzas and Araujo (1998 and 2000).

"distributor policy" that is still quite rare, but that seems to be a prerequisite for effective and efficient distribution in the future:

> "We'd sooner cut off our right arm than sell directly and bypass dealers ... We won't turn on dealers in bad times to avoid short-term pain ... When we see particular dealers not performing well, we jump in and help ... We want dealers to succeed."
>
> (Fites, 1996)

Change and Stability in Distribution Networks

This chapter has shown that distribution has become increasingly important for both suppliers and users. A major factor in this is that the supply-side of customers has moved to the top of their management agenda. To improve performance in these operations, customers are constantly imposing new requirements on the distribution solutions of their suppliers. These diverse demands put very different requirements on the distribution capabilities of suppliers and also on the type of relationships that are appropriate. Our analysis has revealed two crucial dimensions of distribution relationships: the level of involvement with individual users, and the level of complexity of the distribution arrangements between them. Complexity is a critical dimension because different users will make different trade-offs between costs and benefits. Choosing the right level of involvement is also a strategic issue because although high involvement can produce benefits, it is costly and does not always pay off.

It is even more important from a strategic point of view that distribution relationships evolve to meet new conditions. Networks are never static and both customers and suppliers need to continuously monitor the kind of relationships they have. The requirements of users change over time because of the shifts in their problems and in their perceptions of the available offerings. Some suppliers may resist these new conditions and be unwilling to change, which in turn might lead to the dissolution of some of their relationships. For example, in the information technology network the demand for hardware, software, services, advice and delivery and other aspects of supplier relationships has all changed. Many users now have very little need uncertainty when buying a standard-performance PC, when compared to those buyers making their first purchases. In contrast, even these low uncertainty buyers are likely to feel much less comfortable when buying products such as net-servers, which might be completely new to them. Overall, it is likely that the number of low need-uncertainty customers will grow and hence the demand for easier, more convenient, more flexible and lower cost solutions. In turn, suppliers will change the technology of their offerings, which in turn will allow them to satisfy requirements that users had not previously thought of.

As distributors grow larger, they may try to alter their relationships with users by building the reputation of their own brands as a rival to those of manufacturers. Some distributors may evolve towards more integrated, higher-service relationships at correspondingly higher prices. Others may become low-cost box-shifters or may adapt to the requirements of particular types of customers. Similarly, manufacturers will seek economies of scale in both production and distribution operations. Some users will be too insignificant or unprofitable for some manufacturers and these users may have difficulties in finding the solutions they want.

Some manufacturers will concentrate on developing technologies with wide applications and so will be less in touch with the specific requirements of different end-users. These manufacturers may have to rely on relationships with a few large distributors to handle small volume orders and to construct a package that is tailored to the requirements of each user. Also, as the technological complexity and cost of development of their products increase, these manufacturers are likely to form alliances with other manufacturers to provide inputs into their offerings based on the supplier's own technologies.

These examples of the dynamics of networks involve changes in the actor bonds, activity links and resource ties among the companies concerned. But even in an industry characterised by rapid technological change, reorganisation of distribution can often be slow, difficult and cumbersome because of an inherent tendency of stability of these networks (see, for example, Nieschlag 1954; Stern and Sturdivant 1987; Narus and Anderson 1996). There are a number of factors that together tend to reinforce inertia:

- An industrial distributor may ship dozens of orders to different locations within a single customer every day. Similarly, a supermarket may take several deliveries from a manufacturer each week or even each day. The volumes of products and transactions involved and the effects on profitability of only a marginal cost change tend to produce a culture that concentrates on the *efficient* processing and constant refinement of these many interactions.
- Distribution networks involve considerable investments for all the parties in facilities, warehouses, and in relationships with other companies. Development of these relationships is likely to involve considerable commitment over time, such as that of a motor dealer to its franchise with a particular manufacturer. The long-term nature of these investments is likely to make managers wary of the uncertainty of major changes.
- The number of suitable retailers, distributors, users and suppliers in any network is limited and this will restrict any company's ability to change its network of relationships, or for newcomers to develop the relationships they might want. For example, the long-established and rigid networks in Japan have made it difficult for Western companies to enter.
- The interdependencies in networks make change problematic. If a company tries to introduce a change in a distribution network, that change will affect its immediate counterparts. But other firms in the network will also be affected as well. Their goodwill is likely to be necessary for its success. For example, if a manufacturer tried to increase its use of distributors, rather than delivering directly to retailers, then this would depend on these customers being willing to forgo direct contact. The need to achieve the acquiescence of a number of companies restricts the ability of any one company to achieve change. It is quite common for informal rules and norms of behaviour to be established between the companies involved in distribution networks. These norms often cover things such as which companies should hold and pay for

inventories, or what should be the discount structures to intermediaries. They are often enforced by joint action by groups of companies against any change in status quo. This action is sometimes political and sometimes directly against other companies in the network. For example, conventional drugstores in the USA lobbied against discount druggists and achieved the enactment of so-called "fair-trading" legislation (price fixing) in many states. Small shopkeepers in France and Japan successfully lobbied their governments to change the tax or zoning laws to the disadvantage of large supermarkets. Wholesalers and retailers in many markets prevented manufacturers from delivering directly to other retailers or end-users by threatening jointly to stop all purchases. In extreme cases, these norms can extend to illegal activities such as dividing of sales territories between companies, blacklisting and boycotting rule breakers, or fixing common prices charged to end-users.

In the short term, stability will enhance distribution performance and an absence of change should not necessarily be taken as a sign of inefficiency. The distribution infrastructure and the relationships require substantial investments and so the costs of changing them are very great. In turn, this means that change is unlikely to be attempted unless the potential benefits are considerable. However, in the longer term, the search for efficiency in distribution networks will lead to changes. In particular, technical development will pave the way for new distribution arrangements. Over time, new opportunities will change the trade-off between the costs and benefits associated with a potential change. When this occurs, problems can arise if some of the companies involved are in a position to hinder that change.

So at the same time that short-term efficiency is being promoted by stability, there is always a pressure for change. The potential for adaptations and changes will be seen differently by the companies in the network. Some companies might identify them as opportunities while others might consider them as threats to their existing position and to the stability on which it is based. This is the reason why radical changes in distribution often originate from companies "outside" a restructured network. These innovators have made no investments in the prevailing structure and order, nor do they feel obliged to stick to the established rules of the game.

Conclusion

In this chapter we have presented a network perspective on distribution. The view of distribution in mainstream marketing textbooks has been to see it as a "manufacturer's problem". This problem has usually been expressed as a task that a manufacturer faces to select appropriate distributive outlets to reach and cover its target market and then to channel its goods to the intended end-users efficiently and at minimum logistics cost. A network view of distribution extends this perspective in several ways. The main difference is that the idea of efficient distribution cannot be solely concerned with optimising the output of a manufacturer's factory. Improvement efforts must also take into consideration the conditions on the user side. This view is not entirely new. McVey

(1960) argued that intermediaries could also be seen as purchasing agents for their customers. Today, the input operations of buying firms increasingly tend to form the basis for appropriate distribution solutions.

The examples in this chapter have illustrated some of the alternatives open to end-users in their choice of supplier and some of the reasons for their actual choices. They have also illustrated how manufacturers have a range of new opportunities for restructuring the distribution of their offerings. "Traditional" types of intermediaries are supplemented by new actors emerging through the exploitation of opportunities for specialisation provided through technical development. Suppliers and users therefore are able to recombine the activity structure in the network to develop differentiated distribution arrangements where some represent low-cost relationships while others build on high involvement and adaptations. Therefore, distribution networks nowadays are more differentiated than they used to be. The main determinant of this variety is the increasing resource sharing among groups of specialised actors. Anderson *et al.* (1997) describe these constellations as "networks of value-adding partnerships like confederations of specialists". These networks are based on pooling of complementary skills and resources and have in turn affected the view of resource control. Previous recommendations of resource acquisition based on ownership are now supplemented by a focus on gaining access to distribution resources controlled by others.

The increasing attention to resource sharing and the need for co-ordination of interdependent activities undertaken across company boundaries affects the content of distribution relationships. The discussion in the section on the actor dimension revealed an increasing attention to high-involvement relationships, which is further confirmed by Weitz and Jaap, arguing that "there is a shift in the nature of general marketplace transactions from discrete to relational exchange" (1995: 305). But we should also remember that fruitful relationships are developed not only from being good friends. Reliance on trust and collaborative working does not mean the absence of power and conflict. On the contrary, power is rooted in dependence and the increasing interdependence among activities crossing company boundaries enhances the power base of each firm. In spite of that, firms today are relying on power less than they used to do. Frazier and Antia (1995) explain why these two conditions exist simultaneously, by arguing that the firm's possession of power must be kept separate from the way power is applied. Power can be applied either coercively or in a collaborative way. In distribution contexts where high involvement has little value, it is unproblematic to apply power coercively. However, in contexts where close co-operation might enhance distribution performance, the potential pressure residing in power must be applied in other ways. In these relationships power must be used as a means to establish shared norms and expectations.

As discussed in the section on the actor structure, conflict is an inherent characteristic in all distribution relationships. In fact, the potential for conflict is greater, the higher is the involvement, because in these relationships the parties have to agree on joint investments, adaptations of various types and other strategic issues. The actual impact of the potential conflict is contingent on how power is applied. It is most likely that a coercive approach will have destructive effects. This approach has been the norm in prevailing arm's-length relationships, which explains why conflict has been considered dysfunctional. However, conflict has other effects than being destructive. It is the diversity of goals and convictions that are the prerequisites for innovation and dynamics. Therefore it is crucial that these differences are confronted. In fact, the absence of conflict is likely to reflect that the two companies have not really "clinched" with each other, and really tried to exploit the potential for collaborative action. What is important in high-involvement relationships is that the conflicting issues are handled in a more constructive way than is necessary in arm's-length transactions.

References

Anderson, E., Day, G. and Rangan, K. (1997) Strategic Channel Design. Sloan Management Review, Summer, 59–69.

Alderson, W. (1965) *Dynamic Marketing Behavior: A Functionalist Theory of Marketing*, Homewood, IL: Richard D. Irwin.

Andersson, P. (1992) "Analysing Distribution Channel Dynamics: Loose and Tight Couplings in Distribution Networks", *European Journal of Marketing*, 26(2), 47–68.

Bagchi, P. and Virum, H. (1998) "Logistical Alliances – Trends and Prospects in an Integrated Europe", *Journal of Business Logistics*, 19(1), 191–213.

Bucklin, L. (1965) "Postponement, Speculation and the Structure of Distribution Channels", *Journal of Marketing Research*, 2, 26–31.

Buzzel, R. and Ortmeyer, G. (1996) "Channel Partnerships Streamline Distribution", *Sloan Management Review*, Spring, 85–96.

Carbone, J. (1999) "Reinventing Purchasing Wins the Medal for Big Blue", *Purchasing*, 16 September, 38–62.

Dubois, A. (2003) "Strategic Cost Management Across Boundaries of Firms", *Industrial Marketing Management*. Forthcoming.

Evans, J. and Berman, B. (2001) "Conceptualizing and Operationalizing the Business-to-Business Value Chain", *Industrial Marketing Management*, 30, 135–148.

Evans, P. and Wurster, T. (1999) "Getting Real About Virtual Commerce", *Harvard Business Review*, November–December, 85–94.

Fites, D. (1996) "Making Your Dealers Your Partners", *Harvard Business Review*, March–April, 84–95.

Ford, D., Berthon, P., Brown, S., Gadde, L-E., Håkansson, H., Naudé, P., Ritter, T. and Snehota, I. (2002) *The Business Marketing Course: Managing in Complex Networks*, Chichester: John Wiley.

Ford, D., Gadde, L-E., Håkansson, H., Lundgren, A., Snehota, I., Turnbull, P. and Wilson, D. (1998) *Managing Business Relationships*, Chichester: John Wiley.

Ford, D. and Saren, M. (2002) *Managing and Marketing Technology*, London: Thomson International.

Frazier, G. and Antia, K. (1995) "Exchange Relationships and Interfirm Power in Channels of Distribution", *Journal of Academy of Marketing Science*, 23(4), 321–326.

Herbig, P. and O'Hara, S. (1994) "Industrial Distributors in the Twenty-First Century", *Industrial Marketing Management*, 23, 199–203.

Hulthén, K. (2002) "Variety in Distribution Networks: A Transvection Analysis", Dissertation, Department of Industrial Marketing, Chalmers University of Technology, Gothenburg, Sweden.

Kotler, P. (2000) *Marketing Management: The Millennium Edition*, Englewood Cliffs, NJ: Prentice Hall.

Kumar, N. (1996) "The Power of Trust in Manufacturer-Retailer Relationships", *Harvard Business Review*, November–December, 92–106.

Lambert, D. and Cooper, C. (2000) "Issues in Supply Chain Management", *Industrial Marketing Management*, 29, 65–83.

Lampel, J. and Mintzberg, H. (1996) "Customizing Customization", *Sloan Management Review*, Fall, 21–30.

Lee, H. and Whang, S. (2001) "Winning the Last Mile of E-Commerce", *MIT Sloan Management Review*, Summer, 54–62.

Lewis, E. (1968) *Marketing Channels: Structure and Strategy*, New York.

McQuistion, D. (2001) "A Conceptual Model for Building and Maintaining Relationships Between Manufacturers' Representatives and Their Principals", *Industrial Marketing Management*, 30, 165–181.

McVey, P. (1960) "Are Channels of Distribution What the Textbooks Say?" *Journal of Marketing*, 24, January, 61–65.

Mouzas, S. and Araujo, L. (1998) "Manufacturer-Retailer Relationships in Germany: The Institutionalisation of Category Management", in P. Naudé and P.W. Turnbull (eds) *International Marketing*, Oxford: Pergamon.

Mouzas, S. and Araujo, L. (2000) "Implementing Programmatic Initiatives in Manufacturer-Retailer Networks", *Industrial Marketing Management*, 29(4), 293–304.

Murphy, P. and Poist, R. (2000) "Third Party Logistics: Some User Versus Provider Perspectives", *Journal of Business Logistics*, 21(1), 121–133.

Narus, J. and Anderson, J. (1996) "Rethinking Distribution – Adaptive Channels", *Harvard Business Review*, July–August, 112–120.

Nieschlag, R. (1954) *Die Dynamik der Betriebsformen in Handel*, Schriftenreihe Neue Erfolge Nr. 7, Essen: Rheinish-Westfähliges Institut für Wirtschaftsforschung.

Rosenbloom, B. (1995) *Marketing Channels: A Management View*, Fort Worth, TX: The Dryden Press, Harcourt Brace College.

Rosenbröijer, C-J. (1998) "Capability Development in Business Networks", Doctoral dissertation, Swedish School of Economics and Business Administration, Helsinki.

Stern, L. and El-Ansary, A. (1996) *Marketing Channels*, Englewood Cliffs, NJ: Prentice Hall.

Stern, L. and Sturdivant, F. (1987) "Customer Driven Distribution Systems", *Harvard Business Review*, July–August, 34–41.

Stock, J.R. and Lambert, D.M. (2001) *Strategic Logistics Management*, New York: McGraw-Hill.

Tunisini, A. (1997) "The Dissolution of Channels and Hierarchies", doctoral thesis, Uppsala University, Department of Business Studies, Uppsala.

Weitz, B. and Jaap, S. (1995) "Relationship Marketing and Distribution Channels", *Journal of the Academy of Marketing Science*, Fall, 305–320.

TECHNOLOGY AND BUSINESS NETWORKS

Aims of this Chapter

- To examine the effects of technology on business relationships and networks.
- To discuss the nature and the different types of technology and to examine the role of relationships in the process of technological development.
- To examine the technological content of business relationships and look at the two-way process of influence between technology and relationships.

Introduction

All companies need a wide range of different technological resources to enable them to operate in a business network and to build and fulfil their offerings. The cost and difficulty of developing technologies mean that no single company can ever possess all that it needs. Therefore, companies are dependent on the technologies of others in the network such as their suppliers, customers, distributors, advisors and co-developers. This technological interdependence is a major factor in the dynamics of business networks:

- Companies establish relationships to gain access to the technological resources of others and to exploit their own expensively developed technologies. Without relationships in which to exploit them, a company's technologies (or its other resources) have little or no value.
- Technology is developed in the relationships between companies as well as in the companies themselves. This technology is the result of both companies' investments aimed at making their interactions more efficient and effective. The technology developed within one relationship can often be used by either or both of the companies in their other relationships.

- Technologies developed by companies to solve discrete problems can often be rapidly transmitted, modified and combined with other technologies in different relationships and thus may affect many companies and relationships in distant parts of the network.
- A single technology cannot be used in isolation. Every new technology must be combined with others, both old and new and adapted and refined to solve particular problems. Thus, each technology is "embedded" in the network of business relationships through which it is used. This means that an investment in a technology is simultaneously an investment in a network.

The Nature of Technology

"Technology" is a widely but sometimes loosely used term. Often those using it are referring only to *information* technology, or making reference to so-called "high technology". But information technology represents only one very small part of the impact of all technologies on a network and ideas on what is "high" or "low" technology are meaningless if not considered in relation to a particular network situation. A useful starting point is to say that *a technology is an ability based on scientific knowledge that can be used for commercial purposes*.

From this we can usefully separate technologies into two broad areas, as follows

- *Product technologies* are abilities that enable either or both of the companies in a relationship to *design* the offering that is exchanged between them. Thus they form the basis of a supplier's *problem-solving abilities* and a customer's *demand abilities*. For example, McDonald's product technologies provide it with the ability to design offerings that solve the customer problem of needing to eat speedily. The offerings themselves are not the technologies, but are based on those technologies.[1]
- *Process technologies* are abilities that enable the companies in a relationship to produce or *fulfil* an offering, on time, in the right place to the right specification, at the right price and to do all these things consistently. Process technologies are the basis of the transfer ability of a supplier and a customer. For example, McDonald's have process technologies that enable them to produce their fast-food – fast. For example, they designed a scoop that allows their operators to neatly stack French fries in a carton with only two hand movements. The scoop itself is not a process technology, but is the outcome of technologies.[2]

---

[1] Product technologies are equally applicable in the design of the service, advice or logistics elements of an offering. For example, financial service companies have the ability to design different financial offerings in line with changing government tax regulations. Distribution companies are able to design a logistics package to suit the varying requirements of different client companies.

[2] The abilities of a company to manage its relationships with others and to carry out the tasks of marketing and purchasing can also be usefully considered as technologies. They also are learned abilities that can be applied in different situations and can be located at different points in a network. For a discussion of this see Ford and Saren (2001).

Either or both the customer and the supplier in a relationship may possess the product and process technologies on which their relationship depends, or they may have developed some of these technologies together in their relationship. For example, Intel developed many of the product and process technologies used in the microprocessors that form the basis of their relationships with producers of personal computers. Many retailers have the product technologies that enable them to design the offerings that they wish to buy from their suppliers. They also have the process technologies that enable them to specify the manufacturing methods that will be used to fulfil the offerings. In contrast, Marks and Spencer and one of its suppliers, Coates-Viyella *together* developed the technology to produce crease-resistant cotton goods.

A combination of many different product and process technologies is always needed to satisfy the requirements of a customer. Thus, a car is dependent on many product technologies used in the design of its engine, suspension, body-work and fittings. That design would be of little use to a motorist unless someone had the process technologies to produce it. In other situations a company may develop the design (product technology) of an offering, but either by choice or necessity rely on another company with the appropriate process technology to manufacture it. For example, when Amgen developed Epoetin alfa, its first treatment for anaemia (product technology), it did not have the ability to either manufacture or distribute it, so it launched a 50:50 joint venture with Kirin Brewery which had the manufacturing and distribution presence in major Asian markets (process technology).[3] The integration of different technologies in different companies within a network may be co-ordinated by a third company that has a relationship with end-customers. This is common in the fashion industry. Here retailers co-ordinate the work of independent fashion designers and suppliers that "cut-make-and-trim" garments to those designs for their stores.

In some networks a number of combinations can exist. For example, Boeing has traditionally designed the undercarriages of its airliners itself (product technologies). It has then contracted with US manufacturers (that have the necessary process technologies), to make to that design. In contrast, Airbus has used suppliers that both design and produce undercarriages to its requirements, specified in terms of dimensions and weight of aircraft and landing speed.

Some of a company's technologies will have been acquired on a specific occasion and for a particular purpose, such as when making a large investment to develop a new production facility. When BMW established production for its new Rolls-Royce model, it sited it near the coast in Sussex where it was able to recruit staff experienced in the technologies used to produce similar low-volume, high specification luxury yachts. Companies will acquire other technologies through their day-to-day activities, interactions with customers and the learning that results from them (Von Hippel 1988).

Both companies and relationships integrate different technologies with each other. The connections between business relationships mean that a company is part of a network of companies, each of which has substantive, but different investments in technologies.

---

[3] "Unlocking the Value of Intellectual Assets", *The McKinsey Quarterly*, 1999, 4, 28–37.

The product and process technologies of a company affect its position in a business network and its relationships with other companies around it. A business network as a whole and the positions of companies within it change as evolution occurs in relationships, technologies and in their distribution in the network (Lundgren 1995). For example, traditional microchip producers that both designed and manufactured their offerings are now concentrating more and more on their product technologies. They are leaving production to rapidly growing contract manufacturers, that are strong in process technologies. Similarly, cars are increasingly produced by specialised production companies. Design is often the responsibility of specialist design-houses, leaving traditional "manufacturers" to manage their brands and their relationships with consumers and intermediaries.[4]

The Economic Potential of Technology in Business Networks

The interconnections between different offerings, technologies, relationships and the wider network mean that the economic potential of any single offering, piece of equipment, technology or even of a company is not easy to identify. Of course, it is possible to record the cost of the investments in technology that have been made by a company. But the economic potential of that technology investment depends on how the technology can be developed further or combined with other technologies in the company or in its relationships or in the wider network, for example:

- The value of the product and process technologies that are used to produce an offering will depend on the product and process technologies that are employed in the components used in the production.
- Its value will also depend on the support systems of other companies and the technologies that they use.
- Its value will also depend on the particular problems that the offering is used for and on the technologies of immediate customers and those that are involved elsewhere in the network.

All these technologies and relationships may change, for example:

- The company may establish relationships with new suppliers with different technologies, or develop existing ones with its current suppliers.
- It may develop relationships with new customers with different technologies and different relationships so that the offering is used to solve new problems and the technology is exploited more widely.[5]

---

[4] We refer to these processes of changing companies and activities as distintermediation, reintermediation, aggegation and disaggregation and discuss them in Chapter 8.

[5] For a discussion of the issues in technology exploitation, see Ford and Saren (2001).

In this way each single technology can be used as part of a different "bundle" of technologies, in different or modified relationships and to solve different problems. This process of combination and recombination creates new economic potential from existing technologies and resources. It is also the means by which new technologies are commercialised and through which development requirements become apparent and development takes place.

The essence of development in business networks can be encapsulated in the following processes:

- Re-ordering existing technologies and developing new ones in existing relationships.
- Relating these to technological developments elsewhere in the network.
- Developing new relationships to exploit technology widely by solving different problems, and to provide access to different technologies.

Thus, relationships and technologies define a company's existing position, but they are also the drivers for changing it. The task for a company is clearly to take advantage of the technological resources already created within itself and in its existing relationships. But it must also take advantage of the technological resources created elsewhere in the network and seek to exploit its technological resources in new relationships to solve new problems.

A Network View of Technological Development

Technological development is rather mysterious. The mystery arises partly because we have two separate views of the nature of development, as follows:

- The first view sees development as an art, through which a lonely innovator develops a unique product without any help or equipment. One recent example is of a Finnish teenager who developed a way of erasing compact disks in his home without any advanced tools or facilities.
- The second view sees development as "big science", in which new technologies are developed through large-scale, systematic investment in advanced research in sophisticated laboratories.

Both of these different views of technological development emphasise the importance of a single actor, whether an individual or an organisation as the origin of the innovation. Both of them ignore a critical aspect of development. This involves the *interaction* between different individuals and organisations. This interaction aims to reconcile and meet different objectives, combine the technologies and resources of different actors, and achieve development, such as between a supplier and a customer.

A second aspect of the mystery arises because of different views of the nature of the development process itself:

- When we talk about the "development" of something, we suggest a process that is both definable and observable. Development is focused on end-results that can be furthered through a rational process that, by implication, can be controlled by a single actor.

- However, when we talk about something "developing", we suggest a process where the direction or end-result is much less clear. A developing situation is always uncertain and incomplete. It is never controllable by a single actor, nor can it be subjected to rationalistic planning.

A manager in a business network has to cope with this mystery. He must try to make sense of the developing situation in the surrounding network and search for connections with the development that he wishes to initiate in his own company and in its interactions with others.

A company's attempts to initiate or manage technological development are really attempts to connect its own efforts with those taking place at different points in a network. Business relationships play a crucial role in this process. By focusing on these relationships we can gain a realistic view of the nature of technological development and exploitation. This relationship focus integrates the clearly defined task of *development* in a single company to the more complex process of *developing* in the network (David 1975).

Box 7.1 The KM7 Project: An Illustration of the Development and Exploitation of Technology in Business Networks

The Swedish paper and pulp industry was doing extremely well in the 1970s. Companies were making large profits and the future looked even brighter. One of the companies in the industry was Uddeholm, a traditional, long-established Swedish forest, steel and energy conglomerate. It was a good time to think of investments and equipment as the production unit we are concerned with was old and investment was needed to upgrade the technology.

The initial investment decision

Uddeholm used the services of a respected consulting company when considering its investment choices. The consultants identified two areas for investment that appeared to have a high profit potential: newsprint paper and folding board for use in packaging. The company evaluated these findings against three critical criteria:

- The need to increase the value added by the company. This is a classical issue in all primary industries.
- The need to increase the rate of utilisation of raw material inputs.
- The need to retain the company's hard-earned reputation as a high-quality producer, of which it was extremely proud.

Folding board seemed to be the product area that best fitted these requirements:

- It was used for packaging in the food industry and was considered to be modern and technically advanced.
- Customers had a wide variety of requirements and this gave the company the opportunity both to add high value and to solve complex customer problems.

- It seemed to fulfil the criterion of high raw-material utilisation, because it was possible to use mechanically derived pulp as the raw material. This utilises much more of the wood-content than chemical pulp.

However, a major problem was that Uddeholm had no experience in either the process technology of folding board, nor of marketing it. Despite this, the company took three major steps:

- developing a new board product called Uddex;
- investing a large amount in a new board-making machine called KM7 with a planned capacity of 110,000 tonnes/year;
- building a new thermo-mechanical pulp-mill next to the board machine to produce the necessary pulp.

Competition

Just before the final board meeting to approve the project, the management learned that a competing company had made similar plans and their mill was expected to start production within two years. The company still decided to go ahead, but planned to rush the construction of the new mill so that production would start within three years instead of the original four. The announcement of the decision attracted major interest from the media and within the industry. It was a big venture. A project group was formed and it had to work intensively. The time schedule was tight.

Recession

One year after the investment decision the Swedish forest industry hit a devastating downturn. The crisis affected all companies including Uddeholm and all major markets faltered, including that for folding board. At the same time new calculations for the board-making machine, KM7, showed that the total investment now required was expected to increase by 25%. The situation worried the management and it decided to terminate the project. However, it found out that if it did so, then it would only be possible to recover a small proportion of the investment made. The project had already taken off and there appeared to be nothing else to do but continue. So despite the crisis, the construction of KM7 continued according to plan and was completed in three years. The total investment had now increased to 45% more than originally planned. But there were more costs to follow.

Problems

The KM7 machine was built using new and partly unproven technology of which Uddeholm had no previous experience. It became clear that it would take some time before the specified quality of product could be attained. The product technology behind the new product, Uddex, had been continuously improved during the construction of the plant and it had some obvious advantages compared to competing products. It was launched as the "strongest folding board in the world" and this allowed packaging companies to run their production at a higher speed. However, these companies would have to adapt *their* production in order to take advantage of this benefit. They hesitated to do this because of the quality problems with Uddex and therefore the advantages of the new product could not be realised. Also because of the quality problems, a major part of Uddex production had to be sold as second-rate quality at a low price. At the same time the direct costs of running-in the new plant during its first half year of operation amounted to 20% of the total originally planned investment and expectations for the next year were even worse. The quality problems were expected to take at least another year to solve and KM7 was becoming a "black hole" for Uddeholm.

The recession also affected Uddeholm's other businesses and the company was forced to sell all its forest businesses, including the KM7 project to another traditional forest-products company, called Billerud. This sale was not an isolated event, but was another episode in a long relationship between the two companies, stretching back over 100 years.

We will return to this case later in the chapter to see what happened next. But we can use the story so far to point to two important conclusions about the nature of technological development:

- *Embeddedness*: The first conclusion from the case is that the failure of the investment in KM7 was only partly related to the characteristics of the technology itself. In order for the investment to have achieved its potential, it required investment and adaptation by other companies, including Uddeholm's customers and by changes in its relationships with those companies.

  The *technological potential* of the new board-making machine was determined by decisions that it had taken in the past, when the machine had been designed for a specific purpose with limitations to how else it could be used. The *economic potential* of the technology was determined by how it was used by others. The *economic outcome* of this or any other technological investment is never achieved just because the investment is completed, but only after a number of decisions are taken afterwards by the company's counterparts and others.

  This means that a technological investment cannot be considered in isolation. It is always embedded in wider sets of resources and it is this embeddedness that determines the economic potential of the investment and its outcome. If we look at the case from this point of view, then it is not surprising that Uddeholm ran into problems. It invested in a new technology that required it to build relationships with new customers and for them to adapt their operations. This is a major change for the network to cope with. It illustrates the importance of understanding the embeddednes of a technology when planning and predicting its economic outcomes.

- *Episodes in long-term relationships*: The case explains how Uddeholm solved its financial problems by activating an earlier relationship with Billerud. The take-over can be seen as a special event, but it can also be seen as a logical step in the development of the long-term relationship between the two companies and could even have taken place earlier. If we consider the take-over from some other perspective than this investment, then perhaps it should not have taken place. It was only one out of several probable paths that could have been taken. What is important is that it gave KM7 a new position in the network. KM7 did not have a particular place in the process, nor was it a key issue in the take-over. However, it was heavily influenced by it and to this we will return shortly.

Embeddedness

Embeddedness refers to the many connections between a single technological development and the surrounding network. It determines the economic consequences of any technological investment by a company. As Nathan Rosenberg (1982) suggests, the "growing productivity of industrial economies is the complex outcome of large numbers of interlocking, mutually reinforcing technologies, the individual components of which are of limited economic consequence by themselves".

However, the complexity of these connections is such that they are impossible for a manager to grasp. Managers do need to find a way to cope with these connections and there appear to be two approaches:

- A common approach to this complexity is for the manager simply to focus attention on only a few of the most obvious or important connections between her own and other companies, such as its main customers or suppliers. She then tries to design and manage her technological investment on the basis of this assessment. The aim is to plan investment on the basis of what the chosen connections look like today and how they are expected to change in the near future.
- Alternatively, we would suggest that the manager *interacts with other companies in the process of investment choice*. Interaction can help in two ways. It helps to focus choice on a few connections, but that choice will be based on the perceptions and views of several actors so that they are all embedded in the process! Interaction also helps because it means that the counterparts will be involved in determining and carrying out adaptations *over time*. This is likely to lead to a smoother process of adaptation.

We can examine this interaction a little further by considering the highly simplified network surrounding company A in Figure 7.1. Company A is using three inputs from suppliers B, C and D and it produces three related offerings for customers E, F and G. All the suppliers and all the customers have other customers and suppliers (H, I, J and K). What will happen if A makes a change in its operations, product design or some other technological dimension?

If this change affects A's inputs or outputs, then the effects of A's change will, in turn be affected by the reactions of the three suppliers and/or the three customers. How will these actors evaluate A's change? Their evaluation will relate to their own situation and their view of how it will affect their relationships and their own product and process technologies.

Suppose that A is a manufacturer of hard-disk drives in the information technology industry and has the aim of doubling the capacity of the drives. This might require a small increase in their diameter. Company H may be a customer of one of A's customers and may manufacture computers. It may be trying to reduce the size of its products to enable them

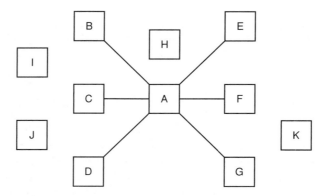

Figure 7.1 A Simplified Network.

to fit better into its customers' equipment. In this case, the value of A's technological investment will be nullified by that of H. If, on the other hand, interaction between A and H leads the computer manufacturer to develop the opportunities presented by the new hard disks, then the value of A's research and development will be increased. The initial investment of A has a value that is dependent on how well it relates to other existing investments and to the extent that new investments made by others will support it.

Issues for managers of embeddedness

The importance of embeddedness raises at least four major issues for managers, as follows:

- *Knowledge*: Any large technological investment is likely to be connected to a wide diversity of other investments among suppliers, customers, competitors or co-developers. This means that managers must develop knowledge beyond that of their technology itself and its immediate application and into quite different companies and areas of application. Furthermore, they must develop mechanisms to scan for future developments and to update this knowledge continuously. Collecting and storing all this knowledge will be very costly for one company and this reinforces the importance of an interactive process of making investment decisions to capitalise on the knowledge of others.
- *Control*: Embeddedness means that a single company never has full control of the use or direction of development of its own technology (Dosi 1982). Because its technology is connected to other actors, coping with the economics of technology means coping with these other actors, who might interpret the technology in quite different ways. So, a particular technological investment might be seen as a limiting factor by one company and as a great opportunity by another. How these other companies actually interpret and act on a technology can be influenced. The extent of this influence will depend on the nature of the relationship between companies and their commitment to the relationship becomes critical.

- *Change*: The way that a company copes with technology in its relationships with others will affect what happens in other connected parts of the network. A change in technological connections between two companies may travel through the network and produce more radical changes elsewhere. For example, changes in the links between electronics producers and makers of cameras leading to higher-performance digital cameras produce enormous changes for producers of film and chemical suppliers and may lead to the demise of retail photo-processors. Thus, even if a change might have been intended to create stability, the dynamics of the sequential coping with connections forces the combination of technologies and actors to change. What might have been a limiting factor at one moment could in the next be a force for expansion.
- *Bundling*: A single technology is of no value until it is combined with others. A product technology, no matter how innovative, has no value to a user unless it can be successfully combined with other, perhaps long-established product technologies and with suitable process technologies, so that offerings can be produced. To satisfy the requirements of any user requires a *bundle* of these different technologies, each of which is embedded in a network of other technologies, companies and the relationships between them. Managers in business networks often face the task of liaising, co-ordinating or managing the links between different companies with the aim of assembling an appropriate bundle of technologies to satisfy a particular set of requirements. This occurs in widely different situations such as those involving prime contractors for major projects and retailers seeking to develop innovative products based on the technologies of their suppliers.

Relationships are needed to handle these managerial issues. It is through its relationships that a company can gain knowledge, or simply rely on the knowledge of a counterpart. Relationships are a way of showing commitment to others, but also a way of generating it from them. Relationships are dynamic and they can be useful in handling inter-related changes. Finally, it is through relationships that the respective technologies of different companies can be brought together to satisfy the requirements of the users of offerings based on them.

Box 7.2 Embeddedness of Technological Development

The following two examples both come from the aerospace industry and illustrate different aspects of the embeddedness of technological development:

Active control of structural resonance (ACSR)

This first case illustrates how technological development is embedded in a complex pattern of internal and external interrelationships, whether or not these are recognised by the company concerned.

Vibration is a major problem in helicopters. Manufacturers try to reduce the problem by using damping material to cushion vibrating parts, but this is never completely satisfactory and involves a considerable weight penalty. The research department of one helicopter company started to develop a system of active control, where each vibration in one direction was countered by an opposing movement from a mechanical actuator. However, the anticipated development costs of the system became too high for the company and work was stopped. Shortly afterwards, the company hit severe vibration problems with a new type of helicopter and development was started again. This time it was undertaken by a different department that was "closer to production" and in co-operation with a manufacturer of mechanical actuators. But it was again stopped when no orders for the new helicopter were forthcoming and it was abandoned. Development only started again when the next generation of helicopters faced similar problems. By this time the company also began to realise that the technology had much wider potential applications if it could be designed into fixed-wing aircraft, military vehicles and trains. The company is now involved in a range of co-operative development projects with companies in these areas.

On-board oxygen supply (OBOGS)

This second case illustrates how the technologies used within any relationship or by any group of companies are not isolated from the surrounding world, but that they and the relationships themselves are embedded in a wider technological and relationship network.

Military aircraft need a system to provide pilots with oxygen at high altitude. This has conventionally been achieved by using compressed oxygen in a tank with a system of pipes, valves and control devices to deliver the oxygen at the correct pressure, volume and temperature. A small number of companies competed with each other to develop the technology to increase reliability and reduce the weight and size of equipment.

In entirely separate companies, and for quite different applications in medical research and bio-technology production, the entirely different technology of molecular filtration was being developed. This technology had strong, but unrecognised, connections with the aerospace industry. One of the oxygen equipment manufacturers became aware of the technology and used it to develop an entirely different approach to its application. This substituted a small scoop on the side of the aircraft to collect the few oxygen molecules at high altitude that were then filtered, collected and delivered to the pilot, thus dispensing with the complicated system of tank, pipes and valves.

The Effects of Relationships on Technological Development

The ways in which technology is developed and used are shaped by interactions between companies in relationships and in the wider network. Relationships are consciously used by companies as a vehicle for technological development and there are now many articles arguing for the importance of co-operative relationships, strategic alliances and joint ventures in development. But all relationships have a technological content and companies have always worked with their suppliers, with customers and with others on issues of technology. What has changed is that the increased awareness of the value of technological co-operation has led many managers to believe that these relationships can easily be managed. However, the interconnections between relationships and technology are complex and require considerable care in their analysis and management.

Relationships have two types of effects on technological development:

- *Interactive effects*: These effects are based on two characteristics of technology itself. The first is that new knowledge often appears at the border between existing bodies of knowledge. This means that interaction between companies with different areas of knowledge can often generate new thinking, as in the example of digital cameras mentioned above. The second is because the economic potential of a technological innovation cannot be judged in isolation, as we have argued above, but it can only be assessed by the support it generates from others and the potential uses that they will put it to.
- *Complementary effects*: These relate to the growing need for companies to specialise in their technological development, as the cost of each generation of new technology increases and the number of technologies required to operate in any application grows. Relationships provide the means for companies to complement their own resources with those of others (Håkansson 1987).

The effects of relationships on technological development may be the result of careful planning and organisation. But they may also arise unintentionally in the day-to-day activities within existing relationships. Because of this, a company's closest counterparts are likely to have the strongest influence on its technological development. This leads to two key questions about these technological relationships, that we will attempt to answer using a study by Håkansson (1989):

1 What sort of technological counterparts is a company likely to have in practice?
2. What are the characteristics of interaction in development relationships?

Technological counterparts

Counterpart companies are very important for a company's technological development. On average, the companies in this study estimated that about 50% of all their development spending was on projects in which external counterparts played a significant role, although there was a wide variation between individual companies.

The most common counterparts were those with which the company already interacted. Customers and suppliers together made up almost three-quarters of the co-operation partners. "Horizontal" units, such as producers of complementary products; competitors; university departments, etc., made up the remainder.

Only 3% of companies' most important relationships were with research institutes. This indicates the relative lack of importance of primary scientific research in the technical development of companies.

A large number of companies had development relationships with nine or more customers. This is because companies in business markets are likely to relate their production to individual customers rather than to produce for stock. When production is based on direct customers' orders, then interaction with them easily develops into technical collaboration. Of course, this large number of separate collaborations can cause major problems if they are not co-ordinated.

In contrast to those companies that had a large number of development relationships, 29% of the companies had none at all. This leads to the questions of how these companies could possibly know about the developments that are taking place in their customers and how these might affect their relationships.

From the study, it is possible to categorise the 123 companies into three distinct groups based on the extent of their development relationships:

- Isolated companies: This group of 29 companies appeared to work as if they were "islands", with very few development relationships.
- Focused companies: This group had many collaborative relationships, but mainly with one type of partner: 28 of the group collaborated mainly with their customers; 13 with horizontal partners and three with their suppliers.
- Broad co-operators: this group of 48 companies were well integrated into their network and worked with a large number of counterparts of different types.

The companies in the sample were as prepared to co-operate with foreign as with home suppliers. Foreign suppliers accounted for 20% of their purchased volume and 22% of the collaborative relationships with suppliers. However, the companies were less likely to have development relationships with overseas customers. These accounted for 32% of sales, but only 18% of collaborators. Horizontal partners were even more concentrated in the same region as the interviewed companies. These results indicate the importance of cultural issues in co-operative relationships, but also show the possibility of international business co-operation. They may also reflect the relative international orientation of Swedish companies when compared to some of their overseas customers.

Characteristics of interaction

Table 7.1 shows the variation in duration of different types of development relationships. Two-thirds of all customer and supplier relationships which include an element of technological development had lasted for longer than five years, and almost half of them for longer than 15 years. It is clear that companies collaborate with well-established and familiar partners from within their portfolios of customers and suppliers. However, horizontal relationships show a somewhat different picture and more than half of these were less than five years old. A possible explanation for this difference is that customer and supplier relationships involve a frequent pattern of goods and payments and technological collaboration evolves through this interaction. Horizontal relationships have no such base and are often established only for a particular collaborative project. If problems arise in the collaboration, then there is no underlying activity to support the relationship.

Most technological collaboration between companies takes place without explicit formalised agreements. Based on our studies we estimate that more than two-thirds of all

Table 7.1 Duration of Development Relationships with Different Types of Partner

Duration (years)	Customers	Suppliers	Horizontal units
0–4	36%	28%	55%
5–14	30%	41%	29%
⩾15	33%	29%	15%
Weighted average	13 years	13 years	8 years

collaborative relationships are non-formalised. Few managers believe in the importance of formal agreements. Instead, they are much more likely to use words like "trust" and "confidence" to describe how these relationships are controlled. Paradoxically, it is the higher-involvement, longer-term relationships that are likely to be the most informal. High-involvement relationships are difficult to formalise, because of their many parameters and the different sources of uncertainty that are involved. This means that formal agreements are only likely to be appropriate in the limited case of co-operation for very specific and clearly definable purposes.

Technological collaboration seems to evolve organically as an integral part of an overall relationship with a customer or supplier, rather than being its starting point, and companies are likely to receive a range of technological advantages from them, both major and minor. Most technologically collaborative relationships are used informally over a long period of time for a number of different purposes. They are part of a company's general resources and are usually well integrated into its internal organisation.

Developmental relationships are costly to establish and time-consuming to nurture. A company's existing, high-investment customer or supplier relationships are an important but often wasted resource for development. Many companies still make only limited use of their partners. Half of the companies in the study collaborated with no more than two of their ten most important customers or suppliers.

The Effects of Technological Development on Relationships

As well as the influence of a company's relationships on its technological development, those relationships themselves will also be affected by the process of technological development. The problem for a manager is that she often does not know where technological development will surface or what effects it will have on her relationships.

The effects of the development of new technologies on relationships

New technologies provide a fruitful basis for the development of relationships. At the start of a relationship they give both parties reasons to make mutual investments and encourage interaction. However, managers face problems when trying to make sense of how to use new technologies in their relationships and which new relationships may be required to effectively exploit a technology. Managers tend to see new technologies in terms of the characteristics and product application of those that are currently in use. For example, radio was initially perceived as a development in wireless telegraphy and the computer as a sort of improved calculating machine. It is often only much later that the full potentialities and direction of a technology become clear. In the case of the computer this only occurred when it was combined with the already existing technology of the keyboard.

Scientific discovery and technological development are often a new combination of already existing ideas. Alternatively, they can be a combination of perhaps one major new idea and a number of existing or new support technologies that are necessary for its success. Often this means that technological innovations fail until the relationships are established to provide access to the vital, existing or new support technologies. For example, Audi have replaced conventional automatic transmissions with a "Multitronic" system. This is not a new technology, but one that was used as long ago as 1900 in France and by Daf in Holland in the 1950s. But in the past the system never worked well enough to achieve standardisation. However, Audi have now combined the original innovative technology with that of other suppliers. It now uses a high-strength metal belt to replace earlier belts of cloth or rubber that could stretch or snap and sophisticated electronics to control the transmission. Similarly, the idea of a car driver being able to choose the ride setting on his car between soft and hard was tried and failed in 1933. It has now been re-introduced by Cadillac, but with a specially designed microprocessor control and special magneto-rheological fluid in the vehicle's suspension. Both of these additions are based on the technologies of its suppliers and accessed through its relationships.

The effects of the development of mature technologies on relationships

Developments in mature technologies also affect relationships between companies, but in this case, there are a number of important institutional factors. For example, the prevailing automotive technology has been gaining momentum for over a century and contemporary society has adapted to the operation of cars with internal combustion engines. Many companies are trying to develop electric vehicles. Even when the critical technological issues have been solved, companies will have to cope with the inertia of the huge existing human and capital investment in current technologies. The prevailing institutions of automotive technology will tend to favour conservative technological innovation and to penalise radical ones.

In many ways technology develops out of local needs and social circumstances. Its impact will be contingent upon the ability of companies to shape it according to the local needs of the users. The successful transfer of an already developed technology from one application to another, or from one country to another, requires that those involved can understand, experiment and evaluate it against the peculiarities of the new context.

Relationships are an essential way of achieving this wider use of technology, but the process of doing so changes relationships themselves. The possibility of adapting technologies for different applications may lead to the development of previously inert relationships between companies that have the technologies and those that understand the applications.

Bringing Relationships and Technology Together

Neither relationships nor the application of technology are ever fixed and each combination of technology and business relationships has the potential for further development. To illustrate this we will return to the KM7 case in Box 7.3 and see how the technology as well as the business relationships were redefined in order to improve the company's situation.

Box 7.3   KM7: From Failure to Success

When we left the KM7 case, the original owner, Uddeholm, had just sold its forest operations to Billerud. The mill had still not reached its projected capacity and sales figures were even worse.

Tetra-Pak

At this point, Tetra-Pak, the rising star of the packaging industry becomes important. Both Billerud and Uddeholm had been the main suppliers of paper-board for liquid containers (can-board) to Tetra-Pak, over 30 years ago. Uddeholm had considered investing in new production facilities for can-board, for which TetraPak was the only customer. However, as they did not want to make the necessary commitment, the plans were dropped and sales to TetraPak decreased. Billerud, on the other hand, had strengthened their position as a supplier.

Product change

In order to exploit the existing investment in KM7, Billerud–Uddeholm resumed discussions with Tetra-Pak. Their task was to develop a new type of can-board that could be produced in KM7. However, there was considerable resistance inside the mill because many staff believed that can-board was a simple product that any company could produce and their previous experience with Tetra-Pak had been negative. Regardless of this, co-operation between Billerud–Uddeholm and Tetra-Pak continued and the company made a further investment in order to switch from producing folding board to can-board and in order to improve its quality. This investment led to a can-board that was both stronger and stiffer. It also produced a surplus of pulp and this was used to improve the economics of the company's production of its fine paper products.

Relationship growth

As the relationship with Tetra-Pak grew stronger, Billerud-Uddeholm became the second largest producer of can-board in the world. Tetra-Pak accounted for 90% of the company's can-board sales and for the first time in its history KM7 was running at profit.

The initial investment in KM7 had been a failure, almost bringing Uddeholm to bankruptcy. The subsequent investments founded on Billerud's relationship with Tetra-Pak turned KM7 to a success story. Not only was the mill converted to making a new, profitable product, but production capacity also almost doubled. Moreover, the conversion to can-board and the production investments also led to new opportunities to exploit other investments in fine paper.

The following are the conclusions on the case:

- *Exploiting technology*: The case illustrates how difficult it is to exploit technology within a structure of relationships, but how important those relationships are for successful exploitation. In this case, it took ten years and some major additional investments in product and process technologies and in relationships before the new mill became successful. These additional investments changed the characteristic of the technologies and made them suitable for a multinational customer.

    The whole process finally produced a totally different product for a different customer, at twice the projected capacity but with sound profits.
- *Investment value*: One important consequence of the complexity of technological development and exploitation is that the ultimate value of any investment in technology is largely determined by other investments. These are not only made by the original company, but also by others both before and, crucially, after the initial investment. A technological resource can become an asset or a liability, depending on these other investments. The same is true for business relationships.
- *Interface between relationships and technology*: The customer's initial lack of trust in the supplier's ability to exploit the new technology and to produce the product successfully meant that they were unwilling to modify their own production. Hence, the benefits of the technology in terms of production speed could not be achieved. In contrast, when KM7 was later converted to produce a new product within an existing customer relationship, this matched the customer's own technology and requirements and the innovation was productive. The take-over of Uddeholm by Billerud made it possible for Uddeholm to tap into the already developed relationship between Billerud and Tetra-Pak, providing an opportunity to introduce innovation. The connection between the technologies of KM7 and Tetra-Pak was of value for both parties individually and in their other relationships. Finally, without the initial investment by Billerud, Uddeholm had nothing to offer in its relationship. The initial investment was necessary to start the process.

Creating Economic Value from Technology

The creation of economic value from technology is a critical managerial task in business networks. There is no single answer to how this can be done and the approaches taken must be specific to each situation. Our discussions in this chapter lead us to identify two dimensions that will influence the process of value creation:

- *Technological content*: This concerns *what* is involved in the process.
- *Business application*: This concerns what the technological content is to be *used for* and *how* it can be used.

Both of these can vary in how well they are known by those involved in the process. In particular, even if the application of a technological innovation is understood, it can still be unclear how that can be achieved.

Figure 7.2 presents these two dimensions in matrix form. Cell 3 occurs when the technological content of an innovation is not well known and the possible business application is unclear. In this situation, the use of the development is likely to be random and where a useful offering occurs or if one occurs at all is likely to be a matter of chance. If anything does appear, it is likely to take a long time before it is of any substantial economic value. This is the situation for the genius inventor who, unfortunately, is likely to die before the innovation generates any money!

At the other extreme, in Cell 2, technological content is well known and there is a common understanding of the application. Here the exploitation of the innovation can be handled as an ordered decision process. A company can forecast the likely reactions of customers and the process of technical development is also likely to be more predictable. This situation is likely to occur when the development involves an existing application with change in a recognised parameter and with technology that does not require corresponding changes in other areas. An example of this was the introduction of solid-state engine management systems to cars.

	BUSINESS APPLICATION	
	UNCLEAR	CLEAR
TECHNOLOGICAL CONTENT – KNOWN	1 SEEK NEW APPLICATIONS FOR KNOWN TECHNOLOGIES, RELATIONSHIPS IMPORTANT	2 ORDERED DEVELOPMENT. SINGLE ACTORS ARE IMPORTANT
TECHNOLOGICAL CONTENT – UNKNOWN	3 DEVELOPMENT IS RANDOM. SINGLE ACTORS ARE IMPORTANT	4 SEEK NEW TECHNOLOGICAL SOLUTIONS FOR KNOWN APPLICATIONS. RELATIONSHIPS IMPORTANT

Figure 7.2   Creating Economic Value in Different Situations.

The other two cells in the matrix describe two development situations that are more frequent than the two extremes we have identified. If technological content is well known but the possible business applications are unknown (Cell 1), then companies are likely to have to seek relationships with companies that will use the development in a different way. The Internet is such a case, where the technological content is to a large degree well known, but its business application is still ambiguous and failure is common. Companies are currently trying to use the content in different ways, often within business relationships, as this co-operation is a useful way to explore new uses.

Another case is when the business use is clear, but the technological content is unknown (Cell 4). In this case there is an obvious requirement of technological development. Here relationships are also important to ensure that the process of developing or redefining technology relates to a business application that may be evolving.

Pharmaceuticals illustrate both situations. Often the disease is known, but what sort of products might cure it is not. Also a product is sometimes conceived and refined, even though its primary function might be ambiguous. For example, the multinational company Astra developed its current major product Losec for the treatment of other diseases, but it proved to be most useful for the treatment of gastric ulcers.[6]

Conclusions

The major conclusion of this chapter is that the way a company creates economic value from technology is to a large extent dependent on its relationships. Relationships are the way that technology becomes embedded in a network of other technologies, companies and individuals through which it is exploited. This conclusion has a number of lessons for both individuals and their companies:

- *Individuals*: The contacts developed by individuals within business relationships are important when a company tries to change from its existing business relationships and technologies. However, these contacts can also make it very hard for a company to achieve change. There will always seem to be thousands of "technical" reasons for these individuals to keep their old relationships and ways of working. Hence, a company's ability to mobilise its own personnel and their personal contacts is very important when it is trying to achieve change. Recruitment of new staff is a useful way of using individual networks to foster innovation. The aim of this is to obtain someone with an already established network within a technological or application area that the company is attempting to enter. This is often much faster and less costly than trying to develop from scratch.
- *Companies*: A manager's own company is perhaps the most natural perspective from which to look at the use of technology, but it can be overly restrictive if it prevents the company from taking a more relational view. No two companies will have entirely

---

[6] Chesborough and Teece (1996) have attempted to structure the situations where a company should attempt to innovate alone or by "networking" with others.

common interests or views and all relationships will involve self-interest by both parties. Yet a certain interest in the other's well-being is a necessary condition for a relationship to develop. If the two parties have their own ambitions, but also listen to each other and are prepared to change and to influence, then we have the conditions for co-evolution. This is what happened in the KM7 case after the merger with Billerud and when Tetra-Pak became involved.

The development and exploitation of technology require creativity, which is often lacking. Too many business relationships are simply not effectively used as vehicles for development and exploitation. Every company should evaluate the technological contribution of its most important supplier and customer relationships at least on an annual basis. This evaluation must be related to its internal technological development and to a wide scanning of the network, preferably on a joint basis. Reactivating existing relationships in this way is likely to produce cheaper and faster results than trying to establish new specialised development relationships. These specialised relationships may still be worthwhile, but they are generally more limited in time and scope than generalised relationships and the companies involved must be clear about their purpose before starting.

The two most common problems in improving the link between technology and relationships concern human and technical resources. The available human resources determine what can be done and how well it can be done. They effectively limit the number and potential of a company's developmental relationships. To develop and maintain them is difficult and requires expensive resources, but it must be a major managerial priority.

The case study showed how the investments in technological resources in KM7 affected the company's relationships. An even clearer example arose in the steel industry. A steel producer found that it could afford to replace its old rolling mill. This was a huge investment for a small company. The new mill was faster and more accurate but needed longer runs in order to be efficient. However, the investment led to considerable problems for the company. The old mill was very flexible and easy to change to meet the different requirements of a number of small customers. Thus, the change meant the end of the company's relationships with its existing customers with special requirements and it had to seek entirely new customers for its the new equipment.

The conclusion is obvious: any technological change can affect a company's relationship possibilities and all changes must be looked at from this perspective.

References

Chesborough, H.W. and Teece, D.J. (1996) "When is Virtual Virtuous?" *Harvard Business Review*, January–February, 65–73.

David, P.A. (1975) *Technical Choice, Innovation and Economic Growth*, Cambridge: Cambridge University Press.

Dosi, G. (1982) "Technological Paradigms and Technological Trajectories", *Research Policy*, 11(3), 147–162.

Ford, D. and Saren, M. (1996) *Technology Strategy for Business*, London: International Thomson.

Ford, D. and Saren, M. (2001) *Technology Marketing and Management*, London: International Thomson.

Håkansson, H. (ed.) (1987) *Industrial Technological Development: A Network Approach*, London: Croom-Helm.

Håkansson, H. (1989) *Corporate Technological Behaviour: Cooperation and Networks*, London: Routledge.

Hippel, E. von (1988) *The Sources of Innovation*, New York: Oxford University Press.

Lundgren, A. (1995) *Technological Innovation and Network Evolution*, London: Routledge.

Rosenberg, N. (1982) "Technological Interdependencies in the American Economy", in N. Rosenberg (ed.) *Inside the Black Box: Technology and Economics*, Cambridge: Cambridge University Press.

MANAGING IN NETWORKS

The Characteristics of Networks

Before examining the model of managing in networks, it is important to make clear some ideas on nature of business networks that will affect that management. We can outline these ideas as follows.

Interaction, interdependence and incompleteness

We started this book by outlining three common myths about the nature of business behaviour and describing our alternative views. These views have an important connection to how managing in networks can be analysed and understood:

- *Problems, interaction and solutions*: The "Myth of Action" sees business as a process of action and reaction. Our view is to see companies as members of a business network consisting of a large number of active heterogeneous companies each interacting with others and seeking a solution to their different problems (Dubois 1998). One important outcome of this approach for managing in networks is that these interacted solutions are likely to affect several of the involved companies (Hertz 1998).

- *Interdependence and limits to discretion*: According to the "Myth of Independence", a company can carry out its own analysis of the environment in which it operates, develop and implement its own independent strategy based on its own resources, taking into account its own competences and shortcomings. Our counter-approach is based on the interaction between companies in relationships. These companies are *interdependent* for sales, supplies, information, technology, development and for access to other companies elsewhere in the surrounding network (Hughes 1987). This means that companies have limited discretion to act or to build independent strategy. The outcomes of their actions will be strongly influenced by the attitudes and actions of those with whom they have relationships. Interaction between interdependent companies involves simultaneous elements of co-operation, conflict, integration and separation in the companies' relationships. A company's position in the network is based on its total set of relationships and that position changes through interaction with other companies in different positions in the network. Interdependence means that the management of a relationship is essentially similar for both of the companies involved in it.
- *Incompleteness*: The "Myth of Completeness" arises from the view that a company is self-sufficient and is able to develop a strategy that marshals its own resources into a unique approach based on its own internal competencies and shortcomings. Our counter-approach is that no company *alone* has the resources, skills or technologies that are necessary to satisfy the requirements or solve the problems of any other and so is dependent on the skills, resources and actions and intentions of suppliers, distributors, customers and even competitors to satisfy those requirements. One important outcome of this is the formation of structures of relationships in networks to provide access for companies to the resources of others.

Making sense of the network

Basically, a network consists of companies and the relationships between them. But the idea of a network is subject to many interpretations. Our view is as follows:

- A network is not restricted to the set of companies with which a single company deals, or even to the companies that they also deal with.
- A network is not confined to the set of companies with which a company has formal or informal agreements about some particular co-operation.
- Any view of a network centred on a single company, or defined by the company itself, is inevitably restricted and biased and gives an incomplete view of the world surrounding that company and the actual or potential influences on it.
- A company-centred view of a network provides a distorted picture of the ideas, problems, pressures and aspirations of the companies that the company includes in its view.
- A company-centred view of the network is likely to be limited to those companies and influences within its immediate horizons. As such, it provides an inadequate basis for understanding the dynamics of the wider world of the network. It hinders the

company's attempts to understand the pressures and opportunities that exist or may exist in the future.

Despite this, the view of a network that is limited to the set of other companies that the single company knows of, thinks of or deals with is implicit in much of the managerial literature. Such a view is often associated with the illusion that the company then controls that network or more simply that it is their own network.[1]

The network surrounding a company is difficult to define and delimit. It has no objective boundaries and its contents will be affected by both the purpose of the analysis and the starting point for that analysis. For example, if we were concerned with issues of the location of technologies in different companies and the processes of technological development and exploitation, then the network we examined would have to include a wide range of companies in different industries, serving different applications of particular technologies. The company that is the focus of our attention would probably have no contact with many of these or even knowledge of them. If we were concerned with issues of logistics, then the network we examined may be much more circumscribed to those companies involved in using or providing logistical services, perhaps of a particular type. But even here, we would have to include companies with no direct relationship with those which our company dealt with, particularly if their role in logistics was different or innovative and if the companies or their methods could affect our focal company. Even if we are concerned with a narrowly defined issue such as component or service supply, we would need to extend our view of the network from that of a single company to that of other principal companies and their relationships. This issue can be seen very clearly when we consider companies on the "boundary" of a network. Such boundaries are essentially artificial, so that if we looked at the network from the perspective of a company on that boundary, we would see that it would be well within a different network with different boundaries and so on.

There is no single, objective network. There is no "correct" or complete description of it. It is not the company's network. No company owns it. No company manages it, although all try to manage *in* it. No company is the hub of the network. It has no "centre", although many companies may believe that they are at the centre.[2] One important consequence of this is that the outcomes of the actions of any company cannot just be related to that single company – many of those outcomes will affect many others in the network.

In fact, all the actors involved in a particular issue in the network will have their own different "picture" of the network.[3] This picture is the basis for their perceptions of what

---

[1] The fallacy of this view can be readily seen when asking a number of companies, listed as being part of a certain company's network if that view coincides with their view of their position. They will often suggest that rather than being in someone else's network, they actually have their own one, of which the first company is simply a part!

[2] The idea that no one company manages the network does not mean that companies cannot hold an important position within it, or be a "strategic center", such as Nike (Lorenzoni and Baden-Fuller, 1995).

[3] The variation in the idea of the network depending on the purpose of the analysis and the position from which it is viewed is the reason why we slip between talking of *the* network or simply *a* network.

is happening around them and of their actions and reactions in the network. Network pictures have a central role in our model, as we will see below.

The Model of Managing in Networks

Having outlined some of the issues that affect our view of networks and management in them, we can now look at the model itself. The model is illustrated in Figure 8.1 and we will examine each of the three basic elements of the model using the IKEA catalogue case for illustration.

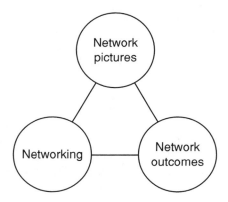

Figure 8.1   A Model of Managing in Networks.

Network Pictures

Network pictures refers to the views of the network held by participants in that network. There is no single, objective network and different companies and the individuals within them will each have a different picture of the extent, content and characteristics of the network, of who is doing what and what does and does not work.[4] This picture forms the basis for their analysis and actions. Their network picture will depend on their own experience, relationships and position in the network and will be affected by their problems, uncertainties and abilities and by the limits to their knowledge and understanding.

In many cases, a common view of the nature and dynamics of a network will be held by a number of participants in it. These common views can lead to inertia in the network and form the basis for joint action for or against change. Broad stereotypes that can affect

---

[4] The idea of a network picture is close to that of "network theory": "An actor's systematic beliefs about network structure, processes and performance and the effects of its own and others' strategic actions" (Mattson 2002).

thinking include the view of the network as a "supply chain" or "distribution channel".[5] More specific stereotypes include the view of "who should do what" and "who should deal with whom" that are common across networks. Sometimes, many participants see a network as something that is controlled by a single powerful company, or that the network is only a group of companies that work together on some specific project. These network pictures arise from interaction and participants' experience in specific relationships and the corporate wisdom of each company.

A common network stereotype involves identifying different "types" of network. But these types are generally the picture of part of the relevant network as seen from a particular perspective, or those held by a particular company. A particular type of network will be quite different if seen from a different perspective. It is important to emphasise that there are no absolute or objective network types and all networks will have different elements, characteristics, possibilities when seen from different perspectives or when parts of the network outside their considerations of any one company are included.

Box 8.1 The IKEA Catalogue and "Green" Paper

IKEA produces more than 100 million copies of its catalogue each year.[6] This requires a lot of paper, approximately 40,000 tonnes per year. IKEA believed that its customers were becoming more environmentally aware and it was keen to show an environmentally friendly image itself. Its catalogue was an obvious place for this and in the early 1990s the company started to investigate the use of "green" paper for the catalogue. This required it to do some active networking.

In this case there was a clear stereotype picture of the network held by the paper producers. In this view, they were the dominant players and they chose which of the existing types of papers they should produce. These choices were based on their existing production structure. They defined the needs of the users in terms of strength, run-ability (for printing), and brightness of the paper. IKEA's network picture was different. They were closer to the final consumer and had a wider picture of the network, of which these consumers were part. They had also noticed an increased interest in environmental issues from these consumers. They felt that they needed a "green" paper. IKEA formulated an environmental policy where it was stated that the catalogue should use a paper based on TCF (Total Chlorine Free) pulp with at least 10% of recycled fibres. The first reaction from the producers, especially the German producer Haindl that had been the main supplier to IKEA, was to refuse. They said, "It is impossible to produce such a paper." At that time there were just a few producers of TCF pulp in Europe and none who could produce a catalogue paper using recycled fibres. IKEA now had to start to mobilise paper producers in a number of countries, as well as suppliers of equipment and chemicals. In other words, it had to expand its picture of the network in order to find a solution.

---

[5] We discussed the effects of the picture of a network as a supplier's distribution channel in Chapter 6.
[6] This case study is taken from Håkansson and Waluszewski (2002).

This example illustrates the importance for a company of examining the network pictures of others. These pictures will be different and may appear "outdated", "unrealistic" or "unfair" to the company, but they are the reality on which these other companies will act or react. In this case, the pictures of the paper producers were based on the importance to them of existing operations, investments and relationships. The example also shows that for a company to create change then its own network picture as well as those of others have to be challenged. But these pictures cannot be changed instantly or completely and change requires both time and a systematic approach.

Networking

This second element of the model is closely related to the network picture held by each individual or company. This affects what they can or might wish to do. Networking encompasses all of the interactions of a company or individual in the network. Networking has the following characteristics, that are summarised in Figure 8.2:

- *Networking is interactive*: Networking by any company affects and is affected by the actions of others. Networking is not something carried out by a single company that "manages its network" or something that is done "to" some other companies. All companies are networking by suggesting, requesting, requiring, performing and adapting activities, simultaneously. The outcome is the result of *all* those interactions! This means that the outcome of any action by a single company is seldom restricted to the company's original aims or wholly in accordance with the wishes of any of the involved companies. Accordingly, companies have to adapt their goals and ambitions continuously.
- *Networking is based on restricted freedom*: All companies in the network have restricted freedom to act. Much of their networking will involve reaction to the actions of others and all of it will have to take into account the reactions of others and will be moderated by these reactions.
- *Networking is not defined by conventional company categories*: All wholesalers, retailers or manufacturers will not behave in a particular way and cannot be treated in common.

- NETWORKING IS INTERACTIVE
- ALL COMPANIES NETWORK SIMULTANEOUSLY
- ALL COMPANIES HAVE RESTRICTED FREEDOM TO ACT
- NETWORKING IS NOT DETERMINED BY TYPE OF COMPANY
- NETWORKING INVOLVES WORKING WITH, THROUGH, IN SPITE OF AND AGAINST OTHERS
- NETWORKING CAN BE BI- OR MULTI-LATERAL
- IT IS NOT BASED ON CO-OPERATION OR COMPETITION ALONE
- IT IS BASED ON COMPANY'S PICTURE OF ITS OWN AND OTHERS' POSITIONS
- IT IS BASED ON ITS VIEWS OF THE LIKELY REACTIONS OF OTHERS
- INCOMPLETE KNOWLEDGE LEADS TO "LEARNING BY DOING"
- NETWORKING COPES WITH THE NETWORK PARADOXES

Figure 8.2 Characteristics of Networking.

From a network point of view all companies are "middle men" that have suppliers and customers. Each will build their activities on those of others and produce an output that will be used by someone else. Each will behave in a unique way.

- *Networking involves combined co-operation and competition*: Networks involve simultaneous combinations of working with, through, in spite of or against others. Also, the classical roles of suppliers, customers and competitors are less clear and sometimes totally blurred. For example, the offering of a supplier may be produced according to the design of a customer. Another customer may make an offering for itself according to the design of a supplier. Two competitors may co-operate to design a new product or buy some of the products that they sell from each other.
- *Position, experience and expectations are central factors in networking*: A company's networking will be based on a view of its own position in the network, the positions of others and their likely reactions. In the same way its networking will be affected by earlier experiences and by the actor bonds, resource ties and activity links between the company and its counterparts. Finally, networking is based on a company's expectations of the effects of its own actions and those of its counterparts. Companies are likely to confront the status quo when they can envision something better.
- *Networking is based on incomplete knowledge*: The inadequacy of each company's knowledge means that "learning by doing" is an important aspect of networking.
- *Networking copes with the network paradoxes*: Finally, companies network to cope with the three paradoxes of business networks, as we discuss below.

The three aspects of networking

We can distinguish between three aspects of networking. Each involves managerial choices for a company and each relates to the three *paradoxes* of networks that we introduced in Chapter 2.

The first aspect of networking: choices within existing relationships

This aspect of networking relates to the first network paradox:

> A company's relationships are the basis of its current operations and development. Yet those relationships also restrict that development.

A company's relationships are major assets and are the basis of its current activities. Without them it could not operate. These relationships arise from investments made by all companies in current practice. Any change in operations may produce benefits, but always involves costs for each company and the loss of the benefits of current ways of working.

A company's relationships are also liabilities that tie it to its current operations. Even though one company may wish to change a relationship, its counterpart will also make investments in the relationship and may resist change.

The first aspect of networking centres on a company's existing relationships and what these really mean for it. It involves choices of when to *confront* the status quo of accepted ways of operating and when to *conform* to particular ways of operating into which it is tied by its relationships.

These choices may have to be made by a company several times each day and are an integral part of its day-to-day interactions with counterparts. Each company will be questioned by its counterparts or will try to initiate changes itself in such things as the content of an offering for a customer, its method of fulfilment, the components bought from a supplier etc. At the same time other aspects of the company's relationships will be held constant, such as the price charged to the customer or the supplier's relationship with an intermediary. Similarly, a company may negotiate a change in the offering it buys from one of its suppliers whilst keeping overall volumes constant. Making the choice between conforming and confronting requires an understanding of the evolution of both the surrounding companies and the relationships between them. Some aspects of this evolution will be positive for each company and some will be negative. Consequently each has to try to enhance the positive ones but also work against the negative ones. This is a continuous process, but it will be especially important when one of the companies tries to achieve a major change. Because this first aspect of networking may appear mundane or routine, it is possible that a lack of understanding or analysis of the minor changes within different relationships may lead to a drift into an unsatisfactory state. Alternatively, the process of confronting the status quo may sour the atmosphere of a relationship.[7] The IKEA case in Box 8.2 illustrates the first aspect of networking.

Box 8.2   Conform or Confront

In the IKEA case, the company wanted to achieve a substantial change in its supply relationship and had to *confront* the supplier. When the supplier refused to co-operate, IKEA had to show that it was serious and had to try to find someone that was prepared to *conform* to its requirements. IKEA tried to find a supplier that already had both the facilities and the experience to work within its requirements for both chlorine-free and recycled paper. But, before changing supplier, IKEA first had to try with the existing one. It found that it was impossible for Haindl to conform because it was also imprisoned by its relationships. Haindl knew that only small amounts of pulp were totally chlorine-free. If it had chosen to fulfil IKEA's demand, then a number of other important German customers would have been very upset as they also wanted to show an environment-friendly approach. Haindl wanted to avoid confronting these other customers.

The connections between existing and new relationships lead us to the second aspect of networking.

---

[7] We have discussed the issue of relationship atmosphere in Chapter 3 in terms of commitment, adaptation and distance.

The second aspect of networking: choices about position

The second aspect of networking relates to the second network paradox:

> It is equally valid to say that a company defines its relationships or that a company is defined by those relationships.

Companies face important choices between accepting their current network position, defined by their existing relationships, or using their existing or new relationships to change that position. A company's existing relationships, its network position and the company itself are the outcome of its past interactions. A company can accept this existing position and actively work to stabilise it by using the first aspect of networking (above) to improve efficiency and effectiveness.

Alternatively, the company can seek to systematically change its position by combining its existing relationships in new ways or by building new relationships.

> The second aspect of networking involves the choice for a company between when to *consolidate* by stabilising and strengthening its existing network position or *create* a new position by changing the combination of its existing relationships or developing new ones.

This second aspect is not simply a choice between whether to keep existing or develop new relationships. Instead, it is concerned with how the company combines its relationships into a network logic. New and existing relationships can be used for *both* consolidation and creation. Thus:

- *New relationships for consolidation and creation*: A company may seek to consolidate its existing position by adding new customers or suppliers that are similar to its existing ones. Alternatively, it may try to change its position by developing new and different relationships.
- *Existing relationships for consolidation and creation*: Existing relationships can be used to create a new network position by, for example, developing new technology in those relationships so as to radically alter their content, or enable new relationships to be developed. Alternatively, the company can simply seek to consolidate its existing position by operating in the same ways as before in its existing relationships, but with increased effectiveness (as in the first aspect of networking).

Box 8.3   Consolidate or Create

IKEA did not initially want to change its network position, it just wanted to get another paper. But due to the reactions from the suppliers it had to change position in order to get a changed product. Earlier IKEA had been one of the larger buyers. It was a respected buyer that was expected to choose between existing types of paper. Now it suddenly demanded something else. In order to follow IKEA, a supplier had to see IKEA in a new position as a "lead user" (von Hippel 1986). IKEA realised this and one of its strongest arguments in its discussions with suppliers was that it used 8–10 of the largest printers in Europe. Thus, anyone coming up with the new paper could, through

IKEA, have that paper tested and used by these printers. IKEA used its existing relationships with printers to "market" itself to the paper producers. At the same time IKEA established contacts with producers of paper-making equipment. Through these contacts IKEA gained a better understanding of the issues involved in producing the new paper. The outcome of this networking was that IKEA did get the new paper that it wanted. But then it ran into the third aspect of networking.

The third aspect of networking: choices about *how* to network

Companies face decisions on networking both within and between their relationships. They also must consider *how* to network with their counterparts and this involves them in facing the third network paradox. This states:

> Companies try to control the network and want the benefits of control, but control has its problems and when it becomes total, it is destructive.

Companies in networks are incomplete and depend on the resources and skills of others. They also depend on the *initiative* of others to generate change and improvement. Companies inevitably try to get their counterparts to do what they want, in such things as the offerings exchanged between them, the price charged, or direction of development or the attention given to counterparts' other relationships. But if counterparts do what the company wants, they are acting on the basis of the company's ideas alone. They may have to disregard their own wishes and wisdom and the relationships will not have the benefit of the initiative of those counterparts. Thus the development of the company's relationships will be limited by the company's own wisdom and its counterparts may become unwilling participants. Hence companies face the choice of when to *coerce* others to do their wishes and when to *concede* to the wishes and initiative of others.

Again, this is not a dichotomous choice. Companies are likely to simultaneously attempt to coerce some counterparts while conceding to others or do both in different parts of each relationship simultaneously. The ability to coerce counterparts depends on the respective capabilities of the companies involved. For example, one company may be able to insist on the technological direction of a particular relationship based on its own technological capabilities whilst the counterpart, based on the volume of business that it transacts may be able to determine the price that is charged. Conceding may not be absolute and may involve informing or persuading, or simply accepting the decisions of the counterpart, with good grace. Conceding is in line with a realistic view of business networks and the restriction on companies' abilities to take decisions for themselves as well as for others. Management in networks is not a linear process of achieving and maintaining control. A company's networking has to take into account a multitude of factors, for example:

- its dependence on others;
- the inadequacy of its picture of the network;

- the diverse perspectives, approaches, requirements and aims of those around it;
- the need to accommodate and work with these others, but to be willing to coerce them when it is necessary and it is able to do so.

In contrast, an approach to networking that is based solely on coercion implies a self-centred view of the network. A company that sees the network in its own terms and only as a way of solving its own problems will fail to understand both the motivations and problems of others, the dynamics of the network and the interface between the well-being of others and itself.

Box 8.4   Coerce or Concede

This choice became an issue in the next phase of the IKEA case. IKEA managed to get an Italian and two Finnish suppliers to produce the new paper. All of them had production difficulties about including the recycled material. But there was also another problem with this material. All Nordic producers have to import recycled paper as all that is collected in the Nordic countries is already used. Thus, waste has to be transported back from Germany and the UK and added to the pulp. Another big user, the Springer Press group realised that this would increase the costs of production. Thus, when Springer formulated its environmental policy a year after IKEA it also included chlorine-free paper, but specified that only suppliers situated in the centre of Europe should include waste in their paper. Instead Springer added "good forestry" as a new demand. This led to a problem for IKEA. If they tried to coerce suppliers to follow their specification for the new paper they would probably be the only company buying it and they would have to pay the full capital, development and operational costs of the suppliers. Another possibility was to downgrade the specification of the paper to one that is easier to use with recycled fibres. IKEA chose to concede to the new situation and encourage the overall development of environmental paper by accepting the lower specification of others.

The three aspects of networking and their connections to the network paradoxes are summarised in Table 8.1.

Network Outcomes

Networking is a universal phenomenon undertaken by all companies simultaneously as they conform/confront, consolidate/create and coerce/concede. This means that every network is continuously producing *network outcomes* for each single participant in the network both individually and collectively. But we can never be sure of a specific outcome for a specific company to a single networking activity because each company is

Table 8.1 The Three Aspects of Networking.

	Choices	Coping	Networking
THE FIRST ASPECT OF NETWORKING	CHOICES ABOUT WORKING WITHIN RELATIONSHIPS	COPING WITH THE FIRST NETWORK PARADOX	CONFORM OR CONFRONT
THE SECOND ASPECT OF NETWORKING	CHOICES ABOUT NETWORK POSITION	COPING WITH THE SECOND NETWORK PARADOX	CONSOLIDATE OR CREATE
THE THIRD ASPECT OF NETWORKING	CHOICES ABOUT HOW TO NETWORK	COPING WITH THE THIRD NETWORK PARADOX	COERCE OR CONCEDE

subject to multiple, simultaneous networking outcomes and networking always affects more than one company. Still less can we say with certainty that the outcomes of a particular networking are positive or negative in terms of revenue or profit, now or in the future.

Because of this, no company can ever operate on the basis of a complete analysis of the outcomes of all the networking in which it is involved. Each company will observe, assess and respond to only a subset of the networking outcomes that affect it, based on its particular network picture.

Despite the difficulties, it is important that companies try as far as possible to decide which networking actions are important for them and examine the different outcomes of these actions. Because network outcomes affect the network pictures of individual actors, they often lead to increased uncertainty. They also form an important basis for each company's own networking. Negative outcomes may lead a company to change some of its networking activities and/or its network picture. Positive outcomes may encourage the company to extend actions to reinforce the outcomes.

A useful way to cope with the multi-faceted and multi-layered nature of network outcomes is to examine them along three dimensions that we have used throughout this book: actors, activities and resources.

Outcomes and actors

An outcome is by definition "for" somebody and the "somebody" can be on three levels: first, it can be for a single actor, either a company, other organisation or an individual. Second, it can be for those in a single relationship, which has its own "substance" and identity. Third, it can be an outcome for a network as a whole. It is important for managers to examine the outcomes of networking on each of these three levels, as follows.

Outcomes for single actors

Network outcomes directly affect each single actor in the network. So each company needs to examine the outcomes of networking for other significant actors, as well as examining outcomes for itself. The financial aspect of these network outcomes is important, but so are others such as what each company learns from the outcome of networking. It is also important for a company to examine network outcomes for single actors *in relation to* other actors in the network. For example, one outcome of networking may be to give a company better access to the resources of other companies, *when compared with those around it.*

Because a company is part of a network, it is subject to multiple outcomes and needs to examine each *in relation to others.* A company must consider how networking within a number of different relationships affect the *individual* outcomes from each. It must also examine the respective outcomes it can expect from within different relationships in its portfolio. Its task is to maximise the value to it from the outcomes from within its portfolio of relationships as a totality.

Box 8.5   Outcomes for Single Actors

The IKEA case illustrates how the outcomes for a single actor are the result of relationships working together. Haindl refused to supply IKEA because it could not combine its existing relationships with other customers with the new type of relationship required by IKEA.

The particular network outcomes that each company focuses on will strongly affect both its network picture and its own networking.

Outcomes for a single relationship

The outcomes of networking for each relationship need to be assessed by those involved in it. The outcomes for a relationship are of two types: the first concerns what is accomplished in the relationship – its effectiveness – and the second is concerned with how well the processes work within it – its efficiency. These outcomes will affect the views of the participants about the direction of the relationship and its value. This overall evaluation is of course subjective, but it is critical for the enthusiasm and involvement of the participants in the relationship.

Companies need to evaluate the value and processes of each of their significant relationships on a regular basis, from their own perspective and that of their counterpart.[8]

---

[8] We discuss the assessment of relationships in Chapter 4.

> **Box 8.6   Outcomes for a Single Relationship**
>
> The outcome for IKEA's relationship with Haindl was a disaster in terms of both what was accomplished and also how the relationship worked. Neither of the counterparts managed to understand the other's views and the relationship broke up. Some time later, Haindl tried to re-establish the relationship but was then turned down.

Outcomes for the network

There are outcomes that can be identified for whole sets of actors and relationships. Change or stability in one or more relationships can lead to wider outcomes in the network as a whole. For example, a technological development in one relationship may change the way that a whole network operates (Dosi 1988; Lundvall 1988; Lundgren 1995). Each company must therefore develop the skills to scan more widely than its immediate relationships and assess the dynamics of the network and of technologies within it.[9]

> **Box 8.7   Outcomes for the Network**
>
> Network change was an outcome of IKEA's dramatic change of supplier relationships and the technological development this led to. The new chlorine-free paper became widely established and this had dramatic effects on a number of both pulp and paper producers.

Network outcomes also have an important collective element. This refers to outcomes that are observed by all the participants and that explain to them how the network operates. In other words, these outcomes contribute to "what everyone knows", or the collective understanding or picture of the network participants.

Outcomes and activities

Network outcomes can also affect how different activities are related to each other. They can restructure a company's relationships, by changing the activities that each of the companies perform and the links between them. Network outcomes can also restructure the network, with new companies and relationships emerging and existing ones disappearing. We can summarise outcomes and activities as follows:

- *Aggregation*: This refers to the network outcome by which a company undertakes some activities internally that were previously undertaken by relationship counter-

[9] For a discussion of technological scanning see, Ford and Saren (2001: 146–50).

parts. Aggregation either restructures an existing relationship or causes it to end. It may also lead to the establishment of new relationships. An example of this is provided by the Danish shoe company Ecco. It previously bought leather, already prepared for making shoes, and sold the finished shoes to independent retailers. It now buys unprocessed cow hides, makes its own leather and shoes and sells them through its own outlets. This restructured Ecco's relationships, ending those with the suppliers of hides and with retailers, but establishing or developing those with leather chemical suppliers.

- *Disaggregation*: This refers to the network outcome by which a company ceases to carry out some activities internally and relies for them on a relationship counterpart. Disaggregation either involves establishing new relationships or extending an existing one. Disaggregation commonly occurs as companies contract out activities to others with which they establish relationships. A well-known example of this outcome is Nike, who now buy in all of the products that they sell from their suppliers.
- *Disintermediation*: This refers to the network outcome through which two companies establish a direct relationship, where none had existed before, or where the companies had previously dealt with each other via an intermediary. In the case of IKEA, they established relationships with producers of pulp and even with producers of paper-making equipment, rather than simply dealing with paper suppliers.
- *Intermediation*: This refers to the outcome by which a new company is established as an intermediary between companies that had previously dealt with each other directly, or when an existing company changes its portfolio of relationships to include intermediaries.

Outcomes and resources

Networking can have outcomes that affect the development and utilisation of resources between companies:

- *Utilisation of resources*: Networking has important outcomes that affect access to and utilisation of resources for companies. These resources include both those in the company itself and in its counterparts. The resources may include existing technology or know-how, offerings, facilities or an organisational unit. Resource effects are especially critical for all capital and knowledge-intensive companies. The access to and efficient utilisation of resources dominated the networking in the IKEA case.
- *Development of resources*: Another type of outcome affects the development of the resources of the companies involved, whether technical, physical or operational. A major type of outcome of networking in the IKEA case was the development and introduction of a new technology of totally chlorine-free paper.

Outcomes affecting both access to and development of resources have important financial implications for the companies involved. In the IKEA case, the financial outcomes were highly positive for the two Swedish pulp-producers that were the first to produce chlorine-free paper, while the financial outcomes were negative for those that were left behind.

Interconnections

Networking, network pictures and network outcomes are all interconnected. None of them automatically precedes the others and each affects and is affected by those others. We can identify some of the main connections as follows.

Between networking and network outcomes

All the dimensions of network outcomes are clearly affected by networking and the aims of networking can often be expressed in terms of various outcomes. However, the connections between the two are not simple or straightforward. Networking is part of the complex and continuous interaction that takes place and the outcomes will often be so blurred that it is meaningless to attribute causality. Companies certainly learn from networking and their subsequent choices in networking are affected by how their network outcomes develop. In this way, outcomes trigger actions and companies "learn by doing", so that much of networking is in practice a process of controlled experimentation.

Between network pictures and networking

A company's networking is affected by its network picture and its view of its position in the network. Sometimes this picture can restrict networking. A company may see its position in the network as "just a wholesaler". This company will be unlikely to innovate by, for example establishing relationships directly with consumers. In contrast, another company may have a broad picture of network dynamics and use this as the basis for innovative networking.

Conversely, a company's network picture is affected by the networking that is happening within the network. For example, experience with different aspects of networking may convince a company of the respective role and influence of important counterparts. A great deal of activity within companies and relationships consists of discussion and bargaining about network pictures – what does the network really look like and what does it mean for us?

Between network pictures and network outcomes

There is a clear connection between network pictures and network outcomes. If outcomes are in line with a company's existing network picture then that picture will be re-inforced. If the outcome is not in line with the company's expectations then it is likely that its network picture will change. Network outcomes are also affected by the company's network picture, as what is seen as the relevant outcome dimensions and indeed what is seen to have happened are determined by the network picture. For example, IKEA's picture of environmental concerns in the network established the criteria by which it networked with its suppliers, while their picture saw relationships as devices to ensure capacity utilisation, with consequently different criteria.

Network pictures provide the frame within which performance is assessed. One of the consequences of unfortunate outcomes is to change the dimensions by which outcome are assessed as these are affected by the development of a new network picture.

Conclusions: Strategy in Networks

This chapter has presented a model of managing in networks. The model has a number of features that are important both for the researcher trying to understand what happens in networks and the manager trying to operate in them. It is based on two basic ideas about networks:

- *Networks are broad*: Our view of the network is broad. The network is not defined by a single company or restricted to the companies with which that company deals. Nor is it something that it established, owns or manages. However, the term is commonly used in each of these senses. We would simply emphasise that any view that is restricted in this way will inevitably lead to difficulties in understanding how the network looks from the perspective of other companies. These companies will act from their own perspective, which will almost certainly include other companies and other types of relationships, rather than that of the "focal" company. Without a broader view, a company will be unable to anticipate the actions and reactions of those around it. Also, a failure to take a broad view of the network will make the company vulnerable to dynamics that have their origin "over-the-horizon" from its normal operations.
- *Networks are complex*: Managing in networks is complex. Each of the companies in a network attempts to manage its individual relationships and to affect others elsewhere in the network, with which it does not deal directly. Each company has limited knowledge and operates on the basis of an evolving, but subjective "network picture". Each has limited discretion and is subject to the simultaneous networking of many other companies, each operating on the basis of its own different network pictures. Each company has to cope with the peculiarities or paradoxes of the network and networking in each is a combination of three aspects; within and between relationships and involving both encouragement and coercion.

The three elements of the model of managing in networks each provide a perspective on strategy, as follows:

- *Strategy and network pictures*: A company's network picture is an important component in strategy development. Strategic analysis will inevitably be based on the company's own picture of the network. Therefore, it is important for the company to reassess that picture and the assumptions, prejudices and illusions on which it is based. This reassessment must be based on learning fully from its experience of its own networking and that of others. Strategic analysis also involves examining the *different* pictures of the network and their position in it, as seen by individuals in different functional areas inside the company. These individuals can often produce a clearer view of the company's position and the problems and motivations of those around it than that seen by senior management, enabling the company to capitalise more fully on its "corporate wisdom".[10] At the same time, differences in the network pictures seen by different functions may limit the company's ability to implement its strategy or to carry through its networking. Building coherence in these network pictures is a major part of the strategic development of a company. Strategic analysis also involves assessing the network pictures of companies with which it has relationships and others that may affect its actions. This emphasises the importance for strategy of taking a wide view of the network, rather than that of immediate customers and suppliers. Each company will act on the basis of its own idiosyncratic picture and attempts to change some of those pictures can be an important part of a company's strategy.

- *Strategy and networking*: Networking involves choices. Some of those choices have to be made on a day-to-day basis, such as which aspect of the company's existing relationships it should confront and to which it should conform. Others, such as choices about attempting to modify the company's position, are likely to be longer term and involve many individual actions, as well as both coercing and conceding to the actions of many others. Also, the interdependence of companies in networks means that a major part of networking involves *reacting* to the actions of others. The need for reaction may arise on a daily basis, but it is important for a company to look behind the attempts of counterparts to confront some aspect of a relationship or to coerce the company. The company must consider if a counterpart's day-to-day networking is part of an attempt to change network positions or is an indicator of a change in a counterpart's valuation of a relationship. Networking involves numerous outcomes in both the short and long term. Thus, a strategic approach to networking requires a company to assess the possible longer-term effects of short-term actions and to consider its own and others' actions as part of those longer-term views. A strategic view of networking also requires a company to evaluate the effectiveness of its own networking and that of others against their respective aims, both explicit and implicit.

- *Strategy and network outcomes*: It is simplistic to see business strategy in a network as a set of company actions with measurable, or even observable outcomes. All companies in a network are networking simultaneously and all companies are subject to a wide range of outcomes both short and long-term, only some of which will be apparent or understood. A significant aspect of strategy in a business network is to choose the outcomes on which the company will focus its attention. This is important because it is easy for a company to either fail to record or examine outcomes or to simply accept those that occur. Strategy and network outcomes require a company to ascertain "real" and accurate network outcomes and assess their value. Strategy also needs to be based on an awareness of the limits to the outcomes that can be achieved by a company's networking and hence to develop a realistic approach to action. For

---

[10] For a discussion of the issue of managing the knowledge or wisdom within a company, see Nonaka and Takeuchi (1995).

example in Chapter 3, we emphasised the difficulty for company of establishing new types of relationships and hence the common need to seek outcomes within existing relationships. This does not mean that companies can do nothing and are simply passive in the network, but it does emphasise the need for realism in the aims, methods and timescales of strategy, a realisation of a company's dependence on others to achieve strategic change and the importance of strategic reaction as well as pro-action.

- *Strategy and the model of managing in networks*: Finally, strategy involves examining the interconnections between each of the elements of the model of managing in networks. First, this requires a company to make explicit and to take advantage of the two-way connections between networking and network outcomes. Thus, companies have to grapple with the complexity of understanding the flood of different outcomes from their own and others' actions, but they also need to understand how their own networking has been influenced by their particular and limited view of (only some) network outcomes. They also need to use networking as a process of "learning by doing" and to analyse network outcomes to inform their learning about the network.

Second, a company must examine the connections between networking and its current network picture. Network pictures are never complete or accurate. Thus, it is important for strategists to examine the effects of these pictures on the networking that they choose. They must also consider whether their pictures are determined less by reality than by the networking they want to do or are used to doing.

Third, a company needs to examine how its network picture affects its view of network outcomes. Questions include how its view of "success" is affected by the limits to its information or its preconceptions of what does and does not "work" in the network. A company also needs to consider how it incorporates the outcomes of its own and others' networking into its network picture and whether that picture is realistic or up-to-date.

Our idea of managing in networks emphasises the complexity and the difficulties involved. It argues for the importance of accepting that complexity and learning how to live with it, rather than attempting to artificially simplify it and operate under the delusion of an inadequate picture. This requires a company to constantly examine the connections between network outcomes and its picture to be sure that its view bears some relationship to reality, rather than simply what it wants to see.

Strategy in business networks is not a linear process of analysis, development and implementation. The complexity and interactivity of a network mean that a company's strategy is more clearly seen as the "pattern in stream of decisions". These decisions are not just its own, but those of its counterparts. Strategy involves action, reaction and re-reaction, based on a company's network pictures, its own and others' networking and the outcomes from this.

References

Cohen, W.M. and Levinthal, D.A. (1990) "Adsorptive Capacity: A New Perspective on Learning and Innovation", *Administrative Science Quarterly*, 35, 128–152.

Dosi, G. (1988) "The Nature of the Innovative Process", in G. Dosi, C. Freeman, R. Nelson, G. Silverberg and L. Soete (eds) *Technical Change and Economic Theory*, London: Pinter Publishers.

Dubois, A. (1998) *Organising Industrial Activities Across Firm Boundaries*, London: Routledge.

Ford, D. and Saren, M. (2001) *Managing and Marketing Technology*, London, International Thomson.

Ford, D., Gadde, L-E., Håkansson, H., Lundgren, A., Snehota, I., Turnbull, P. and Wilson, D. (1998) *Managing Business Relationships*, Chichester: John Wiley.

Håkansson, H. and Ford, D. (2002) "How Should Companies Interact?", *Journal of Business Research*.

Håkansson, H. and Waluszewski, A. (2002) *Managing Technological Development*, London: Routledge.

Hertz, S. (1998) "Domino Effects in International Networks", *Journal of Business to Business Marketing*, 5(3), 3–31.

Hughes, T.P. (1987) "The Evolution of Large Technological Systems", in W.E. Bijker, T. Hughes and P. Pinch (eds) *The Social Construction of Technological Systems: New Directions in the Sociology and History of Technology*. Cambridge, MA: MIT Press.

Lorenzoni, G. and Baden-Fuller, C. (1995) "Creating a Strategic Center to Manage a Web of Partners", *California Management Review*, 37(3), 146–163.

Lundgren, A. (1995) *Technological Innovation and Network Evolution*, London: Routledge.

Lundvall, B-Å. (1988) "Innovation as an Interactive Process: From User-Producer Interaction to the National System of Innovation", in G. Dosi *et al.* (eds) *Technical Change and Economic Theory*, London: Pinter.

Mattson, L.G. (2002) "Reorganisation of Distribution in Globalisation of Markets", keynote address, Culture and Collaboration in Distribution Networks, Inaugural Meeting of the IMP Group in Asia, Perth, Australia, December.

Nonaka, I. and Takeuchi, H. (1995) *The Knowledge Creating Company*, New York: Oxford University Press.

Von Hippel, E. (1986) "Lead Users: A Source of Novel Product Concepts", *Management Science*, 32(7), 791–806.

So What Does It All Mean?

The aim of this final chapter is to try to bring together the words and ideas in the book into a view of some of the things a manager has to deal with in a business market. We will start with a general idea of an approach to business and what that approach might mean for the nature of a manager's job. Because managers in business companies have jobs with conventional titles like marketing or purchasing manager, the chapter then goes on to outline a view of what these jobs involve, within the approach that we take to management in general. We will also try to bring together a view of the task of business strategy.

A View of Markets

The word "market" can cause problems for the business manager. It conjures up an idea of a fixed set of customer companies or of the general "demand" for a particular product or service. It also suggests some kind of abstract whole, made up of anonymous, homogeneous and individually insignificant customers, but the customers of each business company are likely to be individually significant. Many of them will be very well known to their suppliers. Each will have different problems, uncertainties and experience. Each will seek different solutions to those problems and will have different abilities that may help to solve the problems and uncertainties of its suppliers. Similarly, the term "supply market" also points to an undifferentiated group of suppliers of similar products, but suppliers are not homogeneous and neither is what they supply or the problems that they solve for their customers. Also, all of the customers for one set of suppliers in a business market are simultaneously suppliers to another set of customers and so on. In fact all companies are intermediaries between other companies and a final consumer. A further complication is that these companies cannot be separated into neat groups, such as "manufacturers", "wholesalers" or "retailers", etc., with the companies in each group all doing the same things and with each group different from the others. Most "manufacturers" do not manufacture all of what they sell. They rely on suppliers for a large proportion of their offerings. Some buy in all of what they sell. Some manufacturers design their offerings and those of their suppliers, so do some retailers. Some distributors design and specify how the things that they buy should be made, just like some manufacturers.

- This means that managers must not view their activities as generalised approaches to customer or supplier markets, but as individual approaches to a diverse collection of customers and suppliers.

A View of Networks

A way to start to make sense of this complexity is to consider that business companies operate in complex *networks*, made up of themselves and many other companies and the relationships between them. These networks encompass many "markets", each of which consists of the exchanges between numerous pairs of companies. The term "network" can also be confusing, because if all companies are related to many others and so on, where does the network end? Ultimately, of course there is only one network, which is the universe! But saying that isn't a lot of help to a manager. So the network that we must consider consists of all of the companies that are significant *for the particular issue being addressed*. If we were concerned with logistical issues in the operation of an airport, then we would include in the network at least all the companies that used or provided supplies. If we were concerned with security at that airport, then we would have to consider a network composed of many more companies. If we were considering how technological change may affect a particular company, then we would have to look even more widely and include companies that produced quite different offerings to solve quite different problems for quite different customers, but that used technologies that could influence the technologies that we currently used.

A network view means that a company's supplier and customer markets do not exist in isolation. Nor are the other companies that it knows simply units in its linear "supply chain", or its "value chain" or "distribution channel". Restricting the network in this way is essentially self-centred, unrealistic and can only limit understanding. Each of a company's diverse relationships with its suppliers and customers are affected by *their* own relationships with *their* customers and suppliers. Their view of the network will be equally valid and certainly different. Their view will form the basis of their actions, not your view! None of the surrounding companies will have the same set of relationships with others. This means that there are probably more differences than similarities between supposedly similar customers and suppliers. More importantly, it means that a supply or customer market is neither a discrete entity nor homogeneous.

The idea of a network is also different from the idea of a market, where companies can come and go pretty much at will and where no one transaction is related to others in the future or the past. A network is also different from a hierarchy, or organisational structure because the links between those in a network are neither fixed, nor subject to ownership or overall control. A business network is not something that is imposed on the companies in it, nor is it something that can be designed or managed by any one of them. No-one manages the network, but all have to try to manage *in* it.

- A major concern for a manager is to maintain or change the position of her company in the network. Network position consists of the company's relationships and the benefits, costs, rights and obligations that come from them and changing position is likely to involve variation in existing relationships and establishing new ones.

A network is a peculiar organisational form because it does not have a centre or any clear boundaries. Its characteristics are determined by what companies do in and between the relationships that comprise it. These companies will all see the network differently, depending on their individual "network picture". These network pictures are the basis for managerial action in the network.

- This means that it is important for the manager to examine her own network picture and why they see things that way and to try to make sense of the network pictures of others that form the basis for their action.

A View of Managing in Networks

Managing in networks can be examined through the three elements in the model of managing in networks, that we discussed in Chapter 8 and were illustrated in Figure 8.1. The three elements of the model and their implications for managers can be outlined as follows:

Network pictures

Managing in networks cannot take place solely on the basis of the objectively recorded characteristics of the network, such as numbers of companies and sales volume. Instead, the manager must have an understanding of the "network pictures" of significant companies. It is these pictures of the network and of what happens in it and why it happens that form the basis of their actions. A company also needs to examine its own network picture, the validity of the assumptions on which it is based and effects that these have on its actions.

Networking

This consists of the actions of a company in the network. It has three aspects, each of which involve choices that are central to the process of managing in networks:

- *The first aspect of networking*: The manager must choose with which aspects of her current interaction she will *conform* and which she will *confront*.

    Managers face these choices on a day-to-day basis in many aspects of their relationships, such as price, adaptations and fulfilment. Both companies in a relationship will simultaneously confront aspects of their relationship while conforming to others. It is important for the manager to assess her relationships on a continuing basis to monitor those aspects of each relationship that can and should be confronted, those that are satisfactory or which can at least be accepted. She must also consider the overall, long-term effect of cumulative confronting or conforming.

- *The second aspect of networking*: Managing in business networks also involves the evaluation, maintenance and change of the company's network position. This involves choices between *consolidating* some elements of that position and *creating* new elements.

   These choices involve both existing and new relationships. For example, the company could choose to maintain its existing distribution relationships through wholesalers, while at the same time developing new supply relationships to increase the range of its offerings.

- *The third aspect of networking*: Managing in business networks requires an overall assessment of the company's dealings with the surrounding network. This leads to major choices about the extent to which the company will attempt to *coerce* those around it to achieve its ends, or *concede* to their capabilities and initiative in the network.

   For example, a company may insist that its suppliers should produce to its own design and determine where, when or how they should deliver. Conversely, it could concede to their design and logistics capabilities (perhaps developed elsewhere in the network) and hope to gain from their capabilities and wider initiative.

Network outcomes

All companies attempt to manage their relationships and all are networking simultaneously. So it is never possible to completely disentangle specific network outcomes from the complex networking that occurs. Nevertheless, it is important for the manager to examine, as far as possible, the outcomes of her own networking and that of others. This is the foundation of "learning-by-doing", which is a major basis of managing in networks. The analysis of network outcomes can be facilitated by separating them into the outcomes for different actors, activities and resources.

A View of Managing Relationships

This view of managing in networks involves companies in managing both individual and groups of relationships. These relationships provide a company's revenue and the products, services, advice and logistics that are necessary for its operations. They are also the source of much of the technology that must be developed to meet the requirements of the final end-users of a company's output. Relationships are the primary assets of a company, without which it can neither sell nor buy nor develop. Just like other assets, relationships require *continuing investment* by both of the parties, often over a long period of time. Its relationships are important units of analysis for a company when seeking to assess its performance, or when taking decisions about marketing, purchasing, development or investment. It is just as important to consider ways of improving the "rate of return" on investment in its customer and supplier relationships as it is to examine the rate of return on investment in a product or a piece of equipment, although that rate of return might be more difficult to measure.

Managing in business relationships is a multi-level activity. It requires at least the following:

- Each customer and supplier relationship must be managed for clearly thought-out costs and benefits. Some business relationships are individually vital to a company's success or even survival. Others are only important as part of a collectivity of other, similar ones. Some relationships are just trivial.

  The manager must consider what should be the company's own level of resource investment, adaptation and integration in particular relationships and what it should seek, or what it can expect from its counterpart.

- Each relationship must be examined from the company's own perspective and from the perspective of the counterpart. Both companies will have a different idea of the value of the relationship, its place in their relationship portfolio and the commitment to it that they are prepared to make. The manager's task in a successful business relationship is not to do exactly what the other party wants, at whatever cost.

  Relationship management requires a combination of co-operation, confrontation, guile and the pursuit of mutual and self-interest.

- Each relationship must be managed as part of an interrelated portfolio of supplier or customer relationships, from which the parties might look for different benefits and which might be at different stages of evolution.

- Each relationship involves the manager in evaluating how committed she is to the relationship and how committed she wishes to appear to be to her counterpart. She must decide on the investment she is prepared to make in the relationship and the extent to which she will adapt her products, processes or procedures. She must decide how integrated she wishes the two companies to be in their activities and resources and she must determine the work of the individuals who are involved.

  The manager's choices will be profoundly affected by the interdependencies between the companies in a relationship. Some choices will be made as a reaction to those of her counterpart. Others will be limited by the wishes of her counterpart and the effects of all her choices will be influenced by what the counterpart does.

- Each relationship and the things that happen in it are linked to all the relationships of both companies and to those, in which they are not directly involved, in the wider network around them.

  The manager needs to approach each relationship with an eye on that wider context. This might well involve her in acting in a particular relationship in order to achieve an effect elsewhere in the network and being aware that each relationship is subject to multiple effects.

Managing relationships in business networks in the short term is likely to be based on the first aspect of networking, *within* the company's current relationships in its current network position. In the longer term, management is likely to involve the second aspect of networking, comprising changes within a combination of the company's existing and new relationships with the aim of altering the company's network position. All networking, both short- and long-term, involves the company in choices between attempting to coerce the other companies with which it has relationships to act in particular directions and conceding to the wishes, wisdom and initiative of these other companies. Management of relationships requires an awareness of the different skills and technologies in each company and the ability to integrate, use and develop these in different ways.

A View of the Company in the Network

A network view sees a company as incomplete and dependent on the resources and abilities of others. At the same time, a network view also sees a company is much more than its own resources and abilities, because of the access to the resources of others that come through its relationships. This interdependence means that there are no neat boundaries between the activities and resources of a company and those of its customers and suppliers. For example, product design in one company is unlikely to be an independent activity and more likely to be influenced by interaction with particular customers and suppliers. Similarly, one company's operations cannot easily be separated from those of its customers or suppliers and are likely to be influenced by decisions taken in those companies.

A network view does not categorise companies into general types, such as manufacturer, wholesaler or retailer with easily identifiable characteristics. Instead, a network view identifies diversity and sees each business company as defined by its unique and evolving pattern of relationships. It is these relationships that activate its resources and without which they have no value, and it is these relationships that determine how and to what extent it is able to exploit its own resources and those of others. The successful management of diverse business relationships will place particular demands on a company's internal organisation.

But if a company sees the world around it as comprising a homogeneous "market", then it is likely to take a standardised approach to that market and its internal operations are likely to be oriented towards routinisation to achieve efficiency in that approach. On the other hand, if a company does recognise the diversity of individually important relationships then it is more likely to try to develop a *differentiated* approach to each of these. This will need internal operations that are adaptable enough to provide for this differentiation. However, these adaptations are likely to involve increased costs. All companies in business networks must balance the need for standardisation, routine and cost minimisation and the need to adapt and innovate. We can express this balance in terms of the three aspects of networking:

- A company must be organised to achieve efficiency and effectiveness in the first aspect of networking, involving its routine operations and the interaction in its current relationships.
- A company must also be equipped to manage the second aspect of networking involving change and diversity in current and new relationships to alter its network position.

- A company must also be skilled in the third aspect of networking, involving coercing of other companies where possible and appropriate and the understanding, flexibility and subtlety needed to concede and take advantage of the resources, skills and initiative of others.

All the aspects of networking exist simultaneously in a company and the separation between them is not neat. They require a company to adopt different, but parallel organisational characteristics. They also mean that the internal diversity in a company is likely to come increasingly close to the diversity in the world that it faces outside.

A View of Technology in the Network

No company can have all the skills and technologies that are needed to satisfy any customer's requirements. Each is dependent on the technologies of others. This situation becomes more extreme as the cost of developing new generations of technology escalates and as more technologies are needed to operate any single business. This means that some of the most important decisions a manager faces are which technologies her company will retain *internally* and for which it will rely on other companies *externally*, whether those companies she relies on are customers or suppliers. Many companies attempt to retain technologies internally, at crippling cost, when they would be well advised to rely on the technologies of suppliers, customers or others. Other companies abandon their involvement in technologies that are critical for their future and buy-in products or services based on other companies' technologies. This can mean that their own products and processes lose distinctiveness.

These technology decisions are difficult for a manager to take, because planning in most companies is concerned more with the products, services and production processes that are based on its technologies, rather than the underlying technologies themselves. Also, companies often have a poor idea of the technologies they actually have and of how good they are when compared to those of their competitors. Interaction with other companies is likely to be the manager's most effective way of assessing her company's technologies and taking decisions about them. Another difficulty for the manager is that decisions on technology, once taken, are difficult or even impossible to reverse, at least in the short term. Despite this, many decisions with long-term technology implications are made solely to achieve short-term cost savings and without regard to the longer-term strategic requirements of the company. When a company has decided to rely on the technologies of a supplier to develop products for its use, or asked a customer to advise it on a production method, then its relationship with that company will become the sole source of those technologies. This dependence increases the need for effective management of its relationship with that company and for appropriate integration to ensure that the company gains the full benefits of those technologies and its own.

The pressures of cost and the range of required technologies mean that a company is increasingly likely to develop technology *within* its relationships. When these technologies have been developed, then it is through relationships with other companies that the technologies will be exploited.

The successful operations of companies in business networks are not based on their own internal technological strengths. Instead, it is their skills in managing relationships with a number of others that are important, as well as their ability to *bundle* together these technologies to supply an offering that meets the requirements of a particular set of users. A network view of technology is not company-bound. A company's technologies only have value when they are combined with those of other companies.

- The manager's task is not to develop new technology in splendid isolation over a long period of time. Instead, she needs to examine and match her own technologies with those of other companies. With those other companies she has to synthesise or develop technologies and bring them to new applications, often in a different form.

Technological threats and opportunities can arise anywhere in a very wide network and the manager will need good antennae to spot them and an organisation that can respond quickly. This will mean that the manager must be concerned with different means of acquiring technology as well as her own R&D and with different means of exploiting it, other than in her own products or processes. This acquisition and exploitation will take place within the company's relationships.

A View of Strategy in the Network

Each aspect of a company in a network is embedded in the surrounding network: its operations; its technology and other resources and its relationships. However, many companies develop strategy without a realistic view of the likely responses, counter-moves and independent actions of others. The manager in a business network must take a view of strategy that emphasises action, reaction and re-reaction by different parties. Strategy in business networks is not just about the company acting against others, but also often acting with, or through them.

Understanding the importance to a company's strategy development of other companies' actions leads us to appreciate the limits to its freedom to act independently. The manager in a business company is constrained by the companies on which she depends and also by the ideas and actions of the many individuals in her own company who are involved in interaction with others. The strategy that emerges in a company is the outcome of all these interactions, rather than just her actions. So in a very tangible way, a company's strategy is at least in partly determined by other companies.

The strategist in a business network must cope with the inherent paradoxes of the network, as follows:

- *The first network paradox*: A company's relationships in the network are the key to its current activities and its development, but at the same time these relationships can act to restrict that development.

  A strategic approach to this paradox is necessary if a company is to manage the choices between conforming to these restrictions and confronting them to achieve change.

- *The second network paradox*: Managing in the network involves managing relationships and so it is logical to say that the company's relationships are the *outcomes* of its decisions. Yet when we look at companies we see that it is equally valid to say that the companies themselves are the outcome of the relationships that they have.

  The strategist must be able to take both views of her position if she is to make sound decisions about when to accept her company's current network position and work within it and when to create a new position by changing the structure of its existing and new relationships.

- *The third network paradox*: All companies have to try to achieve control over their dealings with those around them, but this control can lead to problems for the company and complete control would be destructive. This is because each company depends not only on the resources of others, but also on their knowledge and initiative.

  Major strategic choices facing a manager in a network are when to coerce others in the network to achieve their own aims and when to concede to the wishes and actions of others. These choices can dramatically affect the scope, atmosphere and importance of a company's relationships. They will also have a major effect on the resources in which it will have to invest.

Strategy in networks needs to build on a company's current network position and its relationship assets, both individually and collectively. If it is to be realistic, strategy is unlikely to include detailed plans or prescriptions, but will be much more concerned with overall direction, range and the parameters against which future choices, actions and reactions can be set.

This overall direction needs to be expressed in terms of its portfolio of customers and the value that it will choose to offer within that portfolio. Strategic choice in a business network will be as much about changing the nature of existing relationships within that portfolio as it is about seeking new ones to add to it. Value has at least two dimensions when considering a company's overall direction. The first is concerned with the benefits that it will offer *in* its relationships and what it will expect in return. The second is more fundamental and is concerned with the value that it puts *on* each relationship itself. The value of a customer or supplier relationship is measured by its potential that can be exploited and the investment that will be required to fulfil that potential. The company must also take a view of the value that the other party puts on each relationship, which almost certainly will be different.

The complexity of interaction between many individuals in the companies in a business relationship and the interdependence between those companies influence the process of strategy development. The process needs to be built on the implicit knowledge of the many individual actors who interact with counterpart companies, since the strategy will be both the outcome and be implemented through their interaction. This means that to move a company in a particular direction requires co-ordination of these interactions and the commitment of those involved. However, the evolution of a company's strategic direction is not the outcome of its own deliberations, choices and actions alone, but is also dependent on the corresponding commitment, acquiescence, initiatives and counter-moves of others. For this reason, the strategy development process is a continuous process and not something that can take place at regular and discrete points in time like a three-year plan.

A View of Distribution

The network approach that we have taken in this book leads to a different view of the nature of distribution, on a number of levels, as follows:

- On one level, distribution can be seen as the important activity required to make offerings available to end-users, involving considerations of transport and warehousing and the use of intermediaries to reach end-users.
- On a second level, we are led to a view of distributors as companies that join the networks of other companies together. This then raises the important question for managers of how a company can monitor these complex networks and when and how it should intervene, in them directly or indirectly.[1]
- Our analysis of distribution networks points up the variety of ways in which different companies operate in them and the danger of trying to separate those companies into neat categories of manufacturer, distributor or retailer, etc. Every company is simultaneously a user, a producer and a third party to the relationships of others. Each company will have a different picture of the network and of their operations within it. Inevitably, this leads them to develop diverse combinations of resources and activities, each with implications for companies around them.
- Our view of a distribution network cannot be separated from a view of the network as a whole. An examination of the seemingly narrow area of distribution links can lead a manager to new insights on the nature of the network as a totality. This sees the network as encompassing a wide variety of companies, each with evolving relationships in which offerings are designed, produced, delivered, stocked, transformed and combined with others.
- For the manager, this network view leads to a realisation of the simultaneous change and stability in distribution and the need to be aware of her indirect as well as direct inter-company relationships. It also highlights the importance for a company of the ways in which networks evolve to meet the changing requirements of often distant end-users.
- Finally, it also emphasises that this evolution is unlikely to be achieved with an adversarial approach to important relationships and it highlights the need for an increase in distribution relationship co-operation.

A View of Marketing and Purchasing

Perhaps most of the readers of this book will either currently work in marketing or purchasing or have aspirations to do so. Many of the issues addressed in the book concern

---

[1] The issue of intervention in distribution networks is a classic example of the third network paradox.

managers in these functions, whether they recognise this or not. However, we have rarely mentioned the two functions separately and have been careful not to express business relationships as being exclusively of concern to them. This is for a number of reasons. Our view of networks highlights the complexity of the relationships between the many organisations in them. These relationships involve interaction between many different actors and functional areas. It is important that supplier–customer relationships are not seen as comprising just the interactions between a salesperson and a buyer. In business networks, marketing is not just what marketers do and purchasing is not just what buyers do.

Networks involve simultaneous co-operation and conflict within groups of suppliers and customers, as well as between the suppliers and customers themselves. Our view is a long way from the conventional one in which the seller tries to "win" an order at the best price, while the buyer tries to wring the last possible concession from him. Thus, we do not see the two functions on opposite sides of a negotiating table within a solely adversarial or zero-sum context.

Our approach to business networks emphasises the similarities between the tasks facing the two managers. Some of these are as follows:

- Both purchasing and marketing people have to manage individual relationships and portfolios of relationships and are concerned with how these relationships are linked to their company's other indirect relationships.
- Both are concerned with their company's current and potential network position.
- Both have to interact with each other and with numerous other functions in their own and each other's companies.
- Both are concerned with integrating their own company's technologies with those of others.
- Both have to carry out a combination of routine order administration and strategic roles.
- Finally, both functions exist in the same company and need to work with each other. A company is where a supply and customer network come together and each is mutually interdependent.

However, one obvious difference between them is that despite a growing realisation of the importance of purchasing, its status and influence within companies and the financial rewards its practitioners receive still tend to be lower than those for marketing. This is partially because it is easier to observe the short-term effects of marketing success, but also because the separation of the routine from the strategic is often clearer in marketing than purchasing and so it is less likely to be seen as an administrative, internal service function for other departments.

The tasks that are conventionally set for the two functions and the ways in which they are rewarded frequently impede, rather than help, the successful long-term management of business relationships within complex networks. A partial redefinition of some of these tasks might be useful.

Purchasing

The rewards of purchasing staff have traditionally been based on their success in reducing the prices that they pay for the offerings that they buy, although this has changed somewhat in the recent past. Price or "cost" reduction is a predictable purchasing preoccupation, but a network view of purchasing leads to a different idea of the role of price. Price only indicates the direct costs of procurement. Purchasing also needs to be concerned with the less direct relationship handling costs that the company faces.

More importantly, a network view emphasises that the network offers the skills, technologies and resources that are needed to satisfy the requirements of different end-users. Purchasing's role is to scan this network for the resources that the company needs to complement its own. It must manage the interaction through which both companies' resources and activities can be effectively brought together. This means that purchasing must be involved in the company's choices about which technologies it should retain and for which it should rely on others. These choices are both long-term and strategically vital, but frequently poorly addressed or taken within a single function such as R&D. It is frequently argued that purchasing needs "early involvement" in new product development. This network view of a company's technology emphasises early involvement by purchasing in decisions on the technologies on which a company's offerings are based and the processes by which they are fulfilled.

The role of the purchasing function must extend far beyond that of choosing a supplier against a specification issued by another function. Purchasing must initiate and develop supplier relationship and portfolio strategies. Its units of analysis have to be the relationship and the portfolio and not the product, service or the order. This wider view means that purchasing needs to change from being reactive to the requirements of other functions, to being proactive in managing its suppliers. It also needs to switch from an overwhelming concern with cost reduction to a much greater concern with competitive advantage, achieved through changes in network position and more effective use and integration of its own and its suppliers' technology.

Marketing

The marketing function in a business company is frequently evaluated on the basis of the volume of sales it makes and the profit margins it achieves on those sales, but these provide an inadequate view of marketing's function in a business network. Also, an emphasis on short-term sales or profits can actually divert the company away from building the long-term relationships and network position that are necessary to enhance and exploit its technologies and to build future sales volume.

The realities of business networks have implications for the market research function within marketing. Business marketing research is often concerned with finding commonalities in the requirements of potential customers. Frequently the commonalities that it searches for and the questions that it asks are in terms of the characteristics of the products of the client company and of the competitors that it identifies. However, a network view emphasises that business purchases are made to solve problems, not to obtain better products. There is great variety in these problems and in their potential solution and these solutions may come from a range of different companies and within a variety of relationships. A business marketer's research must be based on the examination of problems, relationships, network structure and dynamics and this will require the marketer to capitalise on the understanding of those in sales and other areas who interact with counterparts and who are the holders of its technologies and skills. It is this understanding that has to form the basis for developing and implementing marketing strategy.

In the same way as with purchasing, a network view also changes our ideas of the approach that marketing must make to questions of price. The price that marketing attempts to achieve must be a measure of the long- and short-term relationship benefits it provides for a specific customer *and* the current and potential benefits to the supplier itself, in the things that it learns, or the benefits it receives in its other direct or indirect relationships. The price also has to be adjusted for the relationship costs that are incurred by both the customer and the supplier, such as the adaptations and investment they will have to make.

Our view of business networks means that a marketing manager must take a much wider view of her approach to dealing with customers. The marketer must be able to analyse and develop her actions in terms of the three aspects of networking. This analysis will make clear the extent to which her activities are confined to working within her existing relationships, the extent to which she is involved in changing the network position of her company and the extent to which she is seeking to control the surrounding network and the extent to which this is appropriate. Marketing in business networks involves a combination of the different aspects of networking. However, many marketers largely confine themselves to working within the existing relationships of their company, or they desperately try to find new customers without relating these to the company's existing portfolio, abilities or network position. Similarly, many marketers attempt to control their network of distributors or to coerce customers without a realistic assessment of their network position.

The marketing manager must also consider the *outcomes of her networking*, rather than simply the sales or margins that she achieves. These outcomes are always difficult to decipher and are interconnected with the outcomes of the networking of many other companies, but analysis of them provides the basis for understanding the actions of others and for developing future actions in the network:

- *Outcomes and actors*: The marketer must not restrict the examination of her actions to their immediate effect on the single customer to which they were directed, but also consider their outcomes for the longer-term relationship with that customer, with other relationships, including her own suppliers and their effect on the wider network as a whole.
- *Outcomes and activities*: Relationships in networks involve adaptations and the integration of the activities of the companies involved in them. Because of this, the marketer must consider the outcomes of her own actions and those of her counterpart on the operations of both of the two companies. For example, the acceptance of a single order may involve both companies in changes to their offerings and operations, or may lead to the restructuring of the wider network.
- *Outcomes and resources*: Finally, marketers must consider the outcomes of their own actions and those of their customers in terms of the resources of both companies. The

establishment of a new relationship or even an individual sale may have a significant effect on the utilisation of the resources of both companies. It may also lead to or require the development of those resources, sometimes in directions that do not relate to either company's overall strategies.

Marketing management in business markets is about managing a portfolio of customers and about changing network position. It is not just about selling, but about orchestrating the interaction of many others in both companies. It is not just about products and services but also about the technologies on which they are based.

Marketing is the way that a company brings the benefits of its own and other companies' technologies to its customers and integrates them with their own ...

... now doesn't that sound like a job you could be proud of?

INDEX

Index compiled by Annette Musker